Daniel Solin

SAMS Teach Yourself

Qt™ Programming

in 24 Hours

SAMS

A Division of Macmillan USA
201 West 103rd St., Indianapolis, Indiana, 46290

Sams Teach Yourself Qt™ Programming in 24 Hours

Copyright © 2000 by Sams

International Standard Book Number: 0-672-31869-5

Library of Congress Catalog Card Number: 99-067307

Printed in the United States of America

First Printing: May 2000

03   02   01   00   4   3   2   1

Trademarks

Warning and Disclaimer

ASSOCIATE PUBLISHER
Michael Stephens

EXECUTIVE EDITOR
Rosemarie Graham

ACQUISITIONS EDITOR
William E. Brown

DEVELOPMENT EDITORS
Clint McCarty
Tony Amico

MANAGING EDITOR
Charlotte Clapp

PROJECT EDITOR
Andy Beaster

COPY EDITOR
Bart Reed

INDEXERS
Greg Pearson
Sheila Schroeder
Deborah Hittel

PROOFREADERS
Gene Redding
Tony Reitz

TECHNICAL EDITOR
Benjamin Briandet

TEAM COORDINATOR
Pamalee Nelson

INTERIOR DESIGN
Gary Adair

COVER DESIGN
Aren Howell

COPYWRITER
Eric Borgert

PRODUCTION
Timothy Osborn

Contents at a Glance

Contents

About the Author

DANIEL SOLIN is the president of Solin Linux Consulting (www.solin.org), a consulting firm specializing in Linux business solutions, web solutions, and graphical interfaces. Whenever he has some spare time, he also works as a C/C++ teacher, trying hard to convince his local youngsters the advantages of Object-Oriented programming. However, since he has been working for Macmillan USA, almost half a year, Daniel has forced his other projects to step aside (happily, that is).

He has also been involved in a few other Macmillan USA projects: *Slackware Linux Unleashed*, *Caldera OpenLinux Unleashed*, and *Debian Linux Unleashed*. However, he has always been a dedicated Slackware fan, so he was most involved in the Slackware title.

Daniel first got in touch with Linux in 1994. At that time, he was running on an ancient version of the UNIX clone Minix on his home PC, and fell directly in love with this Finnish product called Linux. After a few years of happily running on Linux, Daniel heard about the GUI library, Qt. He downloaded, compiled, installed, and fell in love once again. One of his first Qt projects was Tarman, a graphical interface for managing Slackware's tgz packages. A simple but useful little program. So, to see a GUI program from the old days (the 20th century), point your browser to www.solin.org/tarman.

Oh, I almost forgot. Daniel actually fell in love a third time too (this time, it was for real). That was when he met his lovely Linda, who he lives with in Ludvika, Sweden. Daniel can be reached at daniel@solin.org.

Dedication

This book is dedicated to Linda who was so understanding when I didn't do much else than stare at my screen. I also thank her for looking so interested when I talked about my work, although I know she was not interested at all.

Acknowledgments

I would like to make this acknowledgment a tribute to all the hard working and tremendously helpful people at Macmillan USA. Without their help and support, this book would have been possible.

A very special thanks goes to my Acquisitions Editor, William Brown, for being so helpful through the whole development process. William got me started and was also very helpful whenever I was unsure about something in the development process. Since this was my first book, I needed some extra help with certain things and William helped me with all this.

Special thanks also goes to my Development Editors, Clint McCarty and Tony Amico. Their technical knowledge and experience was of great value. They always offered a helping hand and corrected me whenever I got things wrong.

Many thanks goes to Rosemarie Graham, the Executive Editor, for overseeing the development process. She always strived hard to make the work go as smoothly as possible and her helpful words made her an invaluable part of this book.

Other people at Macmillan USA that I didn't have actual contact with but I also owe many thanks to include Michael Stephens, my Publisher, and my Copy Editor, Bart Reed, who made my "not always so good" English understandable. I also want thank Michael for inviting me to do another book with him.

However, there are many other people at Macmillan USA that I don't know by name, but anyway had a hand in the production. I want to thank them too.

Despite all the people involved in this title, I also owe many thanks to Don Roche, Acquisitions Editor at Macmillan USA. He wasn't really involved in this book, but it's actually because of him that I got the opportunity to write it. Don contacted me in May of 1999 and wanted me to write some chapters in a book titled *Slackware Unleashed*. And after that, he has fed me with exciting work. If it wasn't for Don, I would probably never had got in touch with Macmillan USA at all. Thanks Don!

It should be mentioned, that in the very beginning of the writing, I got the flu, and because of this, my work got delayed quite a bit. Despite all of this, everyone at Macmillan USA kept on track and I didn't hear anything but encouraging words from all of them.

Thanks also goes to Eirik Eng at Troll Tech, for letting me use their program examples whenever I needed inspiration.

Tell Us What You Think!

As the reader of this book, *you* are our most important critic and commentator. We value your opinion and want to know what we're doing right, what we could do better, what areas you'd like to see us publish in, and any other words of wisdom you're willing to pass our way.

As an Associate Publisher for Sams, I welcome your comments. You can fax, email, or write me directly to let me know what you did or didn't like about this book—as well as what we can do to make our books stronger.

Please note that I cannot help you with technical problems related to the topic of this book, and that due to the high volume of mail I receive, I might not be able to reply to every message.

When you write, please be sure to include this book's title and author as well as your name and phone or fax number. I will carefully review your comments and share them with the author and editors who worked on the book.

Fax: (317) 581-4770

Email: michael.stephens@macmillanUSA.com

Mail: Michael Stephens
Sams Publishing
201 West 103rd Street
Indianapolis, IN 46290 USA

Introduction

How people use computers has changed quite dramatically through the years. What began with cryptic commands on a black screen has in the last 10 years developed into a more or less completely graphic-based environment, where the keyboard plays a less important role. Not many people even consider using a text-based program these days. Therefore, graphical user interfaces are required to create successful programs for today's users.

This book will teach you how to create easy-to-use graphical programs in a step-by-step manner, from the most basic features, to the more advanced ones. The 24 lessons in this book are filled with logical explanations, examples, and instructions that make learning Qt programming easy.

There are a few different so-called *toolkits* you can use to create graphical programs in Linux. However, the one you will learn to use in this book, *Qt*, is one of the more popular ones. Because of Qt's Object-Oriented hierarchy, its good structure, its well-developed widgets, and the fact that it includes many other functions than just for creating graphical interfaces, makes it a good choice for beginners as well as experts. Qt is also the toolkit used by the well-known desktop environment, *KDE*, and is therefore, along with the *Gtk+* toolkit, forming a standard for graphical programs in Linux. Qt's advantage over Gtk+ is, however, the fact that it's not just available for UNIX/Linux, but also for Microsoft Windows. This means that a Qt program written in Linux is actually a valid Microsoft Windows program as well!

By reading this book, you'll be amazed how easy it can be to develop graphical programs for both Microsoft Windows and Linux/UNIX at the same time!

PART I
Getting Started with Qt

Hour

HOUR 1

Introduction to Qt

This initial hour is an introduction to the Qt library. We'll discuss the benefits of Qt—that is, what makes it a better choice compared to other GUI design libraries such as Motif, Gtk+, wxWindows, and Xforms.

You'll also be taught how to use the Qt Reference Documentation. This is a very important information resource when working with Qt. Although this book tells you most of what you need to know about Qt, it doesn't cover every single aspect of the library. Therefore, you'll need to check with the Qt Reference Documentation every now and then.

Finally, you'll learn how to create, compile, and run a very simple Qt program. This is to give you an introduction to the actual programming development, which we'll focus on after this first hour.

Choosing the Qt Library

A GUI toolkit (or GUI library) is a set of buttons, scrollbars, menus, and many other objects that you can use to build graphical user interfaces (programs). On UNIX systems, there are many such GUI libraries available. One of these is the Qt library—a GUI toolkit based on the C++ programming language. Because Qt is based on C++ (instead of C), is fast, is easy to use, and has good portability support, it's the best choice for when you want to create GUI programs for UNIX and/or MS Windows.

Portability

Qt isn't available just for UNIX systems; it's also available for MS Windows. If you're a professional programmer (since you're reading this book, I assume you're not, but let's pretend you are) who creates programs for a living, your goal must be to reach out to as many users as possible so that they have a chance to buy/use your product. If your main platform is MS Windows, you could probably use the standard library, the Microsoft Foundation Classes (MFC), quite happily. However, then you would miss millions of UNIX users around the world. On the other hand, if your main platform is UNIX, you could use any other toolkit, such as Gtk+ or Xforms. But then you would miss millions (if not billions) of MS Windows users. Therefore, the best choice would be a GUI toolkit that's available for both MS Windows and UNIX, right? The answer is, of course, Qt.

Ease of Use

As stated earlier, Qt is a C++ toolkit. It consists of hundreds of C++ classes, ready for you to implement in your programs. Because C++ is an object-oriented programming (OOP) language, and Qt is built on C++, Qt also has all the advantages of OOP. You'll learn more about OOP in Hour 2, "Object-Oriented Programming," of this book.

If you're still not convinced that Qt is the best choice. Give the other toolkits a chance as well. Then you can decide which toolkit suits you best.

Speed of Operation

Qt is very easy to use, but it's also very fast. These two facts usually don't mesh. When talking about other GUI toolkits, *easy* often means *slow*, and *hard* often means *fast* (or, from the other side, *slow* means *easy*, and *fast* means *hard*). When talking about Qt, though, *fast* and *easy* go hand in hand. The credit for this goes to the hard-working Qt developers; they've spent a lot of time optimizing their product.

Another thing that makes Qt faster than many other GUI toolkits is how it is implemented. Qt is a GUI emulation toolkit. This means it doesn't use any native-toolkit calls at all. Qt emulates both the MS Windows and Motif (the standard GUI library for commercial UNIX) look and feel by using the low-level drawing functions on the respective

1

platforms. This, of course, increases the speed of the program. Other toolkits, such as wxWindows, that are also available on multiple platforms use either API layering or API emulation. These methods both use the native toolkit in one way or the other and often make your program slower.

Installing the Qt Library

Installing Qt is an easy process. This section describes how to install Qt on UNIX/Linux systems. To install Qt on MS Windows, you must either purchase a license from Troll Tech or ask for an evaluation version. More information on how to do this can be found at www.troll.no.

Compiling and Installing the Qt Source Distribution

Perhaps the best course of action is to simply download the latest version of Qt Free Edition (2.0.2 at the time of this writing) from www.troll.no and then compile it yourself. By doing this, you make sure the library is installed correctly and that your version of Qt includes the latest features and improvements from Troll Tech.

You'll find the distribution file at ftp.troll.no in the /qt/source subdirectory. At the time of this writing, the latest version is found at ftp.troll.no/qt/source/qt-2.0.2.tar.gz and is about 4MB in size. When you download the distribution, make sure you get the latest version (the one with the largest version number). Figure 1.1 shows a Netscape window pointed at the ftp.troll.no ftp archive.

FIGURE 1.1

In Netscape, enter the address, as shown, in the Address field and hit Enter. Then right-click the latest distribution file and select Save Link As.

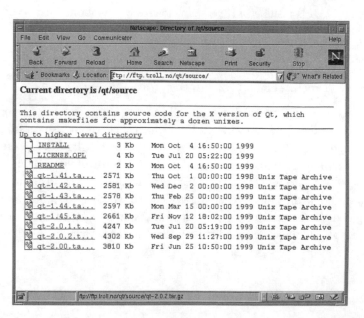

The download now starts. When the download window disappears from the screen, the download is complete, and you're ready to install.

Start by moving your newly downloaded file to /usr/local. Now, from /usr/local, execute the following command:

```
# tar xvfz qt-2.0.2.tar.gz
```

 Be aware that when you read this, a newer version of Qt has most likely been released. This means that the filename probably doesn't exactly match qt-2.0.2.tar.gz; it has probably changed to something such as qt-2.1.0.tar.gz or qt-2.1.1.tar.gz.

This command will unpack the file into a subdirectory. The name of this directory also depends on which version you're installing. In this case, it's /usr/local/qt-2.0.2. When all files has been unpacked, you can delete or move the distribution file:

```
# cd /usr/local
# rm qt-2.0.2.tar.gz
```

In the next step, you have two options to choose from. You can either move your /usr/local/qt-2.0.2 directory to /usr/local/qt or create a symbolic link from /usr/local/qt, which points to /usr/local/qt-2.0.2. It really doesn't matter which you choose to do. (I personally prefer a symbolic link so that I can easily see which version of Qt is installed.) Here's how to create a symbolic link:

```
# ln -s /usr/local/qt-2.0.2 /usr/local/qt
```

To move (rename) the directory, launch the following command:

```
# mv /usr/local/qt-2.0.2 /usr/local/qt
```

Next, you need to define a few shell variables. This is done from one of your startup files (exactly which one depends on which shell you're using). If you're using bash, ksh, zsh, or sh, you can either do this globally (which will affect all users) from /etc/profile or individually (which will only affect yourself) from $HOME/.profile or $HOME/.bash_profile, depending on your Linux/UNIX distribution ($HOME represent your home directory). After you've decided whether you want these variables to become global (a good choice if you want all users on the system to be able to use Qt) or individual, add the code found in Listing 1.1 to the corresponding file.

LISTING 1.1 Qt Variables for bash, ksh, zsh, and sh

```
 1: QTDIR=/usr/local/qt
 2: PATH=$QTDIR/bin:$PATH
 3: if [ $MANPATH ]
 4: then
 5:         MANPATH=$QTDIR/man:$MANPATH
 6: else
 7:         MANPATH=$QTDIR/man
 8: fi
 9: if [ $LD_LIBRARY_PATH ]
10: then
11:         LD_LIBRARY_PATH=$QTDIR/lib:$LD_LIBRARY_PATH
12: else
13:         LD_LIBRARY_PATH=$QTDIR/lib
14: fi
15: LIBRARY_PATH=$LD_LIBRARY_PATH
16: if [ $CPLUS_INCLUDE_PATH ]
17: then
18:         CPLUS_INCLUDE_PATH=$QTDIR/include:$CPLUS_INCLUDE_PATH
19: else
20:         CPLUS_INCLUDE_PATH=$QTDIR/include
21: fi
22: export QTDIR PATH MANPATH LD_LIBRARY_PATH LIBRARY_PATH
23: export CPLUS_INCLUDE_PATH
```

If you're using csh or tcsh, /etc/csh.login is used for global settings and $HOME/.login is used for individual settings. Add the code in Listing 1.2 to one of these files.

LISTING 1.2 Qt Variables for csh and tcsh

```
 1: if ( ! $?QTDIR ) then
 2:     setenv QTDIR /usr/local/qt
 3: endif
 4: if ( $?PATH ) then
 5:     setenv PATH $QTDIR/bin:$PATH
 6: else
 7:     setenv PATH $QTDIR/bin
 8: endif
 9: if ( $?MANPATH ) then
10:     setenv MANPATH $QTDIR/man:$MANPATH
11: else
12:     setenv MANPATH $QTDIR/man
13: endif
14: if ( $?LD_LIBRARY_PATH ) then
15:     setenv LD_LIBRARY_PATH $QTDIR/lib:$LD_LIBRARY_PATH
16: else
17:     setenv LD_LIBRARY_PATH $QTDIR/lib
```

continues

LISTING 1.2 continued

```
18: endif
19: if ( ! $?LIBRARY_PATH ) then
20:     setenv LIBRARY_PATH $LD_LIBRARY_PATH
21: endif
22: if ( $?CPLUS_INCLUDE_PATH ) then
23:     setenv CPLUS_INCLUDE_PATH $QTDIR/include:$CPLUS_INCLUDE_PATH
24: else
25:     setenv CPLUS_INCLUDE_PATH $QTDIR/include
26: endif
```

When you've added either Listing 1.1 to /etc/profile or $HOME/.profile or Listing 1.2 to /etc/csh.login or $HOME/.login, log out and then log in again to activate the changes.

When that's done, use cd to change to /usr/local/qt (which is either a symbolic link or a real directory). From here, you'll now start the actual compilation. But first, you must run the configure script. This is a script that changes the "makefiles" (files that tell the compiler how to compile the source) so that they suit your system. The output from configure will look something like this:

```
# ./configure

Build type:    linux-g++-shared

Compile flags:    -I$(QTDIR)/src/3rdparty/zlib -I$(QTDIR)/src/3rdparty/libpng
Link flags:
GIF supports:  no

Creating makefiles...

Qt is now configured for building. Just run make.
To reconfigure, run make clean and configure.
```

Note that if you execute configure without any arguments, the makefiles are configured only to build shared libraries and don't include GIF image support. If you want static libraries as well, add the -static option to configure. If you want GIF support, execute configure with the -gif option. Therefore, to include GIF support and build static libraries, execute configure as follows:

```
# ./configure -gif -static
```

To see all the options for configure, enter the following command:

```
# ./configure --help
```

When `configure` has finished, run `make` to start the compilation. Here's how:

```
# make
```

Now you'll see a lot of cryptic information scrolling up the screen. This is information about what's being compiled and how it's being compiled. Don't let this bother you. Instead, go drink a cup of coffee while you wait. When the following message is shown, the compilation is finished:

```
The Qt library is now built in ./lib
The Qt examples are built in the directories in ./examples
The Qt tutorials are built in the directories in ./tutorial

Enjoy!   - the Troll Tech team
```

Installing Qt RPM Packages

If you're using an RPM-based (RedHat Package Manager) Linux distribution, such as RedHat, SusE, OpenLinux, or TurboLinux, Qt is most likely included in the distribution as a binary RPM package. To check whether Qt is already installed on your system, issue the following command at a prompt or an `xterm` window:

```
# rpm -q qt
```

If this command lists two packages—one similar to `qt-<version>` and one similar to `qt-devel-<version>`—you're all set. If the command lists only the `qt-<version>` package, you need to install the Qt development package from your distribution CD. If neither of the packages is listed, you need to install both from your distribution CD. To do that, use `cd` to go to the directory containing your distribution `rpms` and execute the following command:

```
# rpm -Uvh qt*
```

Now you're ready to start creating Qt applications, which is exactly what you'll do in the next section.

A Simple Program Example

It has become a tradition among programmers to always introduce a new library by demonstrating the so-called *Hello World* program. Although these Hello World programs are very simple (regardless of the libraries or toolkits they were created with), they give you a good introduction and understanding of how the libraries basically work. In this section, you'll look at a Hello World program built using Qt. You'll find the source code for this program in Listing 1.3.

LISTING 1.3   Hello World with Qt

```
 1: #include <qapplication.h>
 2: #include <qwidget.h>
 3: #include <qpushbutton.h>
 4:
 5: int main( int argc, char **argv )
 6: {
 7:     QApplication a( argc, argv );
 8:
 9:     QWidget mainwindow;
10:     mainwindow.setMinimumSize( 200, 100 );
11:     mainwindow.setMaximumSize( 200, 100 );
12:
13:     QPushButton helloworld( "Hello World!", &mainwindow );
14:     helloworld.setGeometry( 20, 20, 160, 60 );
15:
16:     a.setMainWidget( &mainwindow );
17:     mainwindow.show();
18:     return a.exec();
19: }
```

Much of the code speaks for itself. However, let's look at the program line by line to make sure everything is clear.

Lines 1 to 3 includes three so-called *header files*. These files include various declarations and, by including those declarations, you can use certain parts of the library in your program. In this case, the definitions for the `QApplication`, `QWidget`, and `QPushButton` classes are included. The use of header files is not Qt specific, though, so you're probably already familiar with it.

Line 5 tells you that the definition of the `main()` function starts here. All C/C++ programs must include exactly one `main()` function. The `main()` function is always executed first. Two arguments for `main()`—int `argc` and char `**argv`—are also declared. These two arguments are built-in functions in C++ that make working with command-line arguments easy.

On line 7, an object of the class `QApplication` is created. Just as all C/C++ programs need exactly one `main()` function, Qt programs need to contain exactly one `QApplication` object. Also, `argc` and `argv` are given as arguments to the constructor of the `QApplication` object. This is done to let Qt process command-line arguments, such as `-geometry`.

Line 9 creates a new `QWidget` object, called `mainwindow`. You can think of a `QWidget` object as a window on which you can place other objects, such as buttons. Lines 10 and 11 set the minimum and maximum sizes of `mainwindow` to 200 pixels wide by 100

1

pixels high. When you set the maximum and minimum sizes of the window to the same value, this means the window (mainwindow) cannot be resized.

Line 13 creates a QPushButton object called helloworld. Also, a direct call is made to one of QPushButton's constructors. The first argument tells the constructor to label the button "Hello World!". The second argument makes mainwindow the button's parent widget. This means the button will be placed on mainwindow.

Line 14 sets the geometry of helloworld. The first two arguments tell where the button's upper-left corner will be placed on the button's parent widget (mainwindow). This is done relative to the upper-left corner of the parent widget. Therefore, in this case, the button's upper-left corner will be placed 20 pixels to the left and 20 pixels down relative to mainwidget's upper-left corner. The last two arguments set the width and height of the button (in this case, 160 pixels wide by 60 pixels high). You think this sounds difficult? Relax, when you get used to it, nothing in the world will be more obvious to you.

Line 16 tells the QApplication object to set mainwindow to the program's main widget. When the main widget is killed (closed), the entire program is finished. This is useful if you have a program of more than one window.

Line 17 calls mainwindow's show() function. As you may have guessed, this means mainwindow is to be shown on the screen. You don't need to call helloworld's show() function; this is because helloworld is automatically shown when show() is called for its parent widget (mainwindow).

Line 18 passes the control over from main() to Qt. In exec(), Qt receives and processes user and system events and passes these on to the appropriate widgets. exec() will return when the application is closed. Figure 1.2 shows the compiled result of Listing 1.3.

FIGURE 1.2

A very simple Qt pro-
gram: a small window
with a Hello World!
button on it.

That wasn't so hard, was it? In fact, everything you'll learn from here on will be based on this example.

Compiling and Running a Qt Program

You've installed the Qt library and even looked at a simple Qt program. Now you'll learn how to compile and run a Qt program.

Compiling on UNIX Systems

First, you'll need some valid source code to compile. I suggest you use the code from Listing 1.3. Save the file on your hard drive, use cd to go to the directory containing the file, and issue the following command:

```
# g++ -lqt 01lst03.cpp -o 01lst03
```

Here, g++ is the C++ compiler. However, this could be gcc or c++ or something similar on your system. -lqt means that you want to link with the Qt library libqt.so in the /usr/lib/qt/lib directory. 01lst03.cpp is the source file you want to compile. -o means that the following string is what you want to call the binary file (the program).

You might get an error such as the following when you try to compile the program:

```
can't load library 'libqt.so.2'
```

If so, make sure you've added either Listing 1.1 or Listing 1.2 to one of your startup files, and also make sure you've logged out and logged in again to make these changes active. If this is done and you still get the error message, try to add /usr/local/qt/lib to your /etc/ld.so.conf file and then run the ldconfig program:

```
# ldconfig
```

If it still doesn't work, check LD_LIBRARY_PATH by executing the following command:

```
# echo $LD_LIBRARY_PATH
```

If the output from this command doesn't include /usr/local/qt/lib, enter the following command (if you're using bash, ksh, zsh, or sh):

```
# export LD_LIBRARY_PATH=$LD_LIBRARY_PATH:/usr/local/qt/lib
```

Otherwise, if you're using csh or tcsh, enter this command:

```
# setenv LD_LIBRARY_PATH /usr/local/qt/lib:$LD_LIBRARY_PATH
```

Now, try to compile again. If it works, make sure you add /usr/local/qt/lib to LD_LIBRARY_PATH from one of your startup files.

Next, to run the program, issue the following command from the directory containing your newly compiled program:

```
# ./01lst03
```

Note that you could call the program whatever you like. In this example, the program is called 01lst03 just to show that it was compiled from the file 01lst03.cpp.

Compiling on MS Windows Using Visual C++

The first thing you need to do to be able to compile Qt programs on MS Windows systems is to install the Qt library. You do this just like you do any other piece of Windows software, so no further description is really needed. However, the actual compilation of programs can be a little more complicated, because you need to change some settings in your IDE (Integrated Development Environment—for example, Visual C++ from Microsoft).

When the Qt library is installed correctly, start Visual C++. Click the Project menu and choose Settings. In the window that appears, select the Link option. In the Object/Library Modules text field, enter the following:

```
qt.lib user32.lib gdi32.lib comdlg32.lib imm32.lib ole32.lib uuid.lib
➥ wsock32.lib
```

Then close the window by clicking the OK button. You'll find this window in Figure 1.3.

FIGURE 1.3

This is the linking configuration window in Visual C++.

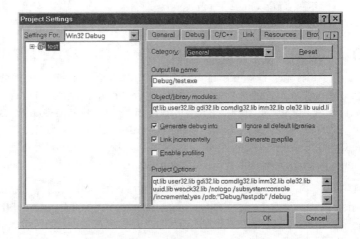

You also need to tell Visual C++ where to find the Qt library and header files. To do this, select Options from the Tools menu. In the window that appears, select Directories. In the directory-configuration menu, look for Show Directories For and select Include Files from this menu. In the middle, you now see a big area where all the include directories are listed. Now, double-click below the last directory and enter `c:\qt\include` (if you installed Qt under `c:\qt`). Then, select Library Files from the same menu and add the directory `c:\qt\lib`, just as you did with the include files directory. Finally, click on the OK button to make the changes active. Figure 1.4 shows this window.

This is the window where you add (and remove) directories that Visual C++ will search to find libraries and header files.

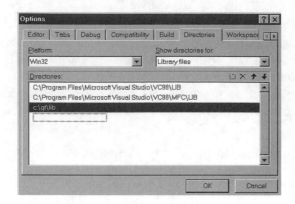

Now, you should be able to compile Qt-based programs. Test this with the example from Listing 1.3. Press F7 to start the compilation. If you get any error messages, go through the preceding steps and make sure you did everything right. Also make sure all variables for Visual C++ and Qt are set correctly.

Using the Qt Reference Documentation

The Qt Reference Documentation is one of the reasons why Qt has become so popular. It's a superb piece of work and will be a great help for you when you need to check on something about the library. The Qt Reference Documentation is very well structured and it's therefore simple to find whatever information you're looking for. You should use the Qt Reference Documentation as often as you can. If you don't, creating Qt applications will be harder and more time consuming.

So, why write a book about Qt if this excellent documentation is already available? Well, although the Qt Reference Documentation is really good, much of the documentation is more like a reference (just as the title implies) than documentation. If you're not familiar with GUI development already, you'll probably need more in-depth explanations than what's offered in the Qt Reference Documentation. This book offers just that.

The Qt Reference Documentation is included in the Qt distribution, in the doc subdirectory. Here, you'll find the HTML version; however, a printable PostScript version can be found at www.troll.no. To open the Qt Reference Documentation, start your Internet browser and point it to the file index.html in the doc subdirectory. You should now see the HTML page shown in Figure 1.5.

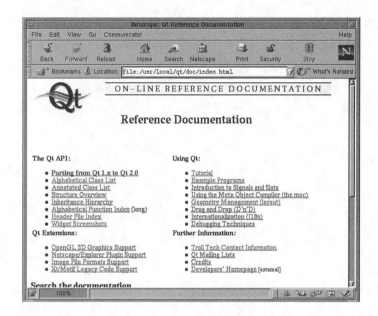

FIGURE 1.5
The Qt Reference Documentation's main page.

The links on the main page take you to different parts of the Qt Reference Documentation. These parts together make a complete reference for the whole Qt library. It is important that you are familiar with each of them and, when there's something you need to know, can find it easily. Table 1.1 describes each one of the sections in the Qt Reference Documentation. You are encouraged to study this table to get an overview of how the Qt Reference Documentation is organized.

TABLE 1.1 Parts of the Qt Reference Documentation

Part	Description
Porting from Qt 1.x to Qt 2.0	Here you'll find information about how to port your Qt applications based in version 1.x of the library to version 2.0.
Alphabetical Class List	Lists all Qt classes in alphabetical order. Each class name is actually a link to a detailed description of the class.
Annotated Class List	Lists all classes but also includes a short description of each one. This is good when you're new to Qt and don't know which class to use for a certain task.
Structure Overview	An overview of Qt's building blocks, sorted by type. For example, if you want to know what dialog boxes you have to choose from, this is the right place to look.

continues

TABLE 1.1   continued

Part	Description
Inheritance Hierarchy	Here you'll find which classes are related to each other.
Alphabetical Function Index	A long, long list of all the functions included in Qt.
Header File Index	Lists all Qt's header files. Here, you can also view the include files.
Widget Screenshots	Screenshots of all Qt widgets. This is really useful.
Tutorial	The great Qt tutorial—a must read!
Example Programs	An index of all sample programs that come with Qt. These programs are very helping when you need a real-life example.
Introduction to Signals and Slots	Signals and slots make your program interact with the users. Without them, your program isn't of much use. Here, you'll find a good introduction to them.
Using the Meta Object Compiler	The meta object compiler makes creating slots and signals easy. Here, you'll find information on how to use it.
Geometry Management	After you read this section (and Hour 11, "Using Layout Managers," of this book), laying out widgets in your program will be easy.
Drag and Drop	This section provide information on how to implement drag-and-drop capabilities in your Qt programs.
Internationalization	Here you'll find information on how to internationalize your programs.
Debugging Techniques	This section offers good advice on how to fix problems with your Qt programs.
OpenGL 3D Graphics Support	OpenGL is a method for creating three-dimensional graphics. The Qt extensions for OpenGL programming are discussed here, although very briefly.
Netscape/Explorer Plugin Support	Plug-ins are small helper applications for Internet browsers. The browser uses plug-ins to deal with certain files. You can write plug-ins using Qt, and that's what is covered in this section.
Image File Formats Support	Wondering how to implement support for a certain image format in your Qt application? If so, look here.
Xt/Motif Legacy Code Support	Here you'll find information on how you can easily use old Motif code with Qt.

When you're new to Qt, the Annotated Class List is maybe the most interesting part. As stated, this includes a short description of all Qt classes. It's a great resource whenever you need to find a class to perform a particular task for you. The alphabetical class list is good to have when you know the name of the class you're looking for and need further information about it.

Let's now look at a standard class reference. Click on the Alphabetical Class List link. You'll see a long list of all Qt classes. From here, click the QPushButton link. You're now presented with a standard description of the class. All class descriptions in the Qt Reference Documentation look like this (see Figure 1.6).

FIGURE 1.6

The QPushButton class description page.

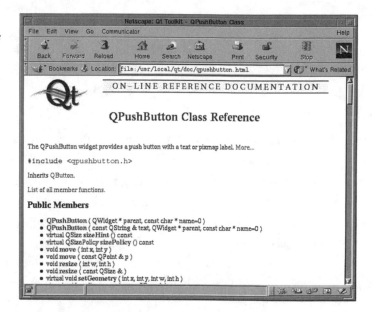

The first thing you find on this page is a list of all public members in the class. Each function is actually a link to a more detailed description of the function. Next is a list of all public slots and protected members (functions). These are also links to detailed descriptions of the slots and member functions.

After this, you find a detailed description of the whole class. In the QPushButton class, you find out that this class is a button widget that can hold a pixmap or text label. You'll often find a screenshot of the widget here as well.

The other parts of the documentation—Qt Extensions and Using Qt—maybe aren't that useful at this level. They'll be of much more use to you later when you know how the library works and have more experience in Qt programming.

Summary

At this point, you know what benefits Qt has to offer, how to install it, and how to write a very simple program, Also, you've learned how to compile a Qt program. Actually, the compilation process is pretty much the same no matter how big and complex your program is, so follow this procedure to compile all your programs from now on. However, the larger the project will become, the more files there will be to compile. And, later you will also be introduced to a tool called MOC that often needs to be used. You've also been introduced to the Qt Reference Documentation; make sure you understand how to use it and why to use it.

It's very important that you fully understand everything in this first hour so that you have all the basic knowledge required to follow the upcoming hours. The next hour will introduce you to object-oriented programming. After you work yourself though that hour, you can start writing real object-oriented Qt programs.

Q&A

Q Why do I get an error message stating that the `make` command can't be found?

A You need to install `make`. It comes with your Linux/UNIX distribution.

Q Why do I get an error message stating that no compiler can be found?

A You have to have a C++ compiler, such as `egcs`, installed to compile Qt.

Q Why do I get an error message stating that some library or package is missing during the compilation?

A Try to find out which package or library is missing and then install it. If it's not included with your distribution, try to search for it on the Internet. If you're using Linux, a great resource for Linux programs is `www.freshmeat.net`.

Q I prefer to have a printed version of the Qt Reference Documentation. Is there any printer-friendly version?

A Yes, a PDF version can be found at `www.troll.no`.

Workshop

You're encouraged to work through the following questions and exercises to help you retain what you've learned in this hour. Working through these questions will help you understand all the basic Qt issues.

Quiz

1. What is Qt?

2. What advantages does Qt have over other similar products?

3. What is a `QPushButton` class?

4. How is the `QWidget` class used?

5. What does `a.setMainWidget( &mainwindow );` mean?

6. Where do you find the Qt Reference Documentation?

Exercises

1. Write a program based on Listing 1.3. Test different geometry parameters. For example, try to make the program twice as big, including the button.

2. Compile your modified program and then run it. If you don't like the result, change some of the geometry parameters and recompile.

3. Add another button to the program in Listing 1.3. You can either make the `QWidget` object bigger to make room for another button or you can make the existing button smaller. Recompile and then run the program.

4. Change the text on the button. Remember to recompile every time you've made a change to the source code.

Hour **2**

Object-Oriented Programming

Unless you're totally new to programming, you've probably heard of object-oriented programming (OOP). This is a programming method that makes many aspects of programming much easier. OOP presents many new programming ideas and is actually a whole now way of looking at programming. Although it's based on the same "low-level" programming features (such as `if`, `for`, `do`, and `while` statements), OOP is a new way of programming.

OOP uses classes to describe certain data forms. Classes are quite similar to C's structures. However, classes can also hold functions and more specifically specify how the class members (such as functions or variables) can be accessed. More about this later in this hour.

OOP isn't language specific; there's actually many object-oriented programming languages out there. However, by far the most popular one is C++, which is based on the old C language. Qt is a C++ class library for creating GUI programs. Qt uses all features of OOP and, for you to be able to use Qt successfully, you need a basic knowledge of object-oriented C++ programming. Therefore, you need to study this hour thoroughly and, if you feel you need more information, you should read *C++ Primer Plus*.

Before we begin, you should note that some parts of the code examples in this hour pertain to things I've made up—such as the calculations of a car's top speed and its weight. Don't take these too seriously!

Understanding Classes

As stated earlier, C++ uses classes to describe certain types of data. You'll now learn how to work with and create simple classes.

It must be said that C++ classes is a very large subject. People write whole books (often much thicker than this one) about just OOP and classes. So, this section can't in any way cover all aspects of classes, but just the most trivial facts that you need to know for getting started. However, the goal of this book is to teach you to create GUI applications with Qt. And, this section is enough for that.

A Class Example

Suppose you want to create a class that describes a car—a class where data such as the car's weight, length, width, top speed, horsepower, and so on can be stored. If you create a class for this, you get a special type of data that can store this information. Here's one solution:

```
class car
{
public:
    int weight;
    int length;
    int width;
    int topspeed;
    int horsepower;
};
```

If you've worked with C's structures, you know that this class declaration looks pretty much like a structure declaration. However, already at this initial stage, at least two differences can be defined. First, the class keyword is used instead of the struct keyword.

Also, the keyword `public:` is used to specify that all the following variables will be accessible from outside the class as well as from within the class. In other words, you'll be able to change and work with these variables from your program. You'll find an example of this defined class in Listing 2.1.

LISTING 2.1   A Sample Use of the car Class

```
 1: #include <iostream.h>
 2:
 3: class car
 4: {
 5: public:
 6:     int weight;
 7:     int length;
 8:     int width;
 9:     int topspeed;
10:     int horsepower;
11: };
12:
13: void main()
14: {
15:     //Create a object of the class:
16:     car a_car;
17:
18:     //Read the weight of the car from the keyboard:
19:     cout << "Define the car's weight!\n:";
20:     cin >> a_car.weight;
21:
22:     //Read the length of the car from the keyboard:
23:     cout << "Define the car's length!\n:";
24:     cin >> a_car.length;
25:
26:     //Read the width of the car from the keyboard:
27:     cout << "Define the car's width!\n:";
28:     cin >> a_car.width;
29:
30:     //Read the car's top speed from the keyboard:
31:     cout << "Define the car's top speed!\n:";
32:     cin >> a_car.topspeed;
33:
34:     //Read the car's horsepower from the keyboard:
35:     cout << "Define the car's horse power!\n:";
36:     cin >> a_car.horsepower;
37:
38:     //Print out that car's data:
39:     cout << "\n\nThis is the car's data:\n";
40:     cout << "\nWeight: " << a_car.weight;
41:     cout << "\nLength: " << a_car.length;
```

continues

LISTING **2.1**   continued

```
42:        cout << "\nWidth: " << a_car.width;
43:        cout << "\nTop Speed: " << a_car.topspeed;
44:        cout << "\nHorse Power: " << a_car.horsepower;
45:        cout << "\n";
46: }
```

Note that this example would have worked just the same if a structure was used instead. However, if you want to make a class just a bit more "intelligent," you need to extend it with some features specific to classes. Let's say you want the class to be able to make calculations based on the car's data. Then you need to add member functions that can do this for you. You can't add functions to a structure, but you can add them to a class. An example of how this could be done is shown in Listing 2.2.

LISTING **2.2**   The *car* Class with Member Functions

```
 1: #include <iostream.h>
 2:
 3: class car
 4: {
 5: public:
 6:      car();
 7:      void printdata();
 8:      void printweight();
 9:      void printtopspeed();
10: private:
11:      int length;
12:      int width;
13:      int horsepower;
14: };
15:
16: car::car()
17: {
18:      //Read the length of the car from the keyboard:
19:      cout << "Define the car's length!\n:";
20:      cin >> this->length;
21:
22:      //Read the width of the car from the keyboard:
23:      cout << "Define the car's width!\n:";
24:      cin >> this->width;
25:
26:      //Read the car's horsepower from the keyboard:
27:      cout << "Define the car's horse power!\n:";
28:      cin >> this->horsepower;
29: }
30:
```

```
31: void car::printdata()
32: {
33:     //Print out that car's data:
34:     cout << "\n\nThis is the car's data:\n";
35:     cout << "\nLength: " << this->length;
36:     cout << "\nWidth: " << this->width;
37:     cout << "\nHorse Power: " << this->horsepower;
38:     cout << "\n";
39: }
40:
41: void car::printweight()
42: {
43:     //Print out the car's weight to the screen:
44:     cout << "Weight: " << (this->length * this->width * 100 );
45: }
46:
47: void car::printtopspeed()
48: {
49:     //Print out the car's top speed to the screen:
50:     if( this->horsepower <= 200 )
51:     {
52:         cout << "\nTop Speed: " << (this->horsepower * 1.2 ) << "\n";
53:     }
54:     if( this->horsepower > 200 )
55:     {
56:         cout << "\nTop Speed: " << (this->horsepower * 0.8 ) << "\n";
57:     }
58: }
59:
60: void main()
61: {
62:     //Create an object of the class and call the member functions:
63:     car a_car;
64:     a_car.printdata();
65:     a_car.printweight();
66:     a_car.printtopspeed();
67: }
```

2

This listing presents a few new programming methods that needs to be explained. These methods are discussed in the bulleted list below. They are of great essence to object-oriented C++ programming, and you should therefore make sure you follow this discussion.

- First, you see a pretty strange function in the class declaration. It's name is `car()` (always the same as the class name), it doesn't take any arguments, and it doesn't have a return type. This function is called the *constructor*. It's called when you create an object of the class. In Listing 2.2, the constructor is called on the following line:

```
car a_car;
```

The constructor and the other member functions are declared under `public:` to make them accessible from outside the function. If they weren't declare under `public:`, you wouldn't be able to call them from `main()`.

- The data types (the variables) are declared under the keyword `private:`. This makes the variables accessible only from within the class (that is, you can't change or access the data from outside the class). By doing this, you make the program safer and less error prone. This programming method is called *data hiding* and is widely used among C++ programmers.

- The way of declaring the member functions probably looks new to you. You use the `::` operator to tell which class the function belongs to (in this case, `car::`).

- Also, the `this` pointer is used to access members of the current class. The `this` pointer represents the object, which when you write the class definition you don't know the name of yet. However, in this simple example, you could leave out the `this` pointer and simply enter the name of the variable; then the program would assume you meant the variable of the current object. (I just included it to show how it can be used.) However, the `this` pointer will become very useful later, when you need to access a parent widget that's not yet created. Sound complicated? If so, grab a good C++ book. There you'll find in-depth explanations of how this works.

Make sure you understand how to access functions and variables from a class or a structure. If the object of the class or structure is a *real* object, you use the dot (.) operator. If the object is a pointer, you use the `->` operator.

The method used in Listing 2.2 to make the actual data *private* so you can work with this data through member functions is one of the reasons OOP is both safer and easier to work with than procedural programming. Because the data is processed only within the class, the risk that something unwanted will happen to the data is much less.

As mentioned, you can add a constructor to your class that will handle everything you want to be done every time you create an object of the class. C++ also includes something called a *destructor*. It's used to free memory that was allocated in the constructor, and it's executed when the object is finished or deleted. The destructor must be named `~<class name>()`. Therefore, in the current example, the constructor should be named `~car()`. Then, you just define it as any other member function and use the `delete` keyword to free up memory. However, you need to use dynamic memory allocation to make this work. Listing 2.3 changes the program in Listing 2.2 to also include a destructor.

LISTING 2.3   The car Class with a Destructor

```
 1: #include <iostream.h>
 2:
 3: class car
 4: {
 5: public:
 6:      car();
 7:      ~car();
 8:      void printdata();
 9:      void printweight();
10:      void printtopspeed();
11: private:
12:      int *length;
13:      int *width;
14:      int *horsepower;
15: };
16:
17: car::car()
18: {
19:      //Allocate memory dynamically for the data.
20:      length = new int;
21:      width = new int;
22:      horsepower = new int;
23:
24:      //Read the length of the car from the keyboard:
25:      cout << "Define the car's length!\n:";
26:      cin >> *this->length;
27:
28:      //Read the width of the car from the keyboard:
29:      cout << "Define the car's width!\n:";
30:      cin >> *this->width;
31:
32:      //Read the car's horsepower from the keyboard:
33:      cout << "Define the car's horse power!\n:";
34:      cin >> *this->horsepower;
35: }
36:
37: car::~car()
38: {
39:      //This function will be called when to object is finished,
40:      //we free up memory with the delete keyword.
41:      delete length;
42:      delete width;
43:      delete horsepower;
```

continues

LISTING 2.3   continued

```
44: }
45:
46: void car::printdata()
47: {
48:     //Print out that car's data:
49:     cout << "\n\nThis is the car's data:\n";
50:     cout << "\nLength: " << *this->length;
51:     cout << "\nWidth: " << *this->width;
52:     cout << "\nHorse Power: " << *this->horsepower;
53:     cout << "\n";
54: }
55:
56: void car::printweight()
57: {
58:     //Print out the car's weight to the screen:
59:     cout << "Weight: " << ( (*this->length) * (*this->width) * 100 );
60: }
61:
62: void car::printtopspeed()
63: {
64:     //Print out the car's top speed to the screen:
65:     if( *this->horsepower <= 200 )
66:     {
67:         cout << "\nTop Speed: " << ( (*this->horsepower) * 1.2 ) << "\n";
68:     }
69:     if( *this->horsepower > 200 )
70:     {
71:         cout << "\nTop Speed: " << ( (*this->horsepower) * 0.8 ) << "\n";
72:     }
73: }
74:
75: void main()
76: {
77:     //Create an object of the class and call the member functions:
78:     car a_car;
79:     a_car.printdata();
80:     a_car.printweight();
81:     a_car.printtopspeed();
82: }
```

As you can see, the new and delete keywords are used to allocate and deallocate memory. Note that you also need the * operator to access the actual data. If you leave out the * operator, the program will just find a memory address (because you're working with pointers). This is basic C stuff, though, so you should already know about it.

How Class Inheritance Works

Another great thing about OOP is that it makes your old code reusable. *Class inheritance* makes it possible for you to build new classes based on old and tested ones. You can add needed features to the class but still be able to use your old and (hopefully) stable code.

Let's go through an example of how this could be done. Suppose you want to modify the class from the previous section so that you can use it to store information about a truck as well. This truck happens to be a truck that hauls ore, so you want to store information about how much ore the truck is actually loaded with. To see how this is done, refer to Listing 2.4.

LISTING 2.4 A truck Class Based on the car Class

```
 1: #include <iostream.h>
 2:
 3: //First, we need to include the code for the car class:
 4: class car
 5: {
 6: public:
 7:      car();
 8:      ~car();
 9:      void printdata();
10:      void printweight();
11:      void printtopspeed();
12: private:
13:      int *length;
14:      int *width;
15:      int *horsepower;
16: };
17:
18: car::car()
19: {
20:      //Allocate memory dynamically for the data.
21:      length = new int;
22:      width = new int;
23:      horsepower = new int;
24:
25:      //Read the length of the car from the keyboard:
26:      cout << "Define the length!\n:";
27:      cin >> *this->length;
28:
29:      //Read the width of the car from the keyboard:
30:      cout << "Define the width!\n:";
31:      cin >> *this->width;
```

continues

LISTING 2.4   continued

```
32:
33:     //Read the car's horsepower from the keyboard:
34:     cout << "Define the horse power!\n:";
35:     cin >> *this->horsepower;
36: }
37:
38: car::~car()
39: {
40:     //This function will be called when to object is finished,
41:     //we free up memory with the delete keyword.
42:     delete length;
43:     delete width;
44:     delete horsepower;
45: }
46:
47: void car::printdata()
48: {
49:     //Print out that car's data:
50:     cout << "\n\nThis is the data:\n";
51:     cout << "\nLength: " << *this->length;
52:     cout << "\nWidth: " << *this->width;
53:     cout << "\nHorse Power: " << *this->horsepower;
54:     cout << "\n";
55: }
56:
57: void car::printweight()
58: {
59:     //Print out the car's weight to the screen:
60:     cout << "Weight: " << ( (*this->length) * (*this->width) * 100 );
61: }
62:
63: void car::printtopspeed()
64: {
65:     //Print out the car's top speed to the screen:
66:     if( *this->horsepower <= 200 )
67:     {
68:         cout << "\nTop Speed: " << ( (*this->horsepower) * 1.2 ) << "\n";
69:     }
70:     if( *this->horsepower > 200 )
71:     {
72:         cout << "\nTop Speed: " << ( (*this->horsepower) * 0.8 ) << "\n";
73:     }
74: }
75:
76: //Then we create a new class based upon car:
77: class truck : public car
78: {
79: public:
80:     truck();
```

```
81:      ~truck();
82:      void printoreload();
83: private:
84:      int *ore_load;
85: };
86:
87: truck::truck()
88: {
89:      //Allocate memory for our new data member:
90:      ore_load = new int;
91:
92:      //Read the ore load from the keyboard:
93:      cout << "Define the ore load!\n:";
94:      cin >> *this->ore_load;
95: }
96:
97: truck::~truck()
98: {
99:      //Free up memory allocated in the constructor:
100:      delete ore_load;
101: }
102:
103: void truck::printoreload()
104: {
105:      //Print out the truck's ore load:
106:      cout << "Ore load: " << *this->ore_load << "\n";
107: }
108:
109: void main()
110: {
111:      //Create an object of the class and call the member functions:
112:      truck a_truck;
113:      a_truck.printdata();
114:      a_truck.printweight();
115:      a_truck.printtopspeed();
116:
117:      //We also want to call the truck specific function printoreload():
118:      a_truck.printoreload();
119: }
```

When you run this program, you soon realize that the constructor from the car class is also executed. This way, you don't need to rewrite a whole new constructor to read in all data from the keyboard. Instead, you can just create another constructor with the truck-specific features you want the truck class to have. Therefore, you save yourself a lot of work.

You don't need to create the variables created in car again but rather the variables you want the new class to be extended with. Also, you don't need to redefine the member functions for calculating the vehicle's top speed and weight.

Next, let's discuss the following line a little further:

```
class truck : public car
```

This is where you define which class the new class will inherit (in this case, `car`). You use what is known among C++ programmers as *public inheritance*, which basically means that what's defined as public in the base class will also be public in the new class, and what's defined as private in the base class will be private in the new class as well. If you changed the `public` keyword to `private`, *private inheritance* would be used instead. Private inheritance makes all functions private in the new class, including the public functions. However, public inheritance is by far the most used inheritance method, including when you're working with Qt.

How Qt Uses OOP

Almost all aspects of OOP are included in Qt in one way or another. In this section, we'll go through some examples of how Qt uses OOP. Although Qt is a fully object-oriented library, you don't actually need to know every single aspect of OOP to master it. This section will teach you the most critical aspects that are required to fully understand the Qt library.

Using Class Inheritance with Qt

Earlier in this hour, you learned about how to use class inheritance to build upon existing code. When creating Qt applications, you'll use class inheritance a lot. In fact, a big part of writing Qt applications consists of writing custom classes based on the existing Qt classes. You'll find a very simple example of this in Listing 2.5.

LISTING 2.5   A Simple Example of Class Inheritance with Qt

```
 1: #include <qapplication.h>
 2: #include <qwidget.h>
 3:
 4: class myclass : public QWidget
 5: {
 6: public:
 7:     myclass();
 8: };
 9:
10: myclass::myclass()
11: {
12:     this->setMinimumSize( 200, 200 );
13:     this->setMaximumSize( 200, 200 );
14: }
```

```
15:
16: int main( int argc, char **argv )
17: {
18:   QApplication a( argc, argv );
19:   myclass w;
20:   a.setMainWidget( &w );
21:   w.show();
22:   return a.exec();
23: }
```

2

This is exactly what you did in the earlier example. You use public inheritance to inherit the members from the QWidget class. A new constructor is created to define the maximum and minimum sizes of the widget (the class). Note that you could also leave out the this pointer; it's just included for clarity. The result of the code in Listing 2.5 can be found in Figure 2.1.

FIGURE 2.1

A simple class based on QWidget.

Creating Objects and Accessing Methods

Because Qt is a class library, you'll of course need to know how to create objects of the classes provided in Qt. You saw how to do this in the basic example in Hour 1, "Introduction to Qt." However, when creating your own classes, you do this slightly differently. In fact, this method was already described earlier in this hour, but now we'll go though an example using Qt classes. You also need to know how to access the methods (members functions) included in the classes. You find an example of this in Listing 2.6. It's well commented so that you fully understand how to write an object-oriented Qt program.

LISTING 2.6 An Example of Object-Oriented Qt Programming

```
1: #include <qapplication.h>
2: #include <qwidget.h>
3: #include <qpushbutton.h>
4:
```

continues

LISTING 2.6   continued

```
 5: //First, we describe the class; which method
 6: //and other members it shall include.
 7: class myclass : public QWidget
 8: {
 9: public:
10:     myclass();
11: private:
12: //Locate memory-space for a QPushButton object:
13:     QPushButton *b1;
14: };
15:
16: //Define the constructor:
17: myclass::myclass()
18: {
19:     //We leave out the this-pointer, the default
20:     //is the current object anyway:
21:     setMinimumSize( 200, 200 );
22:     setMaximumSize( 200, 200 );
23:
24:     //Allocate memory for the QPushButton object.
25:     //We pass two arguments to the class's
26:     //constructor. The first is the label of the
27:     //button, the second is the button's parent
28:     //widget. Here the this-pointer is really
29:     //useful!
30:     b1 = new QPushButton( "Hello", this );
31:     //Here we access the method setGeometry()
32:     //to set the geometry of the button.
33:     b1->setGeometry( 20, 20, 160, 160 );
34: }
35:
36: int main( int argc, char **argv )
37: {
38:     //Create an QApplication object:
39:     QApplication a( argc, argv );
40:     //Create an object of our new class:
41:     myclass w;
42:     //Access the QApplication::setMainWidget
43:     //method:
44:     a.setMainWidget( &w );
45:     //Call the show() method of w (myclass):
46:     w.show();
47:     //Pass control to the Qt library:
48:     return a.exec();
49: }
```

You should now have a basic understanding of how to write object-oriented Qt programs. A picture of the program in Listing 2.6 is shown in Figure 2.2.

FIGURE 2.2

A very simple Qt program written in object-oriented style.

Summary

This hour presented you with a lot of new and sometimes complicated information. If so, you should read a good C++ book to help you fully understand the logic of object-oriented programming. Although you won't need to be a OOP expert to successfully work with the Qt library, you will find it easier to understand the more complicated aspects of the library if you spend some extra time learning about the OOP aspect of the C++ language. As you begin to feel more comfortable with OOP, you'll soon discover the benefits you can gain by using all the new features C++ has to offer.

Q&A

Q My compiler can't compile my OOP code. It whines about missing .h files. What is wrong?

A You need an OOP compiler, such as egcs, to compile an OOP program. You also need to have the C++ library and header files installed. These are things that come with your compiler or distribution.

Q Why do I get an error message about the return type of the constructor when I try to compile an object-oriented program?

A You've probably forgot to add a semicolon (;) after the last bracket (}) of your class declaration.

Q When I try to compile a Qt program, I get a lot of errors about missing references. What's wrong?

A You probably forgot to add the -lqt flag when you tried to compile the program.

Q I get the error message `base operand of '->' has non-pointer type 'car'`. What's wrong?

A If the object is a pointer, you use the -> operand to access its members. Otherwise, you use the . operand.

Q **When compiling a program, I get the warning** `initializing non-const` `'bool &' with 'int *' will use a temporary.` **What's wrong?**

A You probably tried to access a variable that's actually a pointer. You need to use the * operator to access the actual data.

Workshop

You're encouraged to work through the following questions and exercises to help you retain what you've learned in this hour. Working through these questions will help you understand how OOP works.

Quiz

1. What does OOP stand for?

2. What is a class?

3. What is an object?

4. What is a method?

5. What is class inheritance?

6. Why do you need OOP knowledge to use Qt?

Exercises

1. Write a class describing an Internet surfer. The class should store the surfer's gender, age, education, and time spent on the Internet per week. Let the constructor take care of reading information from the keyboard.

2. Change the program from the preceding exercise so that it uses dynamic memory allocation. Also, add a destructor to the class that frees up memory with the `delete` keyword.

3. Write a program based on Listing 2.2. Use class inheritance to add a function that calculates the car's area based on its width and length and then prints the result to the screen.

Hour 3

Learning the Qt Basics

In this hour, we're going to go through the very basics of Qt programming. Perhaps wanting to create actual GUI programs is what made you grab this book. If so, you'll find this to be an exciting hour.

You're going to create your own class based on the QWidget class. This class will become your *main* window; it's the foundation on which you'll add other Qt objects.

Creating Your First Main Widget

The first thing you need to do when you're ready to write a new Qt program is to create a main widget. You can think of the main widget as the working space on which you'll add buttons, scrollbars, labels, and so on. Your program can actually consist of many such widgets, but you can only use one main widget. What makes the main window different from other Qt widgets is that, if the main widget is terminated, the entire program is finished.

Make sure you understand what a widget really is. A *widget* is a graphical (and rectangular) object, such as a button or a scrollbar. An empty window is also a widget. However, when you refer to the *main* widget, that's most likely the main window, although it could be some other widget. The main window can also be referred to as the *top-level widget*.

The most common way of creating a main widget is to create a custom class that's based on either the QWidget or QDialog class. In this book, you'll mainly use the QWidget class. You'll base your custom class on QWidget using public inheritance. You'll create a new constructor, in which you'll define the window's look by calling a few member functions (methods). You looked at this briefly in Hour 2, "Object-Oriented Programming," but we'll go through this in more detail now. An example of this method is included in Listing 3.1. Here, an empty window will be created and shown onscreen. Its size is set to 200 pixels by 120 pixels. Also note that the maximum and minimum sizes are the same, so you'll not be able to resize this window.

LISTING 3.1 Your First Main Widget

```
 1: #include <qapplication.h>
 2: #include <qwidget.h>
 3:
 4: //In the class declaration, we only need
 5: //to include a new constructor. The other
 6: //methods are inherited from QWidget:
 7: class MyMainWindow : public QWidget
 8: {
 9: public:
10:         MyMainWindow();
11: };
12:
13: MyMainWindow::MyMainWindow()
14: {
15:         //Set the maximum and minimum size
16:         //of the window (widget). We don't
17:         //need to use the this-pointer,
18:         //because C++ defaults to the current
19:         //class anyway:
20:         setMinimumSize( 200, 120 );
21:         setMaximumSize( 200, 120 );
22: }
23:
24: void main( int argc, char **argv )
25: {
26:         //Create the required QApplication-
```

```
27:          //object. Pass on the command-line-
28:          //arguments to the QApplication-object:
29:          QApplication a(argc, argv);
30:          //Create a MyMainWindow object, and then
31:          //set it as the main widget:
32:          MyMainWindow w;
33:          a.setMainWidget( &w );
34:          //Paint the MyMainWindow object and all
35:          //its child widgets to the screen:
36:          w.show();
37:          //Pass over control to the Qt library:
38:          a.exec();
39: }
```

After you've compiled this source using g++ -lqt infile -o outfile, you need to execute the outfile. Figure 3.1 shows what appears on your screen.

Figure 3.1

The class
MyMainWindow, created
in Listing 3.1.

Now, try to resize the window. What happens? You can't resize it! Lines 20 and 21 cause this. They define the maximum and minimum sizes of the window to the same value; therefore, you can't resize the window. Also note that the this pointer is left out on those two lines. You can include it if you like. Some programmers think that code is easier to understand if it's included.

Now, try to change the values on lines 20 and 21. For example, change the maximum size to 400 pixels by 240 pixels. Now, you can resize the window from 200 pixels by 120 pixels to 400 pixels by 240 pixels. Also, if you change the minimum value to 100 pixels by 60 pixels, you'll also be able to make the window smaller.

You can use the QWidget::setGeometry() function to define the window's size as well as its placement on the screen. Listing 3.2 includes an example of this.

Listing 3.2   A Main Window Using the setGeometry() Function

```
1: #include <qapplication.h>
2: #include <qwidget.h>
3:
4: class MyMainWindow : public QWidget
```

continues

LISTING 3.2   continued

```
 5: {
 6: public:
 7:         MyMainWindow();
 8: };
 9:
10: MyMainWindow::MyMainWindow()
11: {
12:         setGeometry( 100, 100, 200, 120 );
13: }
14:
15: void main( int argc, char **argv )
16: {
17:         QApplication a(argc, argv);
18:         MyMainWindow w;
19:         a.setMainWidget( &w );
20:         w.show();
21:         a.exec();
22: }
```

With the `QWidget::setGeometry()` function, you set the window's size and position it at the time it appears onscreen for the first time. However, it's fully possible to move and/or resize the window after it appears. In Listing 3.2, the window's top-left corner will appear 100 pixels to the right and 100 pixels down, relative to the top-left corner of the screen (this is represented by the first two arguments given to `QWidget::setGeometry()`). The last two arguments represent the window's size when it appears onscreen. In this case, 200 pixels wide and 120 pixels high. So, if you wanted the window to appear 200 pixels to the right and 350 pixels down relative to the top-left corner of the screen, and if the window should be 400 pixels wide and 300 pixels high, you would make the following call to `setGeometry()`:

```
setGeometry( 200, 350, 400, 300 );
```

Figure 3.2 shows how the window from Listing 3.2 will appear onscreen; Figure 3.3 shows how it might look after you've resized and moved it.

By studying these two methods of defining a window's geometry, you can see that both have positive and negative aspects. If you don't give the user of your program the capability to resize the window, you must live with the risk that the window won't fit his or her screen. On the other hand, if you do let the user resize the window, it will be much harder for you to make the objects on the window look good. However, the window doesn't have any child widgets (objects) yet, so this hasn't been a problem.

FIGURE 3.2

This figure shows how the window from Listing 3.2 will appear onscreen.

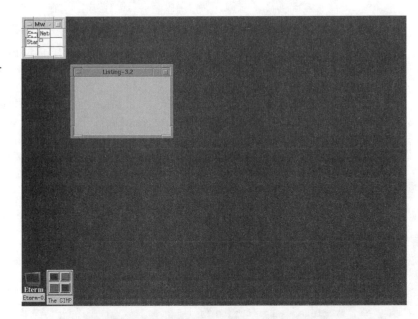

FIGURE 3.3

This figure shows how the window from Listing 3.2 might look if you resize it and move it around.

3

Adding Objects to the Main Widget

Your window (program) won't be of much use if you don't add objects to it that the user can interact with. An empty, blank window can't do much. Therefore, you'll now learn how to add objects to your newly created window. This is not a hard task, though—you just need some basic C++ knowledge to do it. For example, the this pointer is very important when you're adding objects. Actually, this task is quite impossible without it. Therefore, make sure you know what the this pointer is and what you can do with it (see Hour 2, "Object-Oriented Programming," for an explanation of the this pointer).

Adding a Button

To begin, let's add a simple button to the window. The button will not do anything; it will just be visible and clickable. Let's also add some formatted text to the button. See Listing 3.3 for an example.

LISTING 3.3   A MyMainWindow Object with a Button on It

```
 1: #include <qapplication.h>
 2: #include <qwidget.h>
 3: //We include qpushbutton.h to be able to
 4: //use the QPushButton class:
 5: #include <qpushbutton.h>
 6: //We also include qfont.h to be able to
 7: //format the button label:
 8: #include <qfont.h>
 9:
10: class MyMainWindow : public QWidget
11: {
12: public:
13:     MyMainWindow();
14: private:
15: //Locate memory for the button:
16:     QPushButton *b1;
17: };
18:
19: MyMainWindow::MyMainWindow()
20: {
21:     setGeometry( 100, 100, 200, 120 );
22:
23:     //Here we create the button. We give two arguments
24:     //to the constructor, the fist represents the
25:     //label text, the second represents the button
26:     //parent widget. Here, the this-pointer is very
27:     //useful!
28:     b1 = new QPushButton( "Button 1", this );
29:     //Since b1 is a pointer, we use the -> operator.
```

```
30:      //We set the button's geometry by calling the
31:      //QPushButton::setGeometry() function:
32:      b1->setGeometry( 20, 20, 160, 80 );
33:      //Set the buttons label font:
34:      b1->setFont( QFont( "Times", 18, QFont::Bold ) );
35: }
36:
37: void main( int argc, char **argv )
38: {
39:      QApplication a(argc, argv);
40:      MyMainWindow w;
41:      a.setMainWidget( &w );
42:      //Since b1 is a child widget of w, both b1 and w
43:      //will be shown when we make the following call:
44:      w.show();
45:      a.exec();
46: }
```

3

That wasn't hard, was it? Note that line 34 is where you format the text on the button. You do this through the `QPushButton::setFont()` function, which takes a `QFont` object as an argument. Also, note that three arguments are given to the `QFont` constructor—the first represents the font, the second defines the font size, and the third indicates that you want the text to be bold. The last argument is known as the *weight* of the text; it defines the boldness of the text (see the `QFont` section of the Qt Reference Documentation for a complete list of all available weights).

Optionally, you can also add a fourth argument to the constructor. This should be a `bool` value that defines whether the text should be italic or not. Consider the following example:

```
b1->setFont( QFont( "Courier", 12, QFont::Light, TRUE );
```

This would set the font to Courier and the size to 12 pixels, make the text light (opposite to bold), and finally make it italic.

> If you think the line
>
> ```
> b1->setFont( QFont( "Times", 18, QFont::Bold ) );
> ```
>
> looks strange, note that the following code works equally well:
>
> ```
> QFont font( "Times", 18, QFont::Bold );
> b1->setFont( font );
> ```
>
> This may be easier to understand.

By compiling Listing 3.3, you create the program shown in Figure 3.4.

FIGURE 3.4

Here's a MyMainWindow class with a QPushButton object on it. The text label is formatted with QFont.

Adding a Label

Although the process of adding a child widget to a window is pretty much the same regardless of the widget you want to add, let's look at how you would add a text label to the window, just to make sure you get the idea. For this, you need to use the QLabel class. See Listing 3.4 for an example.

LISTING 3.4   A MyMainWindow Object with a Button and a Label

```
1: #include <qapplication.h>
2: #include <qwidget.h>
3: #include <qpushbutton.h>
4: #include <qfont.h>
5: //We include qlabel.h to get access to
6: //the QLabel class:
7: #include <qlabel.h>
8:
9: class MyMainWindow : public QWidget
10: {
11: public:
12:     MyMainWindow();
```

```
13: private:
14:     QPushButton *b1;
15:     QLabel *label;
16: };
17:
18: MyMainWindow::MyMainWindow()
19: {
20:     setGeometry( 100, 100, 200, 170 );
21:
22:     b1 = new QPushButton( "Button 1", this );
23:     b1->setGeometry( 20, 20, 160, 80 );
24:     b1->setFont( QFont( "Times", 18, QFont::Bold ) );
25:
26:     //Here we create the label, define the text
27:     //and where in the window the label shall appear:
28:     label = new QLabel( this );
29:     label->setGeometry( 20, 110, 160, 50 );
30:     label->setText( "This is the first line\n
31:             This is the second line" );
32:     label->setAlignment( AlignCenter );
33: }
34:
35: void main( int argc, char **argv )
36: {
37:     QApplication a(argc, argv);
38:     MyMainWindow w;
39:     a.setMainWidget( &w );
40:     w.show();
41:     a.exec();
42: }
```

3

Note that you use the same method you used earlier to add the button. You locate memory for the label in the class declaration and then you create and define the label in the constructor. Line 28 calls the QLabel constructor and gives the this pointer as the argument (that is, it makes the uncreated MyMainWindow object the label's parent widget). Line 29 sets the label's geometry with the QLabel::setGeometry() function. Note that a text label is handled like a rectangular box in Qt, so its geometry can be set just as you would a QPushButton object. Lines 30 and 31 set the text of the label. They also include a \n, which represents a line change. Line 32 tells Qt to paint the text in the horizontal center of the rectangular QLabel box. This program is shown in Figure 3.5.

The QLabel class should be used to show short strings, such as to explain what should be typed in a text box. However, to show longer text, it's not advisable to use QLabel. Then, widgets like the QMultiLineEdit works better.

FIGURE 3.5

A MyMainWindow class with a button and a label on it.

You should now understand the basics of adding widgets to a window. However, wouldn't it be nice if something happened when you clicked the button? Of course it would. Let's do that now.

Adding a Quit Button

One of the things that make Qt so different from other, similar libraries is how its widgets interact with users—that is, how things happen when you, for example, click a button or drag a slider. Whereas most other GUI libraries use so-called *callback functions*, Qt uses signals and slots. Simply speaking, signals and slots are functions that are connected to each other. The signal (which actually is a function) is executed, and the slot (which also is a function) that is connected to this signal also gets executed. You'll find an example in this section.

We'll discuss this topic in depth in later hours. For now, you'll learn how you can add a simple quit function to a button (see Listing 3.5).

LISTING 3.5 Click the Button and the Program Will Exit

```
 1: #include <qapplication.h>
 2: #include <qwidget.h>
 3: #include <qpushbutton.h>
 4: #include <qfont.h>
 5: #include <qlabel.h>
 6:
 7: class MyMainWindow : public QWidget
 8: {
 9: public:
10:     MyMainWindow();
11: private:
12:     QPushButton *b1;
13:     QLabel *label;
14: };
15:
16: MyMainWindow::MyMainWindow()
```

```
17: {
18:     setGeometry( 100, 100, 200, 170 );
19:
20:     b1 = new QPushButton( "Quit", this );
21:     b1->setGeometry( 20, 20, 160, 80 );
22:     b1->setFont( QFont( "Times", 18, QFont::Bold ) );
23:
24:     label = new QLabel( this );
25:     label->setGeometry( 10, 110, 180, 50 );
26:     label->setText( "If you click the button above,
27:             the whole program will exit" );
28:     label->setAlignment( AlignCenter );
29:
30:     //The following line makes the program exit when the
31:     //b1 button is clicked:
32:     connect( b1, SIGNAL( clicked() ), qApp, SLOT( quit() ) );
33: }
34:
35: void main( int argc, char **argv )
36: {
37:     QApplication a(argc, argv);
38:     MyMainWindow w;
39:     a.setMainWidget( &w );
40:     w.show();
41:     a.exec();
42: }
```

The most interesting part of this listing occurs on line 32. Here, the button b1's signal clicked() is connected to the slot quit() of qApp. Now, when you click the button, the QPushButton::clicked() signal will be emitted, the quit() slot of qApp will be executed, and the program will exit. But, what is qApp, then? Well, qApp is a built-in pointer in Qt. It's designed to always point to the QApplication object of the program (a, in this case). It works just like the this pointer: It points to an object that's not yet created. It's a very important part of Qt, and it makes programming in Qt easier. The program in Listing 3.5 can be found in Figure 3.6.

FIGURE 3.6

A MyMainWindow class with an exit button and a label on it. If you click the button, the program will exit.

Summary

In this hour, you learned how to write a simple OOP program using Qt. You added a button and a label to the main window and then implemented a `quit` function for the program. This was done using a single line of code, which shows one of Qt's advantages over other GUI libraries. To create a library that can implement such an advanced feature (which it really is) with such a tiny amount of code is not just impressing—it's quite revolutionary.

So, you're now familiar with OOP, and you can write simple Qt programs with OOP. In the next hour, we'll take an in-depth look at slots and signals.

Q&A

Q When I resize my main window, the objects in it are misplaced and my program no longer looks good. What's wrong?

A You need to use a special method to make the child widgets change as you resize their parent window. We'll discuss this in Hour 11, "Using Layout Managers."

Q I don't understand. What do the arguments to `setGeometry` really stand for?

A This can be a bit confusing at first. You see, pixel (0,0) on a monitor represents the upper-left corner, not the bottom-left corner, as you may be used to. Therefore, if you're using `setGeometry` on the main window, the first argument to `setGeometry` defines how many pixels should appear between the left side of the screen and the window's upper-left corner. The second argument defines how many pixels should appear between the top of the screen and the window's upper-left corner. The next two arguments define the window's width and height in pixels. It's really not hard once you get used to it.

Q My compiler whines about the line that connects the button's signal `clicked()` to qApp's slot `quit()`. What's wrong?

A Make sure the objects you're giving as arguments to the `connect()` function are pointers (addresses). If they're not, you must use the address operator & (add it before an object's name) to get the memory address of the object.

Workshop

You're encouraged to work through the following questions and exercises to help you retain what you've learned in this hour. Working through these questions will help you understand the basics of Qt programming.

Quiz

1. What does the `setMaximumSize()` function do?

2. What does the `setMinimumSize()` function do?

3. What is the `setGeometry()` function used for?

4. What can you do if you include the `qfont.h` header file in your source file?

5. What does the line `MyMainWindow w;` do?

6. Why don't you need to call the `show()` function for each object?

7. What do you do when you enter the `this` pointer as a parent widget?

8. What is `qApp`?

9. Why do you need to make a call to `a.exec()` in `main()`?

Exercises

1. Write a new Qt class based on `QWidget`. Make it 400 pixels wide and 300 pixels high. Add a button to the upper-left corner of the window.

2. Change the program from Exercise 1 so that the button appears on the bottom-right corner instead. (Remember, the entire button must be visible!)

3. Now move the button to the middle of the window.

4. Finally, connect the button's `clicked()` signal to qApp's slot `quit()`. Then make sure it works.

5. Search the Qt Reference Documentation for other signals included with `QPushButton` (hint: It's based on `QButton`). Also, look up which slots are included in `QApplication`.

3

Hour 4

Making Things Happen: Slots and Signals

The way Qt makes the widgets interact with the user differentiates Qt from other GUI toolkits. This user interaction is what GUI applications are all about. By connecting certain user events (for example, a button click) to certain program events (for example, when the program exits), users can control the program graphically and often by using only the mouse.

In other toolkits, using *callback functions* creates the user interaction. However, callback functions can become quite complicated, confusing, and hard to understand (at least most Qt people think so). Therefore, the Qt developers have worked out an alternate method for performing such tasks. This method depends on two Qt-specific functions: *signals* and *slots*. With this new method, you can connect a user event with a program event with one single line of code.

This new way of connecting user events to program events is much easier to use than callback functions. Slots and signals are two strong reasons why you should choose Qt over other toolkits.

In this hour, you'll learn the basics of signals and slots, and you'll look at some of the predefined signals and slots that come with Qt. At the end of this hour, you will learn how to define your own slots and signals. For this, you'll need to use a utility called the Meta Object Compiler (MOC) which will be covered as well.

Understanding Signals and Slots

First, you need to make sure you understand slots and signals. As stated, this technology differs a bit from the more traditional callback functions. After all, the slots and signals technology was developed independently by Troll Tech—it's not a C++ feature. To fully understand the discussions about slots and signals throughout this hour, there are a few terms you need to understand. These terms are detailed in Table 4.1

TABLE 4.1 Slots and Signals Terms

Term	Explanation
User event	Refers to something the user of the program does. For example, the user can click a button or drag a scrollbar.
Program event	Refers to something the program does. An example of a program event is when the program exits after the user clicks the Exit button.
Emitting a signal	Basically means "sending" a signal. For example, when you click a button, the signal `clicked()` is *emitted*. To emit a signal, the keyword `emit` is used.
Internal state	When talking about signals, you might hear the expression "the internal state has changed." This simply means that some data in an object has changed and therefore the object emits a signal.
MOC	The Meta Object Compiler (MOC) is used to build your own signals and slots. It takes care of the Qt-specific keywords (such as `emit`) and makes valid C++ code of them. You'll learn more about MOC in the "Getting to Know the Meta Object Compiler" section later in this hour.

Understanding Slots

Slots are actually normal member functions (functions that are members of a class). However, they have some special features added to them that make it possible to connect signals to them. Every time a signal connected to a particular slot is emitted, the slot (function) is executed. Therefore, when you create your own slots in Hour 8, "Getting to Know the Qt Widgets: Lesson Three," you'll actually write usual members function.

Many Qt classes already include a few predefined slots you can use in your programs. A good example of this is the `clicked()` function included in the `QPushButton` class.

So, slots are actually normal functions. Therefore, they can be called just like other functions.

Understanding Signals

Signals are also member functions. However, they're implemented in a slightly different way (this is described in the "Getting to Know the Meta Object Compiler" section later in this hour).

When something happens inside an object (that is, its internal state changes), it can send out a signal (although it doesn't have to). If this signal is connected to a slot, that slot (function) is then executed. You can connect multiple slots to the same signals; the slots are then executed one by one, in an arbitrary order.

So, signals are a special type of function. They're defined to be emitted when certain events occur. Then, any connected slots are executed.

Using the Predefined Signals and Slots

In the last hour, "Learning the Qt Basics," you used signals and slots when you implemented a Quit button in your program. You connected the button's signal `clicked()` to the slot `quit()` on qApp. By doing this, you made the program execute the slot (function) `quit()` whenever the signal `clicked()` is emitted.

Of course, there are many other signals and slots included with Qt, and there are an infinite number of ways you can use them. This section will give you a good introduction to the predefined slots and signals. It will also show you some ways in which they can be used.

Example 1: `QSlider` and `QLCDNumber`

Slots and signals can be used to create more exciting items than Exit buttons. Although the next example is not fancy, it's definitely more interesting than the Quit button from the last hour. Listing 4.1 will give you some idea of how slots and signals are used.

LISTING 4.1 A Slot/Signal Example

```
 1: #include <qapplication.h>
 2: #include <qwidget.h>
 3: #include <qpushbutton.h>
 4: #include <qfont.h>
 5: #include <qlcdnumber.h>
 6: #include <qslider.h>
 7:
 8: class MyMainWindow : public QWidget
 9: {
10: public:
11:     MyMainWindow();
12: private:
13:     QPushButton *b1;
14:     QLCDNumber *lcd;
15:     QSlider *slider;
16: };
17:
18: MyMainWindow::MyMainWindow()
19: {
20:     setGeometry( 100, 100, 300, 200 );
21:
22:     b1 = new QPushButton( "Quit", this );
23:     b1->setGeometry( 10, 10, 80, 40 );
24:     b1->setFont( QFont( "Times", 18, QFont::Bold ) );
25:
26:     lcd = new QLCDNumber( 2, this );
27:     lcd->setGeometry( 100, 10, 190, 180 );
28:
29:     slider = new QSlider( Vertical, this );
30:     slider->setGeometry( 10, 60, 80, 130 );
31:
32:     //The following line makes the program exit when the
33:     //b1 button is clicked:
34:     connect( b1, SIGNAL( clicked() ), qApp, SLOT( quit() ) );
35:
36:     //The following line connects the slider to the LCD display,
37:     //and makes the display number change as you drag the slider.
38:     connect( slider, SIGNAL( valueChanged(int) ),
39:             lcd, SLOT( display(int) ) );
40: }
41:
42: void main( int argc, char **argv )
43: {
44:     QApplication a(argc, argv);
45:     MyMainWindow w;
46:     a.setMainWidget( &w );
47:     w.show();
48:     a.exec();
49: }
```

In Listing 4.1, the connect() function is used to connect the clicked() signal of b1 to the qApp's quit() slot (line 24). The result of this is that the program will exit when b1 is clicked. On line 38, the valueChanged() signal of slider is connected to the display() signal of lcd. Note that an int value is also sent between the two functions. The result of this is that the value displayed in the display can be controlled by dragging the slider.

> When you make a function call inside a class definition without defining from which class the function comes, C++ believes it's the current class (the one you're about to define). Therefore, it's fully valid to call the connect() function, as is done in the previous example, without defining in which class the function is included.

Compile the program and then launch it. See what happens when you drag the slider. Wasn't that fun? This program is shown in Figure 4.1.

FIGURE 4.1

An example of how you can use slots and signals with a slider and a LCD display.

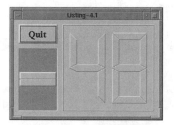

4

As you can imagine, slots and signals can be used for many tasks other than implementing Exit buttons. The next section provides another example.

Example 2: QPushButton and QLineEdit

Now, you're going to use three QPushButton objects to control whether the text in a QLineEdit object should be selected, deselected, or removed. This is done by connecting the clicked() signals of the QPushButton's to the appropriate slots on the QLineEdit object.

The example shown in Listing 4.2 isn't spectacular, but it should give you some inspiration.

LISTING 4.2 Connecting Three QPushButton Objects and One QLineEdit

```
 1: #include <qapplication.h>
 2: #include <qwidget.h>
 3: #include <qpushbutton.h>
 4: #include <qfont.h>
 5: #include <qlineedit.h>
 6: #include <qstring.h>
 7:
 8: class MyMainWindow : public QWidget
 9: {
10: public:
11:     MyMainWindow();
12: private:
13:     QPushButton *b1;
14:     QPushButton *b2;
15:     QPushButton *b3;
16:     QLineEdit *ledit;
17: };
18:
19: MyMainWindow::MyMainWindow()
20: {
21:     setGeometry( 100, 100, 300, 200 );
22:
23:     b1 = new QPushButton( "Click here to mark the text", this );
24:     b1->setGeometry( 10, 10, 280, 40 );
25:     b1->setFont( QFont( "Times", 18, QFont::Bold ) );
26:
27:     b2 = new QPushButton( "Click here to unmark the text", this );
28:     b2->setGeometry( 10, 60, 280, 40 );
29:     b2->setFont( QFont( "Times", 18, QFont::Bold ) );
30:
31:     b3 = new QPushButton( "Click here to remove the text", this );
32:     b3->setGeometry( 10, 110, 280, 40 );
33:     b3->setFont( QFont( "Times", 18, QFont::Bold ) );
34:
35:     ledit = new QLineEdit( "This is a line of text", this );
36:     ledit->setGeometry( 10, 160, 280, 30 );
37:
38:     //The following three lines connects each button to a predefined
39:     //slot on the ledit object. Test the program to find out what
40:     //happens!
41:     connect( b1, SIGNAL( clicked() ), ledit, SLOT( selectAll() ) );
42:     connect( b2, SIGNAL( clicked() ), ledit, SLOT( deselect() ) );
43:     connect( b3, SIGNAL( clicked() ), ledit, SLOT( clear() ) );
44: }
45:
46: void main( int argc, char **argv )
47: {
48:     QApplication a(argc, argv);
```

```
49:     MyMainWindow w;
50:     a.setMainWidget( &w );
51:     w.show();
52:     a.exec();
53: }
```

Figure 4.2 shows this program in action.

FIGURE 4.2

An example of how you can use the slots in a QLineEdit *object with three* QPushButton *objects.*

This example uses the clicked() signal of QPushButton (a very useful signal) and connects it to three different slots included in the QLineEdit class (lines 41, 42, and 43). By doing this, you can control the text in the QLineEdit object by clicking the buttons.

I could write many more sample programs like the ones you've looked at in this hour, but these two examples should be enough for you to understand the general use of slots and signals. Instead of exploring more program examples, you should look at the Qt Reference Documentation. There you'll find information about all the slots and signals included in Qt. Try some of them and see what happens.

Creating and Using Custom Signals and Slots

You will spend much time creating custom slots on when you're writing a Qt program (in other word, slots that you have defined yourself). You can, of course, create your own signals as well. But, because the predefined signals are enough in most cases, that is something you won't have to do often. In this section, you will learn how to create custom slots and signals, and how to use the Meta Object Compiler, which is required for doing this.

Getting to Know the Meta Object Compiler

As mentioned earlier, the signal/slot technique is quite special. Actually, there's also a special programming syntax for creating signals and slots. Your C++ compiler doesn't understand this syntax, so you have to use special tool, called the Meta Object Compiler (MOC), to make this work. This tool scans a source file for the special programming

4

syntax used to create signals and slots and creates valid C++ code out of it (code that your compiler understands). In this section, you will learn how to work with the MOC.

Locating the Meta Object Compiler

The Meta Object Compiler binary, moc, is always located in the $QTDIR/bin directory. So, if the base directory of your Qt installation is /usr/local/qt, all your Qt binaries are located in /usr/local/qt/bin, including moc. This binary was compiled automatically when you compiled the Qt library.

If you added the $QTDIR/bin directory to your PATH variable, as described in Hour 1, "Introduction to Qt," you can execute moc from anywhere on your file system by just entering moc at the prompt.

Using the Meta Object Compiler

After you have defined a slot or a signal in a class declaration (as described later in this hour), you need to let moc read the file and extract valid C++ code from it. Fortunately, using moc is very simple. The syntax is as follows:

```
$ moc infile.h -o outfile.moc
```

This command will read the file infile.h, which should hold the declaration for your Qt class, and declare a few signals and/or slots. moc will then create valid C++ source code from this and place it in the outfile.moc file. It's as simple as that!

To compile your new class, you can either include the moc-file (the file created by moc) in the cpp-file (the file that holds the class definitions) or you can make object-files out of the moc-file and the cpp-file and then link them together, as shown in the following:

```
$ g++ -c outfile.moc -o outfile.o
$ g++ -c infile.cpp -o infile.o
$ g++ -lqt outfile.o infile.o -o MyProgram
```

Both methods (including the moc-file or linking against it) work equally well; chose the method that suits you best. In this book, you will use the former method.

Creating Custom Slots

Whenever you want a custom event to occur when the user does something with your program (like clicking a button), you must create a custom slot that can be connected to the appropriate signal (the clicked() signal, if you're working with buttons). For this, you need to know two things: how to use moc and how to define a slot in a class declaration. After reading the last section, you should know how to use moc. However, you don't know how to define a slot in a class declaration yet, so that's what you're going to learn next.

Declaring a Custom Slot

The first thing you need to do when you want to create a custom slot is to declare it in the class declaration. A slot is actually a usual member function, but you need to use a special keyword so that moc can separate the slot from the other member functions. Consider the following class declaration:

```
class MyMainWindow : public QWidget
{
public:
    MyMainWindow();
};
```

This class holds only a constructor in which you can create and use predefined slots and signals for connecting widgets to events. However, if you want to implement a function that the predefined slots can't achieve, you need to define a custom one. For example, say that the QApplication::quit() slot didn't exist, and you needed to write your own slot that made the program exit. First, you would add the following slot to the class declaration:

```
class MyMainWindow : public QWidget
{
    Q_OBJECT
public:
    MyMainWindow();
public slots:
    MyExitSlot();
};
```

The first thing that probably looks new to you is the call to the Q_OBJECT macro. All Qt classes that hold custom signals and slots must mention this macro, otherwise it won't work. You don't need to know why this has to be done, just remember to include it in your class declaration, and everything will be just fine.

As you also see, a new syntax is used to define that the new function is a slot. Now, when you use moc on this declaration, it will find the line

```
public slots:
```

and consider all functions that declared after this line as slots (until the end of the class declaration is reached, or another section, such as private:, starts). If you want to declare more than one custom slot in the class, you should just list them one by one after MyExitSlot().

Defining a Custom Slot

After you've declared the slot in the class declaration, you need to write the actual slot definition (the function). This is done the same as any other function in the cpp-file. For the example with the MyExitSlot() slot, the cpp-file could look as follows:

```
#include <stdlib.h>
#include <qpushbutton.h>

//The slot:
void MyMainWindow::MyExitSlot()
{
    //Use the exit() function defined in stdlib.h:
    exit(0);
}

//The constructor:
MyMainWindow::MyMainWindow()
{
    //Some code
    //Some code

    //Connect a button to our custom slot:
    connect( MyButton, SIGNAL( clicked() ), this, SLOT( MyExitSlot() ) );
}
```

The interesting part here is the slot definition. As you see, it's a very simple (yet useful) slot that uses the exit() function defined in stdlib.h to make the program exit. If you would write a complete program (with real content in the constructor that would create and place out the MyButton button), and then connected it as done on the next-to-last line in the previous example, the result would be the same as using Listing 3.5 (from Hour 3, "Learning the Qt Basics").

Compiling a Program that Uses Custom Slots

As stated previously, you need to use moc whenever your program uses classes that holds custom slots or signals. You also need to use moc on the example with the MyExitSlot() slot. First, use moc on the class declaration:

```
$ moc ClassDeclaration.h –o ClassDeclaration.moc
```

Then, include the moc-file in the class cpp-file (the file that holds the definitions of the functions):

```
#include "ClassDeclaration.moc"
```

And finally, compile the cpp-file and make sure that you link with the qt-library (of course, you also need to implement a main() function for this to work):

```
$ g++ -lqt ClassDefinition.cpp main.cpp –o MyProgram
```

Optionally, if you prefer to compile the moc-file to an object-file and then link it against the `ClassDefinition.cpp` and `main.cpp` files, that will work equally well, as shown in the following:

```
$ moc ClassDeclaration.h -o ClassDeclaration.moc
$ g++ -c ClassDeclaration.moc -o ClassDeclaration.o
$ g++ -c ClassDefinition.cpp -o ClassDefinition.o
$ g++ -c main.cpp -o main.o
$ g++ -lqt ClassDeclaration.o ClassDefinition.o main.o -o MyProgram
```

In this case, note that you don't need to include the `ClassDeclaration.moc` file in `ClassDefinition.cpp`.

You have now declared, defined, and used a custom slot. Although this was a very simple example, the concept explained here is the same, no matter how long and complex you choose to make your slot definition(s). You will learn more about custom slots and see more examples of how they can be defined and used throughout this book.

Creating Custom Signals

Every now and then, you might need to define your own signals. However, this is something you don't need to do often (and certainly not as often as you need to define your own slots). Therefore, you will just go through this briefly.

The first thing you need to do is to declare the custom signal in the class declaration. Just as slots are declared under `public slots:`, signals should also be declared under a special keyword with the obvious name `signals:`. Therefore, a class declaration holding a custom signal could look something like the following:

```
class MyMainWindow : public QWidget
{
    Q_OBJECT
public:
    MyMainWindow();
    SetValue( int );
public slots:
    ChangeValue( int );
signals:
    ValueChanged( int );
};
```

In this case, a custom signal, `MyCustomSignal()`, is declared. This signal takes an `int` value as argument. A custom slot, `ChangeValue()` is also declared; this function also takes an `int` value as argument. A usual member function, `SetValue()`, is also declared.

As you might have guessed, the `SetValue()` function should call the `ValueChanged()` signal only when a new value is passed to `SetValue()`. Then, by connecting the `ValueChanged()` signal to the `ChangeValue()` slot, the value will be changed if a new value is passed to `SetValue()`. In many cases, this is just unnecessary work, but it demonstrates the use of signals. The implementation of `SetValue()` could look something like the following:

```
void MyMainWindow::SetValue( int value )
{
    if( value != oldvalue )
    {
        oldvalue = value;
        emit ValueChanged( value );
    }
}
```

As you see, the `ValueChanged()` signal will only be emitted if the new value is not the same as the old one. If that is true, `oldvalue` will be changed to `value`, and the `ValueChanged()` signal will be emitted. Note that a signal is not a usual function that is defined like a slot. On the contrary, it is only emitted using the `emit` keyword. The implementation of `ChangeValue()` could look something like the following:

```
void MyMainWindow::ChangeValue( int value )
{
    FunctionForChangingTheValue( value );
}
```

In this code, the function `FunctionForChangingTheValue()` is called to actually change the value. The last thing you need to do is connect the signal and the slot together:

```
connect( this, SIGNAL( ValueChanged(int) ), this, SLOT( ChangeValue(int) ) );
```

The result of this little example is that when the `SetValue()` function is called, it checks if the new value is equal to the old value. If that is not the case, the `ValueChanged()` signals is emitted. And, because the `ValueChanged()` signal is connected to the `ChangeValue()` slot, the `ChangeValue()` slot will be executed whenever the `ValueChanged()` signal is emitted. The `ChangeValue()` slot then uses the `FunctionForChangingTheValue()` for actually changing the value.

Does this feel like a complete mess? Well, you're totally right about that. However, this is something you often have to live with when creating more complex Qt application (and any other GUI application, for that matter). You are encouraged to write code that is as smooth and easy-to-understand as possible. The example you just looked at might not be the best solution when you want to implement a mechanism for changing an int value, but it shows how a signal can be used. And that was, after all, the whole point! Remember to use `moc` on the class declaration whenever it holds any custom signals or slots.

After reading this section about custom signals and slot, you should have a good under-standing of how to create them and how they can be used. As stated earlier, you will find many more examples of how custom slots can be used later in this book, and you will learn more about them as you go through the other hours.

Interesting Features of Slots and Signals

You now basically know how to work with signals and slots. However, there are still a few more interesting features that you might find useful when working with signals and slots, such as disconnecting slots and signals and connecting signals to signals. These features, and a few other, will be covered in this section.

Avoiding Unwanted Information

In Listing 4.1, the slider was connected to the LCD display with the following code:

```
connect( slider, SIGNAL( valueChanged(int) ),
        lcd, SLOT( display(int) ) );
```

Note that both the signal valueChanged() and the slot display() take an int (integer) value as an argument. This basically means that the signal will notice that the slider has been moved as well as tell what the new value is. This int value is sent to the connected slot display() and is then handled to be shown on the LCD display.

However, sometimes a signal gives more information than the slot you want it connected to can take. A good example of this is when you want to know when a toggle button is toggled, but you don't care whether it's toggled on or off. In this case, you can just leave out the corresponding parameter in the slot definition, as shown in the following (note that the receiving object and its slot are made up; they do not exist):

```
connect( togglebutton, SIGNAL( toggled(bool) ),
        anotherobject, SLOT( aslot() ) );
```

You should use this method when you want to connect a signal to a slot and they don't really fit together.

Connecting Signals to Signals

Sometimes, you might find it necessary to connect a signal to another signal. Although this may sound strange, it's completely possible to do. For example, you might want a certain event to occur when you click a button—an event that's easiest to start by calling another signal. In this case, it's a good idea to connect the button's clicked() signal to the signal that will start the event.

When you want to declare a signal to be connected to another signal, just change the third argument of the connect() function, as shown in the following:

```
connect( button, SIGNAL( clicked() ), this, SIGNAL( anothersignal() ) );
```

Now, every time the clicked() signal of button is emitted, it will appear that the anothersignal() signal of the currently-defined class is emitted, too. If you then connect the anothersignal() signal to some slot, that slot (function) will be executed every time clicked() is emitted.

Disconnecting Slots and Signals

It's possible that you'll find it necessary to disconnect a signal from a slot (or a signal from a signal) at some point. This is good to do when you want to disable a function in your program for a while. To accomplish this, you use the QObject::disconnect() function. It expects the exact same parameters as Qobject::connect. For example, if you want to disconnect a clicked() signal from a quit() slot, you use the following line of code:

```
disconnect( button, SIGNAL( clicked() ), qApp, SLOT( quit() ) );
```

If you implement this line in one of the examples that contain a Quit button, you won't be able to terminate the program through the button anymore.

Saving Keystrokes when Using the connect() Function

The connect() function has a feature that can save you a few keystrokes. If you're connecting a signal to a slot of the class that you're currently defining (in a method of that class), you can leave out the object that holds the slot. For example, consider the following example of a method of a class based on QWidget:

```
MyWidget::Mywidget()
{
    //Some code here (including the
    //definition of button1):
    ...
    ..
    .
    //And then the call to connect():
    connect( button, SIGNAL( clicked() ), SLOT( clearFocus() ) );
}
```

In this example, the third argument is left out. The connect() function will then default to the currently-defined object. However, although this method can save you a few keystrokes, it's not advisable that you use it because your code becomes harder to understand. Although I don't recommend that you use this feature, you should still be aware of it because you might see someone else's code that incorporates this shortcut.

Summary

In this hour, you've learned how to make your programs interact with user actions. In fact, this is the whole idea behind GUI programming, so you really need to have a good understanding of this subject to be able to create good programs.

The signal/slot implementation in Qt is really brilliant. Because of this, you shouldn't have had any problems following and understanding the examples in the hour. It's easy to work with slots and signals, and doing so will make your programs easier to understand and less error prone.

However, to build real GUI applications, you need to know more about Qt's building blocks. You'll learn more about these building blocks in the next hour, "Learning More About Qt's Building Blocks."

Q&A

Q My compiler reports that it's not finding the `connect()` function. What's wrong?

A If you call the `connect()` function without defining which class it can be found in, you'll get errors. The call must reside in a method of a class derived from the `QObject` class. If the call is made from an outside function, you must make the call as follows:

```
QObject::connect()
```

Q My compiler reports errors about the arguments I give to `connect()`. What could be wrong?

A The `connect()` function wants pointers to the object, not the object itself. Therefore, you need to make sure you provide the correct arguments.

Workshop

You're encouraged to work through the following questions and exercises to help you retain what you've learned in this hour. By completing these questions and exercises, you'll ensure that you understand how signals and slots work and how to implement them in your programs.

Quiz

1. What is a slot?
2. What is a signal?

3. How do you connect a signal to a slot?

4. Can you connect multiple slots to one signal?

5. When can you call the `connect()` function without specifying in which class it's defined?

6. Is it possible to disconnect a connected slot from a signal?

7. What does it mean to leave out the name of the object holding the slot in a call to the `connect()` function?

8. Is it possible to connect a signal to another signal? If so, how?

Exercises

1. Write a program based on Listing 4.2. Add a button that changes the text in the `QLineEdit` object. (Hint: Use the Qt Reference Documentation.)

2. Try using the `disconnect()` function with Listing 4.2. Disconnect all the connections and recompile the program. What happens?

3. Write a program with two `QPushButton` objects and one radio button (check the Qt Reference Documentation to find which class to use for the radio button). Connect the three objects so that the two `QPushButton` objects can control whether the radio button is checked—one button to check, and one to uncheck.

HOUR 5

Learning More About Qt's Building Blocks

In this hour, you'll look a bit further into what Qt has to offer you when creating GUI applications. You'll learn how to use scrollbars, menus, and file I/O, and you'll also take a look at the useful QMainWindow widget.

The knowledge you'll gain in this hour is essential to Qt programming. You'll gain a better understanding of what Qt has to offer as well as how to basically work with and implement Qt classes in your programs. Actually, all Qt widgets are implemented in a fairly standardized way. Therefore, after you've learned to use a few widgets, you'll most likely feel comfortable implementing most of the other widgets as well. At that point, the Qt Reference Documentation should be enough for you to learn about new widgets.

The first thing you'll learn in this hour is to add scrollbars to your program. This is something most modern GUI applications have to make room for more widgets in a smaller area. Then, you'll go on by getting to know Qt's capabilities of creating menus. Menus are also more or less standard in all modern GUI programs. They are great for presenting program features and options to the user, and they make arranging options and features easier At the end of this hour, you'll find a discussion about the Qt class QMainWindow. This is a class that makes the creation of standard programs easier.

If you've being longing to get started with the real GUI creation, you'll find this hour exciting.

Using Scrollbars

Scrollbars enable you to create applications that are actually too big to fit the screen. In many cases, scrollbars are required for your application to run on all desktops. By learning to use scrollbars, you can make programs that are easier for people to use (since they can see all the widgets, no matter what resolution they use for their desktops). For example, if you create a program optimized for your 1024 pixel by 768 pixel desktop, those who use 800 pixel by 600 pixel or even 640 pixel by 480 pixel desktops will have no chance to get an overview of your program (since their desktops simply are not big enough). So, study this section and make sure your program never will suffer from this problem.

Getting Started with Scrollbars

When you're working with Qt, the easiest way of implementing a scrollbar function is to base your main widget (the main window) on the QScrollView class. By doing this and making a call to QScrollView::addChild for each child widget, you'll automatically create a *scroll-on-demand window* (that is, the window will only add scrollbars if it's too small to show all its child widgets at their original sizes). However, if no scrollbars are needed, no scrollbars will be shown. Listing 5.1 shows an example of this.

LISTING 5.1 An Example of QScrollView

```
1: #include <qapplication.h>
2: #include <qpushbutton.h>
3: #include <qfont.h>
4: #include <qscrollview.h>
5:
6: //We base our new class on QScrollView
7: //instead of QWidget:
8: class MyMainWindow : public QScrollView
9: {
```

```
10: public:
11:     MyMainWindow();
12: private:
13:     QPushButton *b1;
14: };
15:
16: MyMainWindow::MyMainWindow()
17: {
18:     //Set the geometry for the scrollview:
19:     setGeometry( 100, 100, 200, 100 );
20:
21:     b1 = new QPushButton( "This button is not too\n big for the window!",
this );
22:     b1->setGeometry( 10, 10, 180, 80 );
23:     b1->setFont( QFont( "Times", 18, QFont::Bold ) );
24:
25:     //We must call the QScrollView::addChild function
26:     //for each of its child widgets:
27:     addChild( b1 );
28: }
29:
30: void main( int argc, char **argv )
31: {
32:     QApplication a(argc, argv);
33:     MyMainWindow w;
34:     a.setMainWidget( &w );
35:     w.show();
36:     a.exec();
37:}
```

5

Notice that, at line 8, the class is based on QScrollView instead of QWidget. Also notice the call to QScrollView::addChild() on line 27. This call tells QScrollView which widgets to consider when it's determining whether a scrollbar is needed. When a widget based on QScrollView finds that its child widgets added with QScrollView::addChild() don't fit anymore, it adds vertical or horizontal scrollbars (or both) that can be used to see the child widget that is partly or completely *outside* the widget. By basing your widgets (windows) on QScrollView and using the QScrollView::addChild() function, scrollbars will be added to the window whenever needed. Figure 5.1 shows the program in Listing 5.1 in its original form (as it first appears onscreen).

FIGURE 5.1

A simple program based on the QScrollView *class. As you can see, no scrollbars are needed.*

However, there isn't much use for the scrollview function at this point. To make this function visible (and usable), you must resize the window (by dragging one of its corners) so that it becomes too small to show all the child widgets (in this case, only one QPushButton). By reducing the window's width, you should end up with something similar to Figure 5.2.

FIGURE 5.2

If you make the window's width too small to show the whole button, a horizontal scrollbar appears.

As you can see, a horizontal scrollbar now appears, and you can drag it with the mouse to see the hidden part of the button. On the other hand, if you decrease the window's height, you should end up with something similar to what's shown in Figure 5.3.

FIGURE 5.3

By making the window's height too small to show the whole button, you make a vertical scrollbar appear.

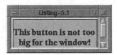

This time, a vertical scrollbar appears. This can be used to see the part of the button that was hidden when you decreased the window's height. Last but not least, you can also decrease both the width and the height of the window. By doing this, you make both the horizontal and the vertical scrollbars appear. This is shown in Figure 5.4.

FIGURE 5.4

If both the width and the height of the window are too small for the button, both the horizontal and vertical scrollbars appear.

What we've just covered here is called scroll-on-demand—that is, scrollbars are not shown if they're not needed. However, you can add scrollbars manually by using the QScrollBar class. (I wouldn't recommend that you do that, though, because it involves unnecessary work—work that's actually done automatically by the QScrollView class.) Therefore, you should just stick with QScrollView, which is easier to implement anyway.

A Real Example

Listing 5.2 shows you an example of when a scrollbar can be useful. This example creates a simple layout with a few buttons and a text area. These widgets are all children to a QWidget object. This QWidget object is added to the scrollview with the QScrollView::addChild() function so that scrollbars will be added to the window when necessary.

LISTING 5.2   A Real Example Using QScrollView

```
 1: #include <qapplication.h>
 2: #include <qpushbutton.h>
 3: #include <qfont.h>
 4: #include <qmultilineedit.h>
 5: #include <qscrollview.h>
 6: #include <qwidget.h>
 7:
 8: //We base our new class on QScrollView
 9: //instead of QWidget:
10: class MyMainWindow : public QScrollView
11: {
12: public:
13:     MyMainWindow();
14: private:
15:     //We create a QWidget object as a child widget
16:     //to the QScrollView object instead:
17:     QWidget *main;
18:     QPushButton *b1;
19:     QPushButton *b2;
20:     QPushButton *b3;
21:     QPushButton *b4;
22:     QPushButton *b5;
23:     QMultiLineEdit *edit1;
24: };
25:
26: MyMainWindow::MyMainWindow()
27: {
28:     //Set the geometry for the scrollview:
29:     setGeometry( 100, 100, 470, 410 );
30:
31:     main = new QWidget( this );
32:     main->resize( 460, 400 );
33:
34:     b1 = new QPushButton( "New", main );
35:     b1->setGeometry( 10, 10, 80, 30 );
36:     b1->setFont( QFont( "Times", 18, QFont::Bold ) );
```

continues

5

LISTING 5.2   continued

```
37:
38:        b2 = new QPushButton( "Open", main );
39:        b2->setGeometry( 100, 10, 80, 30 );
40:        b2->setFont( QFont( "Times", 18, QFont::Bold ) );
41:
42:        b3 = new QPushButton( "Save", main );
43:        b3->setGeometry( 190, 10, 80, 30 );
44:        b3->setFont( QFont( "Times", 18, QFont::Bold ) );
45:
46:        b4 = new QPushButton( "Print", main );
47:        b4->setGeometry( 280, 10, 80, 30 );
48:        b4->setFont( QFont( "Times", 18, QFont::Bold ) );
49:
50:        b5 = new QPushButton( "Quit", main );
51:        b5->setGeometry( 370, 10, 80, 30 );
52:        b5->setFont( QFont( "Times", 18, QFont::Bold ) );
53:
54:        edit1 = new QMultiLineEdit( main );
55:        edit1->setGeometry( 0, 50, 440, 340 );
56:        edit1->setText( "Let's pretend this is a text editor." );
57:
58:        //We must call the QScrollView::addChild function
59:        //for each of its child widgets. Since main holds
60:        //all our other widgets, we only have to insert that
61:        //one:
62:        addChild( main );
63: }
64:
65: void main( int argc, char **argv )
66: {
67:        QApplication a(argc, argv);
68:        MyMainWindow w;
69:        a.setMainWidget( &w );
70:        w.show();
71:        a.exec();
72: }
```

This listing presents a new way of using QWidget: by creating an QWidget object as a
child widget of the class based on QScrollView. In the earlier examples, QWidget has
only been used as a base class, but this example illustrates that it can be used as a child
widget as well. The buttons and the QMultiLineEdit object are then created as child
widgets of the QWidget object, and by doing this you only need to call
QScrollView::addChild() once (to add the QWidget object). If no QWidget object was
used here, you would need to call QScrollView::addChild() for each of the buttons and
the QMultiLineEdit object. Finally, the QWidget object is inserted into the scrollview via
the QScrollView::addChild() function. This program is shown in Figure 5.5.

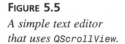

Figure 5.5

A simple text editor that uses `QScrollView`.

Note that no scrollbars are visible at first. However, if you make the window just a little bit smaller, the scrollbars will appear.

The `QMultiLineEdit` class, which is used in this example, has a built-in function for scrollbars. This can save you some work, since you don't have to add scrollbars manually to a `QMultiLineEdit` object. The scrollbars will appear whenever the text shown consists of too many lines or if a line(s) is too long to be fully shown. To see this function in action, click once on the text area and press the Enter button until the vertical scrollbar appears. Then, add text horizontally until the horizontal scrollbar appears. Your window should look similar to the one shown in Figure 5.6.

Figure 5.6

Here you see that `QMultiLineEdit` *also has a scrollbar function. In fact, this program has a total of four scrollbars.*

5

You can certainly see that scrollbars are helpful for creating large applications. What's more, implementing scrollbar functions in your Qt programs isn't hard.

Adding Menus

It's always nice (although not *required*) to have a few pull-down menus at the top of your application. Later in this hour, we'll look at the `QMainWindow` class, which creates the standard menus automatically for you. However, you'll first learn how to create our own, custom menus.

To create pull-down menus, you need to use two Qt classes: `QMenuBar` and `QPopupMenu`. `QPopupMenu` represents the individual menu, and `QMenubar` represents the entire bar of menus. To create a bar with a few menus, you first need to create one or more `QPopupMenu` objects and add entries to them. Then, you need to create one `QMenuBar` object and add the `QPopupMenu` object to it. An example of this can be found in Listing 5.3.

LISTING 5.3 A Simple Menu Example

```
 1: #include <qapplication.h>
 2: #include <qpushbutton.h>
 3: #include <qfont.h>
 4: //We include the header-files we need to
 5: //use the QMenuBar and QPopupMenu classes:
 6: #include <qpopupmenu.h>
 7: #include <qmenubar.h>
 8:
 9: class MyMainWindow : public QWidget
10: {
11: public:
12:     MyMainWindow();
13: private:
14:     //Locate memory for one QPopupMenu and one
15:     //QMenuBar object:
16:     QPopupMenu *file;
17:     QMenuBar *menubar;
18: };
19:
20: MyMainWindow::MyMainWindow()
21: {
22:     setGeometry( 100, 100, 300, 300 );
23:
24:     //Create the popupmenu and add an item to it.
25:     //We also connect the item to the quit() slot
26:     //of qApp. Note that we don't define any parent
27:     //here. That's because we will insert it in the
28:     //QMenuBar object later:
29:     file = new QPopupMenu();
30:     file->insertItem( "Quit", qApp, SLOT( quit() ) );
31:
32:     //Create the menubar and insert the QPopupMenu
```

```
33:     //object in it:
34:     menubar = new QMenuBar( this );
35:     menubar->insertItem( "File", file );
36: }
37:
38: void main( int argc, char **argv )
39: {
40:     QApplication a(argc, argv);
41:     MyMainWindow w;
42:     a.setMainWidget( &w );
43:     w.show();
44:     a.exec();
45: }
```

The menu-creation procedure is very simple. First, you create a QPopupMenu object and insert one item in it (called Quit, in this example). This item is connected to the quit() slot on qApp. Then, a QMenuBar object is created, and a QPopupMenu is inserted into it. The result of this code is a menu bar with a single menu, labeled *File*. The File menu holds one item, called *Quit*. This program is shown in Figure 5.7.

FIGURE 5.7

A window with a menu bar holding a single item.

Of course, to add more items and menus, you follow the same procedure. In Listing 5.4, a few more menus and items are added to the menu bar.

LISTING 5.4   A Menu Bar with More Items Added

```
1: #include <qapplication.h>
2: #include <qpushbutton.h>
3: #include <qfont.h>
4: #include <qpopupmenu.h>
5: #include <qmenubar.h>
6:
```

continues

LISTING 5.4 continued

```
 7: class MyMainWindow : public QWidget
 8: {
 9: public:
10:     MyMainWindow();
11: private:
12:     QPopupMenu *file;
13:     QPopupMenu *menu2;
14:     QPopupMenu *menu3;
15:     QMenuBar *menubar;
16: };
17:
18: MyMainWindow::MyMainWindow()
19: {
20:     setGeometry( 100, 100, 300, 300 );
21:
22:     file = new QPopupMenu();
23:     file->insertItem( "Quit", qApp, SLOT( quit() ) );
24:     file->insertItem( "Open" );
25:     file->insertItem( "Save" );
26:     file->insertItem( "New" );
27:
28:     menu2 = new QPopupMenu();
29:     menu2->insertItem( "Item-2.1" );
30:     menu2->insertItem( "Item-2.2" );
31:     menu2->insertItem( "Item-2.3" );
32:     menu2->insertItem( "Item-2.4" );
33:
34:     menu3 = new QPopupMenu();
35:     menu3->insertItem( "Item-3.1" );
36:     menu3->insertItem( "Item-3.2" );
37:     menu3->insertItem( "Item-3.3" );
38:     menu3->insertItem( "Item-3.4" );
39:
40:     menubar = new QMenuBar( this );
41:     menubar->insertItem( "File", file );
42:     menubar->insertItem( "Menu2", menu2 );
43:     menubar->insertItem( "Menu3", menu3 );
44: }
45:
46: void main( int argc, char **argv )
47: {
48:     QApplication a(argc, argv);
49:     MyMainWindow w;
50:     a.setMainWidget( &w );
51:     w.show();
52:     a.exec();
53: }
```

On lines 22 through 26, the File menu is created and a few entries are added to it. Only one of the entries, Quit, is connected to a slot (qApp->quit()) though. On lines 28 through 38, two more menus are created, and a few entries are added to them. None of these entries is connected to any slot. Then, the actual menu bar is created on line 40, and the three menus are inserted into the menu bar on lines 41, 42, and 43. This program is shown in Figure 5.8.

FIGURE 5.8

Here, a few more items are added to the menu bar. However, they don't have any functionality because they're not connected to any slots.

Now you know how to add menu bars to your applications. Menu bars can add a lot of functionality to your applications and, as you can see, they're certainly not hard to create.

Using The QMainWindow Widget

Through the years of GUI development, programmers have worked out a standard look and feel for graphical applications. This standard mostly applies to Microsoft platforms, but lately it has also been used more and more on UNIX platforms as well. You'll probably want to create applications following this standard to make it easier for users to use your applications. A great help when doing this is the QMainWindow class. It's a class that enables you to add toolbars and menus more easily, and it makes the look and feel of these toolbars and menus more standard. If you want to create standard applications, QMainWindow will save you a lot of work.

Adding Menus, Buttons, and a Central Widget

You'll start by looking at a sample program based on QMainWindow (see Listing 5.5). This program is a virtual text editor. Although it doesn't actually do anything, it looks like a real text editor, with menus, a toolbar, and a large text entry field. This example shows how easily you can create a professional look and feel for your program.

5

LISTING 5.5   A Program Based on `QmainWindow`

```
 1: #include <qapplication.h>
 2: #include <qmainwindow.h>
 3: #include <qpopupmenu.h>
 4: #include <qmenubar.h>
 5: #include <qtoolbar.h>
 6: #include <qtoolbutton.h>
 7: #include <qpixmap.h>
 8: #include <qmultilineedit.h>
 9:
10: //We include a few pixmaps, which
11: //we will use for the buttons on
12: //the toolbar.
13: #include "fileopen.xpm"
14: #include "filesave.xpm"
15: #include "fileprint.xpm"
16:
17: class MyMainWindow : public QMainWindow
18: {
19: public:
20:     MyMainWindow();
21: private:
22:         //We create four menus:
23:     QPopupMenu *file;
24:     QPopupMenu *edit;
25:     QPopupMenu *options;
26:     QPopupMenu *help;
27:         //We create one toolbar
28:         //and three buttons, which
29:         //we will add to the toolbar.
30:     QToolBar *toolbar;
31:     QToolButton *b1, *b2, *b3;
32:         //We create three QPixmap objects,
33:         //one for each .xpm file.
34:     QPixmap openicon, saveicon, printicon;
35:         //At last, we create a QMultiLineEdit
36:         //object. We make this widget the "central
37:         //widget" in the application-
38:     QMultiLineEdit *centralwidget;
39: };
40:
41: MyMainWindow::MyMainWindow()
42: {
43:     setGeometry( 100, 100, 400, 400 );
44:
45:     //Start menu definition:
46:     file = new QPopupMenu( this );
47:     file->insertItem( "New" );
48:     file->insertItem( "Open" );
49:     file->insertItem( "Save" );
```

```
50:        file->insertSeparator();
51:        file->insertItem( "Exit", qApp, SLOT( quit() ) );
52:
53:        edit = new QPopupMenu( this );
54:        edit->insertItem( "Undo" );
55:        edit->insertItem( "Redo" );
56:        edit->insertSeparator();
57:        edit->insertItem( "Cut" );
58:        edit->insertItem( "Copy" );
59:        edit->insertItem( "Paste" );
60:        edit->insertSeparator();
61:        edit->insertItem( "Select All" );
62:
63:        options = new QPopupMenu( this );
64:        options->insertItem( "Preferences" );
65:
66:        help = new QPopupMenu( this );
67:        help->insertItem( "Contents" );
68:        help->insertSeparator();
69:        help->insertItem( "About" );
70:        //End menu definition.
71:
72:        //Start insertion of menus in
73:        //QMainWindow:
74:        menuBar()->insertItem( "File", file );
75:        menuBar()->insertItem( "Edit", edit );
76:        menuBar()->insertItem( "Options", options );
77:        menuBar()->insertItem( "Help", help );
78:
79:        //Define three pixmaps:
80:        openicon = QPixmap( fileopen );
81:        saveicon = QPixmap( filesave );
82:        printicon = QPixmap( fileprint );
83:
84:        //Create a toolbar and add three
85:        //buttons to it. We connect the
86:            //buttons to three slots that not
87:            //exist (but feel free to implement
88:        //them!):
89:        toolbar = new QToolBar( this );
90:        b1 = new QToolButton( openicon, "Open File", "Open File",
91:                    this, SLOT( open() ), toolbar );
92:        b2 = new QToolButton( saveicon, "Save File", "Save File",
93:                    this, SLOT( save() ), toolbar );
94:        b3 = new QToolButton( printicon, "Print File", "Print File",
95:                    this, SLOT( print() ), toolbar );
96:
97:        //Set centralwidget to the
98:        //applications central widget.
```

5

continues

LISTING 5.5   continued

```
 99:     centralwidget = new QMultiLineEdit( this );
100:     setCentralWidget( centralwidget );
101: }
102:
103: void main( int argc, char **argv )
104: {
105:     QApplication a(argc, argv);
106:     MyMainWindow w;
107:     a.setMainWidget( &w );
108:     w.show();
109:     a.exec();
110: }
```

As stated, this program is based on the QMainWindow class. This fact makes the creation of menus and buttons slightly different. For example, you don't need to create any QMenuBar objects; instead, this is taken care of on lines 74 through 77 by the QMainWindow object. On lines 80 through 82, the three QPixmap objects are defined. These pixmaps are then used in the toolbar.

> In Hour 9, "Creating Simple Graphics," you'll learn about another method of using pixmaps. However, including pixmaps as resources (as done in this example) works just fine.

On line 89, the toolbar is created and, on lines 90 through 95, three buttons are created for this toolbar. The arguments given to the QToolButton constructor are described in Table 5.1.

TABLE 5.1   Arguments to the *QToolButton* Constructor

Argument	Description
openicon	The QPixmap object that holds the pixmap to decorate the button with
"Open File"	The text that will appear if you hold the mouse pointer over the button for a few seconds
"Open File"	The text that will appear in the status bar when you hold the mouse pointer over the button (if a status bar exists, that is)
this	The object holding the slot you want this button connected to
SLOT(open())	The actual slot
toolbar	The parent widget

The slots used on lines 90 through 95 are just made up ones. This is why you get error messages when the program starts. These error messages inform you that the defined slots do not exist. The program will work just fine despite this, although nothing will happen when the undefined slots are called.

Line 99 creates the QMultiLineEdit object, and line 100 sets this object to the *central widget*. The central widget, in a QMainWindow-based program, is the widget that all menus, toolbars, and status bars will be added around. The widget you define as your central widget should be the most essential part of your program (as the text area in a text editor). If you were creating a painting program, the central widget would probably be the area where the user should do the drawing. Or, in a Tetris game, the central widget would be the widget where the playing is done (in that case, a widget you've created yourself). This example uses a QMultiLineEdit widget as the central widget, and the program will therefore look just like a text editor. Figure 5.9 shows this program.

FIGURE 5.9

With not very many lines of code, you can create a program with the look and feel of a member of the Microsoft Office suite.

Adding a Status Bar

The status bar is the little bar you usually see at the bottom of many applications. It shows different messages to the user, depending on what the user is currently doing with the application. Adding a status bar to the program in Listing 5.5 is a really simple task. Just add the following line to the class constructor:

```
statusBar();
```

This is a member function of QMainWindow. It creates a simple status bar at the bottom of the window. The program will now look as shown in Figure 5.10.

FIGURE 5.10

Here, a status bar is added the bottom of the window. It's currently showing the status bar message of the Open button.

If you hold the mouse pointer over one of the buttons, a message will appear in the status bar. This message is defined by the third argument you give the QToolButton constructor (in this case, *Open File*). However, you would normally want a more detailed description here, such as *Click This Button to Open a File*.

As stated, the status bar should be used to briefly inform the user about what's going to happen if he performs a certain user event. By displaying a short explanation text in the status bar for each item in the program, you make the program easier to use and understand.

Remember that the status bar also can be used for things other than explanations. For example, you can use the status bar to present the current line number, or the name of the currently open file in a text editor. A status bar improves the functionality of your program. What it can be used for is up to your imagination.

Summary

This hour has brought you a step further along the Qt learning curve. We discussed some of the essential parts of Qt—parts that you'll find very valuable when you're creating easy-to-use GUIs.

You learned how to add scrollbars, menus, toolbars, and status bars. These are items almost everyone wants in an application. All these items improves your program functionality. A scrollbar makes the program easier to use on different desktops and lets the user resize the window so that it suits his screen without missing any part of the program. With menus and toolbars, the features and options of your program can easily be organized, and your program gets easier to understand (and use).

You also looked at the QMainWindow class. QMainWindow is, perhaps, one of Qt's greatest strengths. In fact, QMainWindow should be used in most cases (where the user interface is not too special). By using QMainWindow, setting up a standard GUI gets both faster and easier.

As stated, this hour has covered many of the essential parts of Qt programming. Therefore, to make sure you've understood it all, you should work through the following "Q&A" and "Workshop" sections.

Q&A

Q I'm creating a scrolling window. I've added quite a few objects with the addChild() function. However, the QScrollView class only seems to care about the first object I added. The scrollbars don't appear if the first object isn't affected. What's wrong?

A The easiest thing you can do to solve this is to add your child widgets to a QWidget object and then add the QWidget object as a child widget to QScrollView with the addChild() function. See Listing 5.2 for details on how to do this.

Q I'm creating a menu bar, but the menus I've added don't appear in the window. What's wrong?

A Make sure you add all menus to the QMenuBar object with the QMenuBar::insertItem() function.

Q I'm writing a class based on QMainWindow, but my menus don't appear in the window. What's wrong?

A You must add all menus with the menuBar()->insertItem() function.

Q When I try to compile Listing 5.5, the compiler whines about not finding the pixmap files. What's wrong?

A For this to work, you have to copy the pixmap files fileopen.xpm, filesave.xpm, and fileprint.xpm to the directory you're trying to compile the program from. These files can be found in the examples/application directory of your Qt installation.

5

Workshop

You're encouraged to work through the following questions and exercises to help you retain what you've learned in this hour. Working through these questions will help you understand how the essential Qt classes covered in the hour work.

Quiz

1. What can the `QScrollView` class be used for?
2. Which member function is used to add objects to the `QScrollView` class?
3. What does *scroll-on-demand* mean?
4. What are `QMenuBar` and `QPopupMenu`?
5. When do you need to call the `QMenuBar::insertItem()` function?
6. What are `QToolBar` and `QToolButton`?
7. What is the `QMainWindow` class good for?
8. What is the central widget in a `QMainWindow` object?
9. Do you need to call any special functions to add a toolbar to a `QMainWindow`-based class?
10. What is `QPixmap`?

Exercises

1. Write a program based on `QScrollView`. Create a `QWidget` object and add a few widgets to it (feel free to check the Qt Reference Documentation for some cool widgets you haven't learned about yet). Then, add the `QWidget` object to `QScrollView`.

2. Add a few menus to the result of Exercise 1. Make sure you make the menus child widgets of the `QWidget` object.

3. Start a popular text editor such as `kedit` or Notepad. Try to copy the look of the text editor by writing a program based on `QMainWindow`. Try to make your menus, toolbars, and status bars look as similar as possible to those found in the real text editor. (You might need to check the Qt Reference Documentation.)

PART II
Important Qt Issues

Hour

Hour **6**

Getting to Know the Qt Widgets: Lesson One

In this hour, you'll take an in-depth look at some of the Qt widgets. Specifically, you'll learn the use of buttons, labels, and tables.

Both buttons and labels are used very often in GUI applications. Therefore, you have to know how to use them to create even the simplest programs. Both buttons and labels have a given place in all modern GUI libraries—this is also true in Qt.

Tables, on the other hand, aren't as commonly used in GUI applications, but they can be very functional (if used correctly). Therefore, you should use tables whenever you feel they're needed in your applications. You'll learn more about tables at the end of this hour.

Using Buttons

Buttons are probably the most commonly used GUI object. Qt provides three types of buttons:

- Push buttons
- Radio buttons
- Check buttons

Push buttons are used to make certain events occur, whereas radio and check buttons are used to make some kind of selection.

Push Buttons

The QPushButton class is probably the Qt class you'll use the most when creating Qt applications. You've already created a few push buttons in the earlier hours of this book. However, you'll now take a closer look on how the QPushButton class actually works and which member functions can be useful to you.

As stated, push buttons are created by the QPushButton class. Listing 6.1 shows a simple example.

LISTING 6.1 A QPushButton Example

```
1: #include <qapplication.h>
2: #include <qwidget.h>
3: #include <qpushbutton.h>
4:
5: class MyMainWindow : public QWidget
6: {
7: public:
8:         MyMainWindow();
9: private:
10:        QPushButton *b1;
11: };
12:
13: MyMainWindow::MyMainWindow()
14: {
15:        setGeometry( 100, 100, 200, 100 );
16:        b1 = new QPushButton( "This is a push button!", this );
17:        b1->setGeometry( 10, 10, 180, 80 );
18:        b1->setFont( QFont( "Times", 16, QFont::Bold ) );
19: }
20:
21: void main( int argc, char **argv )
22: {
```

```
23:          QApplication a(argc, argv);
24:          MyMainWindow w;
25:          a.setMainWidget( &w );
26:          w.show();
27:          a.exec();
28: }
```

On line 10, memory is allocated for a QPushButton object. On line 16, the putton is created (that is, one of the QPushButton constructors is executed). Here, the label (first argument) and the parent (second argument) are set for the button. On line 17, exact
placement and size are set for the button. In this case, the button's top left corner is
placed 10 pixels down and 10 pixels left relative to the top-left corner of the button's parent (the actual window). On line 18, the size and style of the label on the button are set,
as discussed earlier. The push button created in Listing 6.1 is shown in Figure 6.1.

FIGURE 6.1

*The push button from
Listing 6.1.*

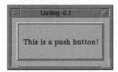

When you want to connect a push button to a certain event, you connect the
QPushButton::clicked() signal to a slot. You can also use the
QPushButton::setPixmap() function to add a pixmap to a button, as follows:

```
QPixmap pixmap( "somepixmap.xpm" );
b1->setPixmap( pixmap );
```

where somepixmap.xpm is the pixmap of your choice. Figure 6.2 shows how a button
with a pixmap can look.

FIGURE 6.2

*A push button with a
pixmap on it.*

6

When working with push buttons, you'll probably also need to use the
QPushButton::setDefault() function. This function is useful if you have multiple buttons in one window. The button that you use setDefault() on will become the default
button—that is, the button that will be clicked when the user presses Enter.

Radio Buttons

Radio buttons should be used when you want the user to make one (and only one) selection out of several choices. You can use the QButtonGroup and QRadioButton classes to create a group of radio buttons, as shown in Listing 6.2.

LISTING 6.2   A QRadioButton Example

```
 1: #include <qapplication.h>
 2: #include <qwidget.h>
 3: #include <qbuttongroup.h>
 4: #include <qradiobutton.h>
 5:
 6: class MyMainWindow : public QWidget
 7: {
 8: public:
 9:     MyMainWindow();
10: private:
11:     QButtonGroup *group;
12:     QRadioButton *b1;
13:     QRadioButton *b2;
14:     QRadioButton *b3;
15: };
16:
17: MyMainWindow::MyMainWindow()
18: {
19:     setGeometry( 100, 100, 150, 140 );
20:
21:     group = new QButtonGroup( "Options", this );
22:     group->setGeometry( 10, 10, 130, 120 );
23:
24:     b1 = new QRadioButton( "Choice 1", group );
25:     b1->move( 20, 20 );
26:     b2 = new QRadioButton( "Choice 2", group );
27:     b2->move( 20, 50 );
28:     b3 = new QRadioButton( "Choice 3", group );
29:     b3->move( 20, 80 );
30:
31:     group->insert( b1 );
32:     group->insert( b2 );
33:     group->insert( b3 );
34: }
35:
36: void main( int argc, char **argv )
37: {
38:     QApplication a(argc, argv);
39:     MyMainWindow w;
40:     a.setMainWidget( &w );
```

```
41:     w.show();
42:     a.exec();
43: }
```

On lines 11 through 14, memory is allocated for one QButtonGroup object and three QRadioButton objects. The QRadioGroup object is then set up on lines 21 and 22. The first argument given to the QRadioGroup constructor (line 21) represents the header for this button group (see Figure 6.3). On line 22, the geometry for this button group is set as usual with the setGeometry() function. Then, the three radio buttons are created and set up on lines 24 through 29. Note that the radio group is used as the parent for these buttons. Also note that the QRadioButton::move() function is used to set the position for these buttons. Although the setGeometry() function could have been used, this is not advisable, since you don't know what height and width these buttons need to have. Finally, the buttons are inserted to the buttons group with the QButtonGroup::insert() function (lines 31, 32, and 33). Figure 6.3 shows the result of Listing 6.2.

FIGURE 6.3

An example of a QButtonGroup object holding three QRadioButton objects.

Note that you can only have one radio button pressed (checked) at a time. This is what makes radio buttons different from check buttons.

The QRadioButton::isChecked() signal is emitted whenever the button is checked (clicked). However, unlike push buttons, radio buttons are usually not used to make a program do something visually but rather are used to make some kind of selection. For example, you could use a few radio buttons to let a user choose the language in a spell checker. Then, the slot connected to the QRadioButton::isChecked() signal wouldn't cause any visual change to the program but instead would make a call to a function that sets the language to the newly selected one.

Check Buttons

Check buttons should be used when you want the user to be able to choose more than one selection out of multiple choices. You can create a group of check buttons using the QButtonGroup and QCheckBox classes, as shown in Listing 6.3.

6

LISTING 6.3   A `QCheckBox` Example

```
 1: #include <qapplication.h>
 2: #include <qwidget.h>
 3: #include <qbuttongroup.h>
 4: #include <qcheckbox.h>
 5:
 6: class MyMainWindow : public QWidget
 7: {
 8: public:
 9:     MyMainWindow();
10: private:
11:     QButtonGroup *group;
12:     QCheckBox *b1;
13:     QCheckBox *b2;
14:     QCheckBox *b3;
15: };
16:
17: MyMainWindow::MyMainWindow()
18: {
19:     setGeometry( 100, 100, 150, 140 );
20:
21:     group = new QButtonGroup( "Options", this );
22:     group->setGeometry( 10, 10, 130, 120 );
23:
24:     b1 = new QCheckBox( "Choice 1", group );
25:     b1->move( 20, 20 );
26:     b2 = new QCheckBox( "Choice 2", group );
27:     b2->move( 20, 50 );
28:     b3 = new QCheckBox( "Choice 3", group );
29:     b3->move( 20, 80 );
30:
31:     group->insert( b1 );
32:     group->insert( b2 );
33:     group->insert( b3 );
34: }
35:
36: void main( int argc, char **argv )
37: {
38:     QApplication a(argc, argv);
39:     MyMainWindow w;
40:     a.setMainWidget( &w );
41:     w.show();
42:     a.exec();
43: }
```

Here, memory is allocated for the button group and the check buttons on lines 11
through 14. The button group is set up on lines 21 and 22, and the check buttons in lines

24 through 29. And, as with the radio button example, the check buttons are inserted into the button group with the QButtonGroup::insert() function (lines 31, 32, and 33). Figure 6.4 shows the result of Listing 6.3.

FIGURE 6.4

An example of a QButtonGroup *object holding three* QCheckBox *objects.*

Just as with radio buttons, you check whether a QCheckBox object is pressed through the isChecked() signal (QCheckBox::isChecked()). As stated previously, check buttons let the user select more than one choice. Therefore, you wouldn't use check buttons in the spell checker scenario described for the radio buttons in the previous section. If you did, the user would be able to select English, French, and German at the same time, and your spell checker would get very confused!

A more realistic example of when check buttons can be useful is when you want the user to select the style of text in a word editor. In this case, it's fully possible to have the bold, italic, and underline attributes selected. If however, you used radio buttons in this case, users would only be able to use one formatting method at a time, and that's not desirable.

Using buttons is straightforward, and you've now learned about the three types of buttons Qt provides. Remember to check the Qt Reference Documentation if you need more information.

Creating Labels

Every now and then, you need to add text to your application in the form of a *label*. Labels are usually used to present brief information or instructions about the widgets in a program. For example, you could use a label to define what should be entered in a text box. In Qt, you implement labels by using the QLabel class and, occasionally, the QLCDNumber class.

6

QLabel

The QLabel class is used for displaying simple text. It's a very basic yet very useful widget. Listing 6.4 shows a simple example.

LISTING 6.4   A QLabel Example

```
 1: #include <qapplication.h>
 2: #include <qlabel.h>
 3:
 4: class MyMainWindow : public QWidget
 5: {
 6: public:
 7:     MyMainWindow();
 8: private:
 9:     QLabel *text;
10: };
11:
12: MyMainWindow::MyMainWindow()
13: {
14:     setGeometry( 100, 100, 170, 100 );
15:
16:     text = new QLabel( this );
17:     text->setGeometry( 10, 10, 150, 80 );
18:     text->setText( "This is a \nQLabel object." );
19:     text->setAlignment( AlignHCenter | AlignVCenter );
20: }
21:
22: void main( int argc, char **argv )
23: {
24:     QApplication a(argc, argv);
25:     MyMainWindow w;
26:     a.setMainWidget( &w );
27:     w.show();
28:     a.exec();
29: }
```

Figure 6.5 shows the program created in Listing 6.4.

FIGURE 6.5

A window with a simple QLabel object.

Notice how the text alignment is set on line 19. This is the standard way of setting alignments in Qt. AlignHCenter and AlignVCenter are Qt definitions. See Table 6.1 for a description of all the definitions for alignment settings.

TABLE 6.1 Definitions for Alignment Settings

Function	Description
AlignTop	Text will be added to the top of the QLabel object.
AlignBottom	Text will be added to the bottom of the QLabel object.
AlignLeft	Text will be added along the left side of the QLabel object.
AlignRight	Text will be added along the right side of the QLabel object.
AlignHCenter	Text will be added at the horizontal center of the QLabel object.
AlignVCenter	Text will be added at the vertical center of the QLabel object.
AlignCenter	This is the same as setting both AlignHCenter and AlignVCenter.
WordBreak	If this function is set, automatic word breaking is used.
ExpandTabs	This function makes QLabel expand the tabulators.

Notice how the arguments to QLabel::setAlignment() are separated by the "or" (|) operator. This method is also used when you want to add more arguments; just separate them with | operators.

> You can also use QLabel to show pixmaps and animation. This is done with the QLabel::setPixmap() and QLabel::setMovie() functions.

QLCDNumber

If you want to show numeric information in your program, the QLCDNumber class is the right choice for you. As QLabel, QLCDNumber is often used to present short information to the user (numeric information, in this case), like the current date. Listing 6.5 shows an example of a program using a QLCDNumber object.

LISTING 6.5 A QLCDNumber Example

6

```
1: #include <qapplication.h>
2: #include <qlcdnumber.h>
3:
4: class MyMainWindow : public QWidget
5: {
6: public:
7:         MyMainWindow();
8: private:
9:         QLCDNumber *number;
```

continues

LISTING 6.5 continued

```
10: };
11:
12: MyMainWindow::MyMainWindow()
13: {
14:         setGeometry( 100, 100, 170, 100 );
15:         number = new QLCDNumber( this );
16:         number->setGeometry( 10, 10, 150, 80 );
17:         number->display( 12345 );
18: }
19:
20: void main( int argc, char **argv )
21: {
22:         QApplication a(argc, argv);
23:         MyMainWindow w;
24:         a.setMainWidget( &w );
25:         w.show();
26:         a.exec();
27: }
```

To begin with, memory is allocated for a QLCDNumber object on line 9. This object is then created on line 15, and the geometry for it is set on line 16.

Then, QLCDNumber::display() is used to set the number to be displayed (line 17). Figure 6.6 shows the result of Listing 6.6.

FIGURE 6.6

A window with a QLCDNumber object.

Other functions you'll find useful when working with QLCDNumber are described in Table 6.2.

TABLE 6.2   Interesting *QLCDNumber* Member Functions

Function	Description
setNumDigits()	Sets the number of digits to be shown.
setBinMode()	Sets the display to binary representation.
setOctMode()	Sets the display to octal representation.
setHexMode()	Sets the display to hexadecimal representation.

Function	Description
setDecMode()	Sets the display to decimal representation (default).
setSmallDecimalPoint()	By passing one of the arguments (TRUE or FALSE) to this function, you can determine whether a possible decimal point will be shown in a position of its own or between two digits. In other words, of you pass TRUE to this function, the decimal point will take up less space than usual.
setSegmentStyle()	With this function, you can change the appearance of the displayed digits. Pass one of the arguments (Outline, Filled, or Flat) to it.
checkOverFlow()	You call this function to check whether a given value will fit in the display. (QLCDNumber also emits a signal, overflow(), which you can connect to a slot that handles the situation appropriately.)

Keep in mind that QLCDNumber is often used along with a QSlider object. See Listing 4.1 from Hour 4, "Making Things Happen: Slots and Signals," for an example of this.

Working with Tables

The QTableView class is provided for creating tables in Qt. It's a useful class, but it's also quite abstract in its definitions. Therefore, you need to derive a new class based on QTableView to make something useful out of it.

Creating a Simple Grid

When creating a class based on QTableView, you need to implement the function paintCell(). This function is not defined in the class; instead, it's used by the class to draw the cells. Therefore, you need to implement a function by this name and let it handle the cell drawing. This may sound hard to you, but that's not the case at all. See Listing 6.6 for a simple example of how to create a grid with QTableView.

When you implement the paintCell() function, you have to use some painting functions from the QPainter class. This class and its methods are covered in detail in Hour 9, "Creating Simple Graphics," and Hour 15, "Learning More About Graphics."

6

LISTING 6.6   A Simple Grid Created with `QTableView`

```
 1: #include <qapplication.h>
 2: #include <qwidget.h>
 3: #include <qtableview.h>
 4: #include <qpainter.h>
 5:
 6: class MyMainWindow : public QTableView
 7: {
 8: public:
 9:     MyMainWindow();
10: private:
11:     void paintCell( QPainter *, int, int );
12: };
13:
14: MyMainWindow::MyMainWindow()
15: {
16:     setGeometry( 100, 100, 300, 300 );
17:
18:     //Set the number of columns:
19:     setNumCols( 6 );
20:     //Set the number of rows:
21:     setNumRows( 10 );
22:     //Set the width of the cells:
23:     setCellWidth( 50 );
24:     //Set the height of the cells:
25:     setCellHeight( 30 );
26: }
27:
28: //Here is the simple implementation of paintCell():
29: void MyMainWindow::paintCell( QPainter* p, int row, int col )
30: {
31:     //Find out height and width of the cells:
32:     int x = cellWidth( col ) ;
33:     int y = cellHeight( row );
34:
35:     //Two lines are enough for creating a cell:
36:     p->drawLine( x, 0, x, y );
37:     p->drawLine( 0, y, x, y );
38: }
39:
40: void main( int argc, char **argv )
41: {
42:     QApplication a(argc, argv);
43:     MyMainWindow w;
44:     a.setMainWidget( &w );
45:     w.show();
46:     a.exec();
47: }
```

This example draws a simple grid with six columns (line 19) and ten rows (line 21). The cells all have the same size: 50 pixels wide (line 23) and 30 pixels high (line 25).

One line 29, the definition of the paintCell() function starts. As you can see, this is a very simple version of the function, consisting of just four lines of code in all. Lines 32 and 33 call the cellWidth() and cellHeight() functions to find out the width and height, respectively, of the current cell (the cell that's about to be painted). Lines 36 and 37 do the actual painting. Note that only the bottom horizontal line and the right vertical line are painted.

> When looking at lines 36 and 37, you might think that the lines are painted at the same position all the time. However, this is not the case—it's taken care of by QTableView. You see, QTableView sets the drawing area of QPainter each time, so (0,0) is the corner of each cell.

Figure 6.7 shows the result of Listing 6.6.

FIGURE 6.7

A simple program based on QTableView.

Adding Text and a Click-to-Select Function

Although a nice grid is created in Listing 6.6, it's not useful yet. You'll most likely want to add some kind of text information to the cells. Text, along with a click-to-select feature, is included in Listing 6.7.

LISTING 6.7   A Table with Text and a Click-to-Select Feature

```
1: #include <qapplication.h>
2: #include <qwidget.h>
3: #include <qtableview.h>
```

6

continues

LISTING 6.7 continued

```
 4: #include <qpainter.h>
 5:
 6: class MyMainWindow : public QTableView
 7: {
 8: public:
 9:     MyMainWindow();
10: private:
11:     void paintCell( QPainter *, int, int );
12:     void mousePressEvent( QMouseEvent * );
13:     int curRow, curCol;
14: };
15:
16: MyMainWindow::MyMainWindow()
17: {
18:     setGeometry( 100, 100, 300, 300 );
19:
20:     setNumCols( 12 );
21:     setNumRows( 20 );
22:     setCellWidth( 80 );
23:     setCellHeight( 30 );
24:
25:     //The following function call makes
26:     //both horizontal and vertical scrollbars
27:     //appear:
28:     setTableFlags(     Tbl_vScrollBar |
29:                        Tbl_hScrollBar );
30:     //This line sets changes the colors
31:     //of the cells:
32:     setBackgroundMode( PaletteBase );
33:
34:     curRow = curCol = 0;
35: }
36:
37: void MyMainWindow::paintCell( QPainter* p, int row, int col )
38: {
39:     int x = (cellWidth( col ) - 1);
40:     int y = (cellHeight( row ) - 1);
41:
42:     p->drawLine( x, 0, x, y );
43:     p->drawLine( 0, y, x, y );
44:
45:     //Add the text "Some Text" to the center of all cells:
46:     p->drawText( 0, 0, (x+1), (y+1), AlignCenter, "Some text" );
47:
48:     //If this is the current cell, draw an
49:     //extra frame around it:
50:     if( (row == curRow) && (col == curCol) )
51:     {
52:         //If we have focus, draw a solid
```

```
53:            //rectangle around the current cell:
54:            if( hasFocus() )
55:            {
56:                p->drawRect( 0, 0, x, y );
57:            }
58:            //If we don't have focus, draw dashed
59:            //rectangle instead.
60:            else
61:            {
62:                p->setPen( DotLine );
63:                p->drawRect( 0, 0, x, y );
64:                p->setPen( SolidLine );
65:            }
66:        }
67: }
68:
69: //This function takes care of your mouse clicks:
70: void MyMainWindow::mousePressEvent( QMouseEvent *e )
71: {
72:        int oldRow = curRow;
73:        int oldCol = curCol;
74:
75:        QPoint clickedPos = e->pos();
76:
77:        //Find out which cell were clicked:
78:        curRow = findRow( clickedPos.y() );
79:        curCol = findCol( clickedPos.x() );
80:
81:        //If it wasn't the current cell, update both
82:        //the current cell and the old cell:
83:        if( (curRow != oldRow) || (curCol != oldCol) )
84:        {
85:            updateCell( oldRow, oldCol );
86:            updateCell( curRow, curCol );
87:        }
88: }
89:
90: void main( int argc, char **argv )
91: {
92:        QApplication a(argc, argv);
93:        MyMainWindow w;
94:        a.setMainWidget( &w );
95:        w.show();
96:        a.exec();
97: }
```

6

In this example, scrollbars are added to the table via a call to the `setTableFlags()` function, and the appropriate arguments are added to it (lines 28 and 29). The color of the cells is changed at line 32.

A few nice features of the `paintCell()` function have also been added. To begin with, a simple text label is added to all cells at line 46. Of course, you probably wouldn't want to add the exact same text to 240 cells, as is done in this example! However, the method is always the same. The `paintCell()` function now also checks whether the cell it's about to paint is the currently selected cell. If the program has focus (that is, it's your currently selected application) and the currently painted cell is the selected one, an extra rectangle will be drawn around it. If the program doesn't have focus, this rectangle will be dashed. Figure 6.8 shows this program in action.

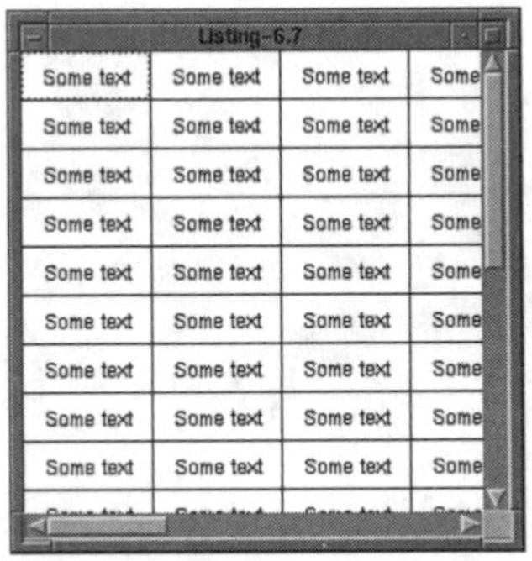

FIGURE 6.8

A table with text in its cells. The upper-left cell is currently selected.

Adding a Header

You'll probably want to add some kind of headers to your tables' rows and columns. This is done via the `QHeader` class. You'll find an example in Listing 6.8.

LISTING 6.8 A Table with a Horizontal Header

```
 1: #include <qapplication.h>
 2: #include <qwidget.h>
 3: #include <qtableview.h>
 4: #include <qpainter.h>
 5: #include <qheader.h>
 6: #include <qlabel.h>
 7:
 8: class MyTable : public QTableView
 9: {
10: public:
11:     MyTable( QWidget *parent = 0 );
12: private:
13:     void paintCell( QPainter *, int, int );
14: };
15:
16: MyTable::MyTable( QWidget *parent ) : QTableView( parent )
```

```
17: {
18:     setNumCols( 5 );
19:     setNumRows( 5 );
20:     setCellWidth( 100 );
21:     setCellHeight( 30 );
22:     setBackgroundMode( PaletteBase );
23: }
24:
25: void MyTable::paintCell( QPainter* p, int row, int col )
26: {
27:     int x = (cellWidth( col ) - 1);
28:     int y = (cellHeight( row ) - 1);
29:
30:     p->drawLine( x, 0, x, y );
31:     p->drawLine( 0, y, x, y );
32:
33:     if( col == 0 )
34:     {
35:         p->drawText( 0, 0, (x+1), (y+1), AlignCenter, "Name" );
36:     }
37:     if( col == 1 )
38:     {
39:         p->drawText( 0, 0, (x+1), (y+1), AlignCenter, "Address" );
40:     }
41:     if( col == 2 )
42:     {
43:         p->drawText( 0, 0, (x+1), (y+1), AlignCenter, "City" );
44:     }
45:     if( col == 3 )
46:     {
47:         p->drawText( 0, 0, (x+1), (y+1), AlignCenter, "Gender" );
48:     }
49:     if( col == 4 )
50:     {
51:         p->drawText( 0, 0, (x+1), (y+1), AlignCenter, "Tel." );
52:     }
53: }
54:
55: class MyMainWindow : public QWidget
56: {
57: public:
58:     MyMainWindow();
59: private:
60:     MyTable *table;
61:     QHeader *header;
62:     QLabel *label;
63: };
64:
```

6

continues

LISTING 6.8 continued

```
65: MyMainWindow::MyMainWindow()
66: {
67:     resize( 500, 250 );
68:
69:     table = new MyTable( this );
70:     table->setGeometry( 0, 100, 500, 150 );
71:
72:     header = new QHeader( this );
73:     header->setGeometry( 0, 70, 500, 30 );
74:     header->setOrientation( Horizontal );
75:     header->addLabel( "Name", 100 );
76:     header->addLabel( "Address", 100 );
77:     header->addLabel( "City", 100 );
78:     header->addLabel( "Gender", 100 );
79:     header->addLabel( "Tel.", 100 );
80:
81:     label = new QLabel( this );
82:     label->setGeometry( 0, 0, 500, 70 );
83:     label->setAlignment( AlignCenter );
84:     label->setText( "Let's pretend this is a real
85:             program that needs to present
86:             personal information in a table." );
87: }
88:
89: void main( int argc, char **argv )
90: {
91:     QApplication a(argc, argv);
92:     MyMainWindow w;
93:     a.setMainWidget( &w );
94:     w.show();
95:     a.exec();
96: }
```

In this example, the MyMainWindow class from Listing 6.7 is renamed as MyTable. This creates a second class in which an object of the MyTable class, called MyMainWindow, is created.

This is the first time you've seen a new class created that wasn't made the main widget. Note that a few things have been added to the MyTable constructor at lines 11 and 16. At line 11, the constructor is defined to take a pointer to a QWidget object as an argument. This argument will represent the parent widget. However, code doesn't need to be written to handle this argument. Instead, it's passed on to the QTableView constructor (line 16).

Now, the `MyTable` constructor is given the `this` pointer as an argument (line 69). This makes the uncreated `MyMainWindow` object the parent widget.

The header is created in lines 72 through 79. This part of the code speaks for itself. Figure 6.9 shows this program.

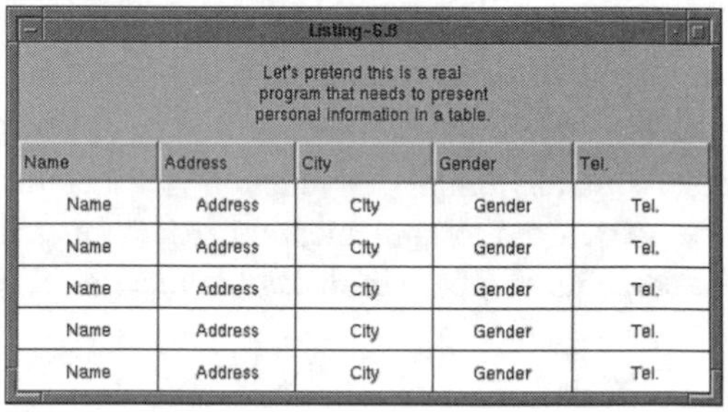

FIGURE 6.9

A table with a horizontal header.

Summary

In this hour, you've learned how to work with buttons, including push buttons, radio buttons, and check buttons. A button is likely to be the widget you use most often in your programs; therefore, the section on buttons is an important one. When you think about, a GUI program wouldn't be much if it didn't have any buttons.

Next, you learned how to implement text and numerical labels. You also learned that, by far, the most used class for labels is `QLabel`. However, you also looked at the `QLCDNumber` class, which you can use to present numerical information. Labels, like buttons, are basic to all GUI libraries.

Finally, you learned how to work with tables. You should make it a point to expand upon what you learned in this hour to see how you can implement tables with Qt. This hour has only presented the basics. Remember, `QTableView` requires you to do a lot of the work yourself. As stated, it's quite an abstract class and therefore needs some work to make it useful. However, this is good because it lets you decide exactly what should be done and which features should be included.

Q&A

Q The label I add to my radio or check button is not visible or only partly visible. What's wrong?

A Make sure there's enough room for the label. Maybe the text is behind some other widget.

Q How come when I'm using a `QLabel` object to show some text, my other widgets (or some of them) disappear?

A A `QLabel` object is a rectangular object (although you can't always see that). It needs room for the entire rectangle, not just the text. Therefore, if you have a `QLabel` object that's 400 pixels wide, but the text in the middle of that object is just 50 pixels, the object will still cover 400 pixels.

Q I don't see how the click-to-select function in Listing 6.7 would be useful at this point. Am I missing something?

A No, you're not missing anything. This function was included just to show you how a feature is added. You need to implement other features (such as one that lets the user change the contents of a cell) to make this function useful.

Workshop

You're encouraged to work through the following questions and exercises to help you retain what you've learned in this hour.

Quiz

1. What are the different types of buttons used for?
2. What signal should be used to check whether a `QPushButton` object is clicked?
3. Which class should be used for arranging buttons?
4. Which function sets the alignment of the text in a `QLabel` object?
5. How do you change the size, font, and style of the text in a `QLabel` object?
6. When creating a subclass based on `QTableView`, which function do you need to implement other that the constructor?
7. Why do you need to implement this function?
8. Which class should be used to create a table header?

Exercises

1. Create a program with three push buttons and three check buttons. Make it possible to control whether the check buttons are checked with the push buttons.
2. Write a program with one signal widget—a `QLabel` object. Add the text *I Think Qt Is A Good, Fast, Professional, And Nice GUI Library* (or whatever you like) to it. Change the alignment to horizontal center and vertical bottom. Make the text size 14 points. Also, use the Times font and make the text italic.

3. Make a table that can be used to show information about computers. Add columns for processor type, processor speed, and amount of RAM. Add headers to the columns and then add a few entries to the table.

6

HOUR 7

Getting to Know the Qt Widgets: Lesson Two

In this hour, you'll continue your Qt widget walkthrough. You'll look at widgets used for making selections, widgets used to arrange other widgets, and widgets used to let the user select a numerical value.

This hour does not present anything revolutionary for GUI development, but it does cover some very useful aspects of Qt that any Qt programmer should understand thoroughly.

Using Selection Widgets

Selection widgets let the user make a selection from a predefined menu of items. This includes list boxes and combo boxes. An example of a selection widget is the font selector in Microsoft Word (a combo box). In Qt, the `QListBox` class is used for list boxes and `QComboBox` for combo boxes.

Working with List Boxes

The QListBox list box widget is generally used to let the user select one or more items from a list. This is usually a text item but can also be a pixmap. You'll find an example in Listing 7.1.

INPUT **LISTING 7.1** A QListBox Example

```
 1: #include <qapplication.h>
 2: #include <qwidget.h>
 3: #include <qlistbox.h>
 4:
 5: class MyMainWindow : public QWidget
 6: {
 7: public:
 8:         MyMainWindow();
 9: private:
10:         QListBox *listbox;
11: };
12:
13: MyMainWindow::MyMainWindow()
14: {
15:         setGeometry( 100, 100, 170, 100 );
16:         listbox = new QListBox( this );
17:         listbox->setGeometry( 10, 10, 150, 80 );
18:
19:         //Start the insertion of items:
20:         listbox->insertItem( "Item 1" );
21:         listbox->insertItem( "Item 2" );
22:         listbox->insertItem( "Item 3" ),
23:         listbox->insertItem( "Item 4" );
24:         listbox->insertItem( "Item 5" );
25:         listbox->insertItem( "Item 6" );
26: }
27:
28: void main( int argc, char **argv )
29: {
30:         QApplication a(argc, argv);
31:         MyMainWindow w;
32:         a.setMainWidget( &w );
33:         w.show();
34:         a.exec();
35: }
```

Here, memory is allocated for the list box widget on line 10. The list box is then created on lines 16 and its geometry is set on line 17. In lines 20 through 25, size items are inserted into the list box using the QListBox::insertItem() function. The argument given to this function represents, as you might have guessed, the label of the list box item. Figure 7.1 shows the result of Listing 7.1.

Note that it's also possible to pass a QPixmap object to the insertItem() function, as shown in Figure 7.2.

When you're ready to start working with a QListBox object, use QListBox::currentItem() to retrieve the position that's currently selected. You can then pass this position number to QListBox::text() or QListBox::pixmap() to get the actual text or pixmap of the currently selected item.

Working with Combo Boxes

If you don't have enough space in your window for a QListBox object, it's a good idea to use a QComboBox object instead. A QComboBox object is quite similar to QListBox in the way it works. Listing 7.2 provides an example.

INPUT   **LISTING 7.2**   A QComboBox Example

```
 1: #include <qapplication.h>
 2: #include <qwidget.h>
 3: #include <qcombobox.h>
 4:
 5: class MyMainWindow : public QWidget
 6: {
 7: public:
 8:         MyMainWindow();
 9: private:
10:         QComboBox *combobox;
11: };
12:
13: MyMainWindow::MyMainWindow()
14: {
15:         setGeometry( 100, 100, 150, 50 );
16:         combobox = new QComboBox( false, this );
17:         combobox->setGeometry( 10, 10, 130, 30 );
```

7

continues

LISTING 7.2   continued

```
18:          //Start the insertion of items:
19:          combobox->insertItem( "Item 1" );
20:          combobox->insertItem( "Item 2" );
21:          combobox->insertItem( "Item 3" ),
22:          combobox->insertItem( "Item 4" );
23:          combobox->insertItem( "Item 5" );
24:          combobox->insertItem( "Item 6" );
25: }
26:
27: void main( int argc, char **argv )
28: {
29:          QApplication a(argc, argv);
30:          MyMainWindow w;
31:          a.setMainWidget( &w );
32:          w.show();
33:          a.exec();
34: }
```

First, memory is allocated for the QComboBox object on line 10. The QComboBox constructor is then executed on line 16. The first argument given the QComboBox constructor determines whether this combo box should be read-write or read-only. If this is set to false, the combo box will be read-only. If it's set to true, the combo box will become read-write (that is, the user will be able to insert items dynamically at runtime). The second argument represents, as usual, the parent of this widget. On line 17, the geometry is set for the combo box. And finally, six items are inserted into the combo box on lines 19 through 24. This is done exactly as with a spin box. Figure 7.3 shows the result of Listing 7.2.

FIGURE 7.3

A QComboBox object with Item 4 currently selected.

You can insert pixmaps to a QComboBox object with the insert() function. However, you can't use pixmaps as items in read-write combo boxes because it's not possible for the user to edit the pixmaps.

Working with Arrangers

If you arrange the widgets in your programs wisely, your programs will look better and will be easier to use. Qt provides a few classes that make arranging widgets easier:

- QGroupBox
- QButtonGroup
- QSplitter
- QWidgetStack

These classes will be covered, one by one, in this section.

 QFrame can also be used to arrange widgets, but it's really more of a base class for creating custom widgets.

Using the QGroupBox Class

QGroupBox is used to draw a frame around widgets. Also, you can add some kind of description at the top of the frame. Listing 7.3 provides an example.

INPUT   **LISTING 7.3**   A QGroupBox Example

```
1: #include <qapplication.h>
2: #include <qwidget.h>
3: #include <qgroupbox.h>
4: #include <qlabel.h>
5:
6: class MyMainWindow : public QWidget
7: {
8: public:
9:         MyMainWindow();
10: private:
11:         QGroupBox *groupbox;
12:         QLabel *label;
13: };
14:
15: MyMainWindow::MyMainWindow()
16: {
17:         setGeometry( 100, 100, 150, 100 );
18:
19:         groupbox = new QGroupBox( this );
20:         groupbox->setGeometry( 10, 10, 130, 80 );
21:         groupbox->setTitle( "A Group Box" );
22:
23:         label = new QLabel( this );
24:         label->setGeometry( 30, 35, 90, 40 );
25:         label->setText( "Add widgets\n here!" );
26:         label->setAlignment( AlignHCenter | AlignVCenter );
```

7

continues

LISTING 7.3   continued

```
27: }
28:
29: void main( int argc, char **argv )
30: {
31:         QApplication a(argc, argv);
32:         MyMainWindow w;
33:         a.setMainWidget( &w );
34:         w.show();
35:         a.exec();
36: }
```

Here, memory is allocated for the QGroupBox object on line 11. The group box is then created and placed on lines 19 and 20. The only thing new to you here is the QGroupBox::setTitle() function (line 21). As you may have guessed, it sets the title of the group box, as shown in Figure 7.4.

FIGURE 7.4

A window QGroupBox object and a QLabel object.

Using the QButtonGroup Class

QButtonGroup is quite similar to QGroupBox. However, it has some special features for arranging buttons. The most common use of QButtonGroup is for arranging radio buttons. Arranging a set of radio buttons in a QButtonGroup ensures that the user can only check (click) one radio button at a time (also known as *making them exclusive*). See Listing 6.2 from Hour 6, "Getting to Know the Qt Widgets: Lesson One," for an example of this.

Although radio buttons are exclusive automatically when you insert them into a QButtonGroup object, you have to make a call to QButtonGroup::setExclusive(true) to make other buttons exclusive.

You'll find examples on how to use this arranger in the "Using Buttons" section of Hour 6.

Using the QSplitter Class

A splitter object makes it possible for the user to control the size of child widgets by dragging the boundary between the widgets that the splitter provides. Qt gives you the QSplitter class for doing this. Listing 7.4 shows an example of this. Here, a splitter is created so that the user can change the size of the two buttons.

INPUT   **LISTING 7.4**   A QSplitter Example

```
 1: #include <qapplication.h>
 2: #include <qwidget.h>
 3: #include <qsplitter.h>
 4: #include <qpushbutton.h>
 5:
 6: class MyMainWindow : public QWidget
 7: {
 8: public:
 9:         MyMainWindow();
10: private:
11:         QSplitter *splitter;
12:         QPushButton *b1, *b2;
13: };
14:
15: MyMainWindow::MyMainWindow()
16: {
17:         setGeometry( 100, 100, 150, 100 );
18:
19:         splitter = new QSplitter( this );
20:         splitter->setGeometry( 10, 10, 130, 80 );
21:
22:         b1 = new QPushButton( "Button 1", splitter );
23:         b2 = new QPushButton( "Button 2", splitter );
24: }
25:
26: void main( int argc, char **argv )
27: {
28:         QApplication a(argc, argv);
29:         MyMainWindow w;
30:         a.setMainWidget( &w );
31:         w.show();
32:         a.exec();
33: }
```

Here, the splitter is created on line 19, and the geometry is set for it at line 20. Then, on lines 22 and 23, two buttons are created and the splitter is used as their parent. By this, a splitter will be inserted between the buttons. This program is shown in action in Figures 7.5 and 7.6.

FIGURE 7.5

The QSplitter program in its original form.

7

FIGURE 7.6

What happens when the splitter is dragged to the right.

As you see, by dragging the boundary to the left or right, you can make the two buttons bigger or smaller.

By default, `QSplitter` doesn't resize the widgets until the user has finished the resizing (dropped the boundary). However, via a call to `QSplitter::setOpaqueSize(true)`, the widgets will be resized as the user drags the boundary.

You can also make a vertical splitter. You do this by making a call to `QSplitter::setOrientation(Vertical)` or by adding an argument to the constructor `QSplitter( Vertical, this )`.

You might also want to define a minimum size for the widgets in the splitter. This is done with the `setMinimumSize()` function. Therefore, in the previous example, you could restrict the user from making the buttons too small for the labels to be fully visible. You can also use `setMaximimSize()` with `QSplitter`.

Finally, you can define whether a widget should be resized when the splitter is resized. This is done with the `QSplitter::setResizeMode()` function.

Using the `QWidgetStack` Class

`QWidgetStack` is used when you have a number of widgets that you want to be visible only one at a time. Listing 7.5 provides an example of this. In this example, you can control which of two buttons should be visible by clicking two other buttons.

INPUT   **LISTING 7.5**   A `QWidgetStack` Example

```
1: #include <qapplication.h>
2: #include <qwidget.h>
3: #include <qwidgetstack.h>
4: #include <qpushbutton.h>
5:
6: //Make sure you place the class declaration
7: //in a header-file of its own, before you run
8: //MOC on it. Then include the moc file in the
9: //file holding the class definition.
10:
11: class MyMainWindow : public QWidget
12: {
13:     Q_OBJECT
14: public:
```

```
15:      MyMainWindow();
16: private:
17:      QWidgetStack *widgetstack;
18:      QPushButton *b1, *b2, *cb1, *cb2;
19:
20: public slots:
21:      void showb1();
22:      void showb2();
23: };
24:
25: void MyMainWindow::showb1()
26: {
27:      widgetstack->raiseWidget( b1 );
28: }
29:
30: void MyMainWindow::showb2()
31: {
32:      widgetstack->raiseWidget( b2 );
33: }
34:
35: MyMainWindow::MyMainWindow()
36: {
37:      setGeometry( 100, 100, 150, 130 );
38:
39:      widgetstack = new QWidgetStack( this );
40:      widgetstack->setGeometry( 10, 10, 130, 80 );
41:
42:      b1 = new QPushButton( "Button 1", this );
43:      b2 = new QPushButton( "Button 2", this );
44:
45:      widgetstack->addWidget( b1, 1 );
46:      widgetstack->addWidget( b2, 2 );
47:
48:      cb1 = new QPushButton( "Raise b1", this );
49:      cb1->setGeometry( 10, 100, 60, 20 );
50:
51:      cb2 = new QPushButton( "Raise b2", this );
52:      cb2->setGeometry( 80, 100, 60, 20);
53:
54:      connect( cb1, SIGNAL( clicked() ), this, SLOT( showb1() ) );
55:      connect( cb2, SIGNAL( clicked() ), this, SLOT( showb2() ) );
56: }
57:
58: void main( int argc, char **argv )
59: {
60:      QApplication a(argc, argv);
61:      MyMainWindow w;
62:      a.setMainWidget( &w );
63:      w.show();
64:      a.exec();
65: }
```

7

In this program, two custom slots are defined (lines 25 through 33), and they're two very simple ones. They call the `QWidgetStack::raiseWidget()` function to make either b1 or b2 visible (lines 27 and 32). These slots are then connected to the `clicked()` signal of the buttons cb1 and cb2 (lines 54 and 55). By doing this, you can control which of the buttons (b1 or b2) should be visible. See Figures 7.7 and 7.8 for how this program looks in action. Note that these two figures are included for illustrative purposes only. This actual function is rarely useful in a *real* program.

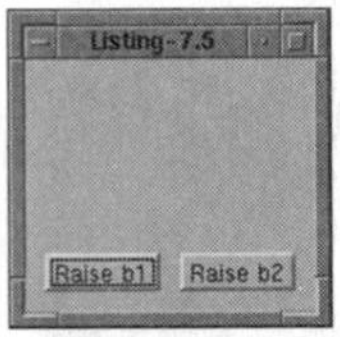

FIGURE 7.7

This is how the program looks when it first appears onscreen.

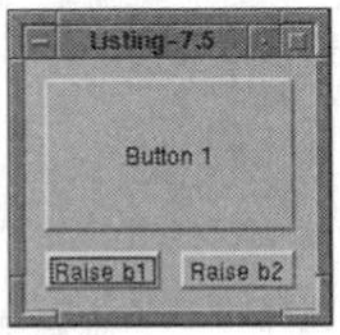

FIGURE 7.8

This is what happens when the button labeled "Raise b1" is clicked.

Of course, you can add more than two widgets to the widget stack. Just remember to have them use the `QWidgetStack::addWidget()` function. As you can see in Listing 7.5 (lines 45 and 46), you should give two arguments to this function: a pointer to the widget you want to add and a unique integer ID you want the widget to have in the stack. This ID can be used as the argument to the `QWidgetStack::raiseWidget()` function instead of a widget pointer.

Sliders and Spin Boxes

In this section, you'll learn how to use the various Qt classes that exist for creating sliders and scrollbars. A slider is a widget that lets the user select a numeric value by dragging a knob with the mouse. A spin box is also used to select a numerical value; however, it's used in a slightly different way (in a spin box, the value is changed by clicking buttons instead of dragging a knob).

Using the `QSlider` Class

If you want to create a slider of any kind, you should use the `QSlider` class. As is the case with all other Qt classes, it's very simple to use. See Listing 7.6 for an example.

INPUT **LISTING 7.6** A QSlider Example

```
1: #include <qapplication.h>
2: #include <qwidget.h>
3: #include <qslider.h>
4:
5: class MyMainWindow : public QWidget
6: {
7: public:
8:         MyMainWindow();
9: private:
10:         QSlider *slider;
11: };
12:
13: MyMainWindow::MyMainWindow()
14: {
15:         setGeometry( 100, 100, 150, 50 );
16:
17:         slider = new QSlider( 0, 100, 10, 50, Horizontal, this );
18:         slider->setGeometry( 10, 15, 130, 20 );
19:         slider->setTickmarks( QSlider::Below );
20: }
21:
22: void main( int argc, char **argv )
23: {
24:         QApplication a(argc, argv);
25:         MyMainWindow w;
26:         a.setMainWidget( &w );
27:         w.show();
28:         a.exec();
29: }
```

As you can see, the QSlider constructor takes quite a few arguments (line 17). The first argument sets the minimum value of the slider, and the second sets the maximum value. The third argument sets the number of steps the slider jumps if you click to the left or to the right of the knob. The fourth argument sets the default value of the slider. The fifth argument sets the orientation of the slider (Horizontal or Vertical), and the last argument is a pointer to the slider's parent widget (as you've probably already guessed).

Line 19 makes a call to the QSlider::setTickmarks() function. The tickmarks are the marks you usually see below a slider. They make it easier for the user to see what value the slider currently has. Figure 7.9 shows you what this program looks like.

FIGURE 7.9

A slider with tick-marks.

7

However, you won't get much use out of a slider without a method that tells you the current value of the slider. Luckily, Qt provides a few functions that make this an easy task. See Table 7.1 for descriptions of these functions.

TABLE 7.1   Useful `QSlider` Member Functions

Function	Description
value()	Returns the current value of the slider.
sliderMoved(int)	This is a signal that's emitted whenever the slider is moved enough that the value is changed. The parameter contains the new value.
valueChanged(int)	This signal is emitted when the user has finished moving the knob (that is, the user has selected a new value). The parameter contains this new value.
sliderPressed()	This signal is emitted whenever the user clicks the knob.
sliderReleased()	This signal is emitted when the user releases the knob after he or she has clicked or dragged it.
setValue(int)	Sets the value of the slider.

Sliders can be used for many tasks. With just a little bit of imagination, you'll be sure to come up with some interesting ideas. You have probably seen many programs where sliders are used to set various numerical values. You should use sliders whenever you find them more suitable than spin boxes, for example, when there is a large range of values to choose from.

Using the `QSpinBox` Class

A spin box is a widget that lets you select a numerical value with the mouse or with the keyboard. It takes up less space than a slider and is, in some cases, easier to use. Listing 7.7 shows an example of a simple spin box.

INPUT   **LISTING 7.7**   A QSpinBox Example

```
1: #include <qapplication.h>
2: #include <qwidget.h>
3: #include <qspinbox.h>
4:
5: class MyMainWindow : public QWidget
6: {
7: public:
8:         MyMainWindow();
9: private:
10:        QSpinBox *spinbox;
11: };
```

```
12:
13: MyMainWindow::MyMainWindow()
14: {
15:        setGeometry( 100, 100, 150, 50 );
16:
17:        spinbox = new QSpinBox( 0, 100, 5, this );
18:        spinbox->setGeometry( 50, 10, 50, 30 );
19: }
20:
21: void main( int argc, char **argv )
22: {
23:        QApplication a(argc, argv);
24:        MyMainWindow w;
25:        a.setMainWidget( &w );
26:        w.show();
27:        a.exec();
28: }
```

Figure 7.10 shows the result of Listing 7.7.

FIGURE 7.10

A simple spin box. The currently selected value is 48.

The QSpinBox constructor takes four arguments (line 17). The first and second arguments set the minimum and maximum values the spin box can have. The third argument is the stepping value—that is, how much the value of the spin box will change when you click one of its arrow buttons. The last argument is, as usual, the parent widget.

QSpinBox also provides you with a few useful functions. See Table 7.2 for descriptions of these functions.

TABLE 7.2   Useful QSlider Member Functions

Function	Description
value()	Returns the current value of the slider.
setValue(int)	Sets the value of the slider.
setSuffix()	Sets a string you want to be shown after the numerical value. For example, this could be Days, Months, Years, or something similar.
setPrefix()	With this function, you can set a string to be shown in front of the value.
setSpecialValueText()	With this function, you can define text that will be shown instead of the minimum value of the spin box. For example, this could be You Must Select a Higher Value.

7

continues

TABLE 7.2   continued

Function	Description
setWrapping()	If you click one of the arrow buttons when the lowest or highest value has already been reached, nothing will happen. However, if you make a call to setWrapping(true), then when you click one of the arrows when the highest (or lowest) value is reached, the value will start over at the lowest (or highest) value.
stepUp()	Simulates a mouse click on the up button.
stepDown()	Simulates a mouse click on the down button.

Spin boxes are very useful for setting a numerical value where the range of values is not too big. On the other hand, if the range is big (say from 1 to 1000), there will be a lot of clicking! In that case, a slider is a better choice. However, as stated, for setting numerical values where the numerical range is smaller (for example when setting the current date), spin boxes are great!

Summary

In this hour, you learned how to use selection widgets. When working with selection widgets (for text strings as well as numerical values), you need to be aware of the provided class methods. Laying out a few selection widgets in a window is not hard; however, you'll most likely also want these selection widgets to have some kind of functionality in your program.

You won't be able to do this if you don't know which signal is emitted when a particular event occurs or which function to call when you want to change the widget in a particular way. Although it's nearly impossible to have all this information in your head, you should at least have a basic understanding of how the selection widgets work, which you've hopefully learned in this hour. In addition, it's an easy task to check the Reference Documentation when you need information about some method.

You also learned about arrangers in this hour. Arrangers are widgets you can use to arrange other widgets. Although you need to put in some extra work to implement arrangers in your programs, you should use them as often as possible. If used correctly, they can make an application look better and be easier to use.

Q&A

Q **I'm working with one of the widgets described in this hour. It's not visible or just partly visible. What's wrong?**

A This is a common problem among beginning Qt programmers. However, the solution is as simple as the problem itself. You see, all Qt widgets have a rectangular form, although they do not always appear to be rectangular. Therefore, a widget often takes up more space than it appears to. When one or more of your widgets doesn't appear onscreen or if parts of them are hidden, the problem is most likely that some widgets are covered by other widgets (widgets that look like they're taking up less space than they actually do).

Q **I get a lot of error messages from my compiler when I'm trying to compile Listing 7.5. What's wrong?**

A You have to split up this code into one `.cpp` file and one h-file (header file). You also have to use the Meta Object Compiler. You need to do this to make your custom slots work. See Hour 4, "Making Things Happen: Slots and Signals," for a more detailed slot description.

Q **When would I need to use the `QSpingBox::setSpecialValueText()` function? Can you give me an example?**

A If you're implementing a function in your new word processor that lets the user change the size of the font, the `QSpingBox::setSpecialValueText()` function can be very useful. As you know, the size of the font cannot be 0. However, it's very possible that the user won't think about this and try to set the size to the smallest value. At this point, if you didn't used the `setSpecialValueText()` function, the user would have set the font size to 0, which would cause some very strange problems. On the other hand, if you used the `setSpecialValueText()` function and set the text to something like *Must be 1 or more*, the problem would most likely not occur.

Workshop

Work through the quiz and exercises in this section to make sure you understand everything covered in this hour.

Quiz

1. What is a selection widget?
2. What two types of text-selection widgets does Qt provide?

7

3. What is the `QSplitter` class used for?

4. What can you use the `QWidgetStack` class for?

5. When would it be useful to use an integer ID instead of a widget pointer when working with a widget stack?

6. Although they're not explicitly referred to as *selection widgets* in this hour, you learned about two selection widgets for numerical values. Can you name them?

7. What advantage does a slider have over a spin box?

Exercises

1. Write a simple program that includes a list box or a combo box. Use a `for` loop to insert a few items into the list box or combo box.

2. Experiment with the `QSplitter` class. Is it possible to insert another arranger to the splitter? Can you insert widgets that have child widgets?

3. Write a program with one slider and one spin box. Connect the two widgets so that when you drag the slider, the spin box value changes accordingly.

HOUR 8

Getting to Know the Qt Widgets: Lesson Three

This is the last lesson of this section. In this hour, you'll learn a few new types of widgets. As usual, this hour will by no means cover all aspects of the classes and functions mentioned. That's why the Qt Reference Documentation is very important when you're learning Qt (as a reference, that is).

There are three new widgets you'll learn to use in this hour: text-entry fields, list views, and progress bars. Text-entry fields are widgets that can handle text input from users. A list view is a very interesting widget that you can use to present data effectively. Progress bars are widgets that inform a user of the state of a task that's performed by the program. These widgets are considered basic widgets, so you'll most likely need them (sooner or later) in your programs.

Using Text-Entry Fields

Text-entry fields are widgets in which you can enter text. For example, in a text editor, the white area where you can write and read text is a text-entry field. Qt provides two classes for creating text-entry fields: QLineEdit and QMultiLineEdit. Both are covered in this section.

QLineEdit

QLineEdit creates a single-line text-entry field. It can be (and should be) used to retrieve short strings from the user, such as a username and password. Listing 8.1 shows a QLineEdit object.

INPUT **LISTING 8.1**   A QLineEdit Example

```
 1: #include <qapplication.h>
 2: #include <qwidget.h>
 3: #include <qlineedit.h>
 4:
 5: class MyMainWindow : public QWidget
 6: {
 7: public:
 8:         MyMainWindow();
 9: private:
10:         QLineEdit *edit;
11: };
12:
13: MyMainWindow::MyMainWindow()
14: {
15:         setGeometry( 100, 100, 200, 50 );
16:
17:         edit = new QLineEdit( this );
18:         edit->setGeometry( 10, 10, 180, 30 );
19: }
20:
21: void main( int argc, char **argv )
22: {
23:         QApplication a(argc, argv);
24:         MyMainWindow w;
25:         a.setMainWidget( &w );
26:         w.show();
27:         a.exec();
28: }
```

However, Listing 8.1 doesn't present anything really new. It just creates and places the widget as usual. However, it does present the use of the new widget QLineEdit. Figure 8.1 shows this program.

8

FIGURE 8.1

A simple program with a QLineEdit object.

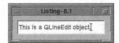

You can set the text of the QLineEdit object manually by using the QLineEdit::setText() function. If you want to retrieve the text that's currently written in the QLineEdit object, you make a call to the QLineEdit::text() function. The signal QLineEdit::valueChanged is emitted whenever the text is changed.

A normal use of QLineEdit is for retrieving a password. Therefore, the QLineEdit class provides a function that makes the text you enter in the field appear as stars. This is the usual way of hiding a password; you've probably seen it in many other applications. By adding the following two lines to the constructor of Listing 8.1, you make the text appear as asterisks and also set the maximum length of the entered text to eight characters:

```
edit->setEchoMode( QLineEdit::Password );
edit->setMaxLength( 8 );
```

Now, when you enter text into the field, it will appear as shown in Figure 8.2.

FIGURE 8.2

A QLineEdit object that shows the entered text as stars. Only eight characters can be entered.

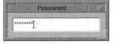

Note that when you've entered eight characters, no more stars appear. This means no more characters can be entered.

When working with QLineEdit, you should also know about the returnPressed() and textChanged() signals. The returnPressed() signal is emitted when the Return or Enter key is pressed. The textChanged() signal is emitted whenever the text is changed. textChanged() also includes the new text.

QMultiLineEdit

QMultiLineEdit is the other text-entry field provided by Qt. You used it in an example earlier in this book. As you probably remember, QMultiLineEdit provides a rectangular area of multiple lines where you can either show text or let the user enter text.

You work with QMultiLineEdit almost exactly as you do with QLineEdit. However, QMultiLineEdit includes a few extra functions for editing the text from within the program. With the insertAt() function, you can insert text at a certain position in the QMultiLineEdit object. QMultiLineEdit takes three arguments: The first is the string you want to insert, the second is the number of the line on which you want to insert text, and the third is the number of the character after which you want to insert text. Therefore, the following code would insert the string Hey! at line 12 after character 37:

```
object->insertAt( "Hey!", 12, 37 );
```

You can also use QMultiLineEdit::insertLine() to insert text. This is a simpler function that takes one or two arguments. Here's an example:

```
object->insertLine( "Hey!", 5 );
```

This line will insert Hey! at line 5. However, if you leave out the second argument, the text will be added to a new line, below the current last line.

You can also remove a line with the QMultiLineEdit::removeLine() function. It takes the line number as an argument.

> Both QLineEdit and QMultiLineEdit can also work with the system
> Clipboard. This is done through the functions cut(), copy(), and paste().

As always, see the Qt Reference Documentation for more information. In this case, you'll find it very helpful because QMultiLineEdit includes so many useful functions. These include setReadOnly() for making the QMultiLineEdit object read-only (useful when you only want to present text in it), text() for retrieving the current text in the QMultiLineEdit object, and clear() to clear all text in it.

Understanding List Views

A list view is one of my personal favorites. It's a widget that can present data in a very nice and easy-to-follow way. Although a list view is a quite complex widget, Qt makes it an easy task to implement one in your program. As you might already have guessed, the class for doing this is called QListView.

A simple example of how you can use QListView can be found in Listing 8.2.

INPUT   **LISTING 8.2**   A QListView Example

```
1: #include <qapplication.h>
2: #include <qwidget.h>
3: #include <qlistview.h>
4:
5: class MyMainWindow : public QWidget
6: {
```

```
 7: public:
 8:     MyMainWindow();
 9: private:
10:     QListView *listview;
11:     QListViewItem *topic1;
12:     QListViewItem *topic2;
13:     QListViewItem *topic3;
14:     QListViewItem *item;
15: };
16:
17: MyMainWindow::MyMainWindow()
18: {
19:     setGeometry( 100, 100, 300, 300 );
20:
21:     //Create the list view:
22:     listview = new QListView( this );
23:     listview->setGeometry( 0, 0, 400, 400 );
24:     //Make the down-arrow visible:
25:     listview->setRootIsDecorated( true );
26:     //Add three columns:
27:     listview->addColumn( "Book" );
28:     listview->addColumn( "Sold Copies" );
29:     listview->addColumn( "Price" );
30:
31:     //Add three items:
32:     topic1 = new QListViewItem( listview, "Topic 1" );
33:     topic2 = new QListViewItem( listview, "Topic 2" );
34:     topic3 = new QListViewItem( listview, "Topic 3" );
35:
36:     //Add three sub-items to each item:
37:     item = new QListViewItem( topic1, "Book 1", "21,000", "$29.99" );
38:     item = new QListViewItem( topic1, "Book 2", "19,000", "$24.99" );
39:     item = new QListViewItem( topic1, "Book 3", "14,000", "$39.99" );
40:
41:     item = new QListViewItem( topic2, "Book 4", "38,000", "$34.99" );
42:     item = new QListViewItem( topic2, "Book 5", "16,000", "$19.99" );
43:     item = new QListViewItem( topic2, "Book 6", "9,000", "$29.99" );
44:
45:     item = new QListViewItem( topic3, "Book 7", "32,000", "$39.99" );
46:     item = new QListViewItem( topic3, "Book 8", "25,000", "$37.99" );
47:     item = new QListViewItem( topic3, "Book 9", "13,000", "$44,99" );
48: }
49:
50: void main( int argc, char **argv )
51: {
52:     QApplication a(argc, argv);
53:     MyMainWindow w;
54:     a.setMainWidget( &w );
55:     w.show();
56:     a.exec();
57: }
```

The process of adding items is quite similar to the menu-creation process. First, the actual list view is created in lines 22 through 29. The call to `QListView::setRootIsDecorated( TRUE )` on line 25 makes sure that the arrow to the left of the top-level items is visible so that the user can make the sub-item visible. Then on lines 27, 28, and 29, the `QListView::addColumn()` function is used to create three columns. The argument given to this function represents the name of the column. On lines 32, 33, and 34, three top-level items are created. This is done with the `QListViewItem` class. The `QListViewItem` constructor takes three arguments; the first is the `QListView` object in which these items should be inserted. The second argument represents the name of the item. On lines 37 through 47, three sub-items are added to each top-level item. Here, another two arguments are added to the `QListViewItem` constructor. These two arguments represent column two and three of the sub-item. The result of this program is shown in Figure 8.3.

FIGURE 8.3

A list view that lists a few books sorted by topic.

Book	Sold Copies	Price
Topic 1		
Book 1	21,000	$29.99
Book 2	19,000	$24.99
Book 3	14,000	$39.99
Topic 2		
Book 4	38,000	$34.99
Book 5	16,000	$19.99
Book 6	9,000	$29.99
Topic 3		
Book 7	32,000	$39.99
Book 8	25,000	$37.99
Book 9	13,000	$44.99

Note that a call to an `insertItem()` or similar function isn't needed. Instead, the parent-child hierarchy is totally relied upon.

If you click one of the column headers, that column will sort the list view.

`QListView` provides many other functions not used in the preceding example. Some of them are described in Table 8.1. To be able to fully control and take advantage of the `QListView` class, you need to learn how to use these functions. Although you probably won't need all of them in every project, it's good to be aware that they exist so that you know what options you have.

TABLE 8.1 Useful `QListView` Member Functions

Function	Description
setColumnsWidthMode()	This method determines how the column's width should be set. It takes two arguments: The first is an integer representing the column in question, and the second is an enum value that can be set to Maximum or Manual. If set to Maximum, the column gets the size of the widest item in the column. If set to Manual, the width is set via setColumnWidth().
setMultiSelection()	Determines whether the user can select one or multiple items at the same time. The function takes a bool value as an argument (TRUE indicates multiselect and FALSE indicates single select).
setAllColumnsShowFocus()	This function can take the argument TRUE or FALSE. If this function is set to TRUE, the focus will be shown in all columns. Test it and you'll see!
setTreeStepSize()	The integer value you give to this function determines how many pixels an item is offset relative to its parent. Don't get it? Try it and see!
setSorting()	This function determines how the sorting should occur. It takes two arguments: an integer representing the column in question and a bool value (TRUE or FALSE). If this function is set to TRUE, the sorting will be ascending. The sorting will be descending if the function is set to FALSE.
itemAt()	This function takes a pointer to a QPoint object as argument. It returns a pointer to the QListViewItem object on that position.
firstChild()	Returns the first item in the list view.
itemBelow()	Returns the item immediately below this item.
itemAbove()	Returns the item immediately above this item.
setSelected()	This function determines whether an item is selected. It takes two arguments: The first is a pointer to a QListViewItem object, and the second is a bool value (TRUE or FALSE). TRUE makes it selected.
setCurrentItem()	Sets keyboard focus to the item the pointer you give as an argument points to.
currentItem()	Returns a pointer to the currently selected item.
selectionChanged()	This function is a signal that's emitted when the selection changes (that is, if you select another item or deselect the current item). It also sends a pointer to the newly selected item.
currentChanged()	This signal is emitted when the current item changes. It also sends a pointer to the new item.

continues

TABLE 8.1   continued

Function	Description
doubleClicked()	This signal is emitted when the user double-clicks an item. A pointer to the double-clicked QListViewItem object is also included.
returnPressed()	This signal is emitted when the user hits Enter or Return. It also sends a pointer to the item that has keyboard focus.
rightButtonClicked()	This signal is emitted when the right mouse button is released (after it has been pressed). This signal also sends three arguments to its slot: a pointer to the item clicked (can be 0), the coordinates to the clicked position, and an integer value representing the affected column.

After studying this table, you probably wonder what the difference between the *current* item and the *selected* item is. The current item can only be one single item at a time; it's the item in focus. However, if you've turned multiselection on with a call to setMultiSelection(TRUE), you can have many items selected at the same time. In this case, you have one *current* item and multiple *selected* items. The current item is one of the selected items, and one particular selected item can be the current item, but it can also be just a selected item.

Now, you'll look at an example that develops the program in Listing 8.2 a bit further. Suppose you want to implement a new function that pops up a description of a book if you double-click its item in the list view. For this, you would create a new slot and connect it to the doubleClicked() signal. Listing 8.3 shows a simple implementation of this function. In this example, the slot MyMainWindow::ShowDescription() is implemented. This slot simply brings up an information window each time you double-click an item. The information window is created by the QMessageBox class covered in Hour 10, "Understanding Qt Dialogs."

INPUT   **LISTING 8.3**   A List View with an Information Feature

```
1: #include <qapplication.h>
2: #include <qwidget.h>
3: #include <qlistview.h>
4: #include <qmessagebox.h>
5:
6: //Remember to make a separate .h file
7: //of the class declaration, and then
```

```
 8: //use the Meta Object Compiler on it.
 9: class MyMainWindow : public QWidget
10: {
11:    Q_OBJECT
12: public:
13:         MyMainWindow();
14: private:
15:         QListView *listview;
16:         QListViewItem *topic1;
17:         QListViewItem *topic2;
18:         QListViewItem *topic3;
19:         QListViewItem *item;
20:    QMessageBox *box;
21: public slots:
22:    void ShowDescription();
23: };
24:
25: //Here is our new slot:
26: void MyMainWindow::ShowDescription()
27: {
28:    box = new QMessageBox( "Book Info", "Here, we could show some short
29:                information text about the book you just
30:                double-clicked on.",
31:                QMessageBox::Information, QMessageBox::Ok, 0, 0 );
32:    box->show();
33: }
34:
35: MyMainWindow::MyMainWindow()
36: {
37:         setGeometry( 100, 100, 300, 300 );
38:
39:         listview = new QListView( this );
40:         listview->setGeometry( 0, 0, 400, 400 );
41:         listview->setRootIsDecorated( true );
42:
43:         listview->addColumn( "Book" );
44:         listview->addColumn( "Sold Copies" );
45:         listview->addColumn( "Price" );
46:
47:         topic1 = new QListViewItem( listview, "Topic 1" );
48:         topic2 = new QListViewItem( listview, "Topic 2" );
49:         topic3 = new QListViewItem( listview, "Topic 3" );
50:
51:    item = new QListViewItem( topic1, "Book 1", "21,000", "$29.99" );
52:    item = new QListViewItem( topic1, "Book 2", "19,000", "$24.99" );
53:    item = new QListViewItem( topic1, "Book 3", "14,000", "$39.99" );
54:    item = new QListViewItem( topic2, "Book 4", "38,000", "$34.99" );
55:    item = new QListViewItem( topic2, "Book 5", "16,000", "$19.99" );
56:    item = new QListViewItem( topic2, "Book 6", "9,000", "$29.99" );
57:    item = new QListViewItem( topic3, "Book 7", "32,000", "$39.99" );
58:    item = new QListViewItem( topic3, "Book 8", "25,000", "$37.99" );
```

continues

LISTING 8.3   continued

```
59:      item = new QListViewItem( topic3, "Book 9", "13,000", "$44.99" );
60:
61:      connect( listview, SIGNAL( doubleClicked( QListViewItem * ) ),
62:           this, SLOT( ShowDescription() ) );
63: }
64:
65: void main( int argc, char **argv )
66: {
67:         QApplication a(argc, argv);
68:         MyMainWindow w;
69:         a.setMainWidget( &w );
70:         w.show();
71:         a.exec();
72: }
```

On line 22, the ShowDescription() slot is declared. The implementation of it can be found on lines 26 through 33. As you can see, the class QMessageBox is used (lines 28 through 31) to create the little information window that pops up if you double-click an item. This is one of Qt's dialog classes, and it will be covered in Hour 10. Figure 8.4 shows this program in action.

FIGURE 8.4

The item labeled "Book 4" has been clicked to make the information box appear. Click the OK button on the informa- tion box to make it dis- appear.

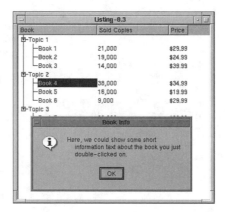

This section should give you some ideas on how you can use a list view in your pro- grams.

Working with Progress Bars

A progress bar is a widget that gives the user information about the program's current state. For example, it can be useful to display a progress bar when the program is about to perform a time-consuming task and you want to give the user a hint about how much time he or she can expect it to take (and also to assure the user that the program has not stopped).

Qt provides the QProgressBar class for creating progress bars. (Another class, QProgressDialog, can also be used for tasks like this. QProgressDialog is discussed in Hour 10. QProgressBar is created and shown just as any other Qt class. However, there are a few other tasks you'll need to perform to make the progress bar act as a progress bar (for example, you'll need to define when the progress bar will be updated). You'll find a simple example in Listing 8.4.

INPUT **LISTING 8.4** A Slider That Controls a Progress Bar

```
 1: #include <qapplication.h>
 2: #include <qwidget.h>
 3: #include <qslider.h>
 4: #include <qprogressbar.h>
 5:
 6: class MyMainWindow : public QWidget
 7: {
 8: public:
 9:         MyMainWindow();
10: private:
11:     QProgressBar *bar;
12:     QSlider *slider;
13: };
14:
15: MyMainWindow::MyMainWindow()
16: {
17:         setGeometry( 100, 100, 200, 90 );
18:
19:     bar = new QProgressBar( 100, this );
20:     bar->setGeometry( 10, 10, 180, 30 );
21:
22:     slider = new QSlider( 0, 100, 10, 0, Horizontal, this );
23:     slider->setGeometry( 10, 50, 180, 30 );
24:
25:     //Connect the progress bar and the slider so
26:     //that the slider controls the progress of the
27:     //progress bar:
28:     connect( slider, SIGNAL( valueChanged(int) ),
29:         bar, SLOT( setProgress(int) ) );
30: }
31:
32: void main( int argc, char **argv )
33: {
34:         QApplication a(argc, argv);
```

continues

LISTING 8.4   continued

```
35:          MyMainWindow w;
36:          a.setMainWidget( &w );
37:          w.show();
38:          a.exec();
39: }
```

In this example, the progress bar's slot `setProgress()` is connected with the `valueChanged()` signal of a slider. By doing this, you can control the progress of the progress bar by dragging the slider. Note that this is not a real-life example. However, the concept is the same if you are implementing this function in a *real* application. You would just make sure to call the `setProgress()` function with the appropriate argument when you reached a certain point.

> The first argument given to the `QProgressBar` constructor at line 19 represents the number of steps the progress bar will take until it reaches 100%. If you want to copy five files, for example, and want the progress bar to go one step further for each copied file, this value should be 5.

This program is shown in action in Figures 8.5 and 8.6. In Figure 8.5, the slider hasn't been dragged, and therefore the progress bar hasn't reached any of its steps, either. In Figure 8.6, the slider has been dragged a bit to the right, and therefore the progress bar has also changed.

FIGURE 8.5

This is how the progress bar program looks when it first appears onscreen.

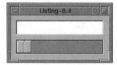

FIGURE 8.6

This is what happens when you drag the slider to the left. At this point, the last value given to the setProgress() function is 73.

Progress bars are simple but yet very useful. If you want your program to perform a very time-consuming task, it's almost required that you provide a progress bar to inform the user about what's happening and how long the task will take.

Summary

Both text-entry fields and progress bars are quite straightforward widgets, and it's clear what you should use them for. On the other hand, this is not the case at all with list views. The QListView class is both powerful and complex. You'll need to study it in depth to have full control over it—and with this control, you'll discover totally new ways of using a list view. QListView is an exciting class (if you think a C++ class can be exciting). Even if you find it hard to understand at first, give it a try!

You've now learned about the Qt widgets. You have learned to use all of Qt's widgets. By studying this section, you have also gotten an understanding of how the widgets work and what they can be used for. The Qt widgets make a complete set of graphical objects that will be enough to build any kind of GUI.

Q&A

Q In Listing 8.3, why do I need to call show() for the QMessageBox object? This isn't done for any of the other objects.

A This is because the QMessageBox object (box) is not a child widget of the MyMainWindow class. Therefore, the call to MyMainWindow::show() in main() does not affect box.

Q I get a lot of error messages from my compiler when I'm trying to compile Listing 8.3. What's wrong?

A You have to split up this code into one .cpp file and one .h file (header file). You also have to use the Meta Object Compiler (MOC) on the .h file and then include the output from MOC in the .cpp file. You need to do this to make your custom slots work. See Hour 4, "Making Things Happen: Slots and Signals," for a more detailed description.

Workshop

As usual, you're encouraged to work through the following questions and quiz. By doing this you make sure you've understood everything described in this hour. What's more, you might learn something that you previously thought was unclear.

Quiz

1. What's the difference between QLineEdit and QMultiLineEdit?

2. Which class should you use to show a text file to the user?

3. If you look only at member functions, what is the most essential difference between QLineEdit and QMultiLineEdit?

4. If you don't use the insertItem() function to insert items to a list view, which method is used?

5. Which signal is emitted when you double-click an item in the list view?

6. Which signal is emitted when you press Return or Enter in a list view?

7. What is a progress bar?

8. When should you implement a progress bar in your application?

Exercises

1. Search the Qt Reference Documentation for a QMultiLineEdit member function that can make the QMultiLineEdit object read-only. What's the name of this function, and how would you call it to set the QMultiLineEdit object as read-only?

2. Create a program with a list view. The list view should include three rows—Country, Capital, and Population—from left to right. Then, create a top-level item for each continent and add sub-items describing a few countries of each continent, along with information about the capitals and population.

3. It's possible that you'll want to use a progress bar but find it hard to implement. Perhaps you find it unclear when to call the setProgress() function. One solution (even though it might not be the best one) is to measure how long the task will take and then create a for loop (or something similar), and with that try to work out an amount of time that you find suitable for the task. For example, suppose your program will perform a task that takes about 30 seconds; try to work out a for loop that calls the setProgress() function at the appropriate times.

HOUR 9

Creating Simple Graphics

When you start your new and shiny GUI program for the first time, you might not realize that the program is in fact made up of a large amount of low-level graphics code. Fortunately, this code is generated by the GUI library (Qt, in this case); therefore, you never need to worry about it.

You might be wondering what *low-level graphics code* is. This is the code that draws your program onscreen. When you create a Qt widget, this widget is drawn onscreen by Qt using your system's simplest functions (functions that only draw lines, rectangles, and such).

As mentioned, Qt handles the low-level code, which creates the predefined Qt widgets. However, sometimes you might need to create custom graphical objects that Qt cannot create for you. In this case, you need some kind of low-level graphics generator that you can use to create custom graphics. Qt provides the QPainter class for this purpose.

In this lesson, you'll learn how to get started working with QPainter. You'll also learn how to implement printing capabilities in your program.

Using the QPainter Class

As stated, QPainter is the class for creating custom graphics with Qt. It's very straight-forward and not difficult to use. You'll start this QPainter section by learning how to create a QPainter object and draw a simple rectangle.

Getting Started with QPainter

For creating custom graphics with QPainter, you need to take a few precautions to ensure that you don't interfere with the drawing handled by Qt itself. What you need to do is to place the drawing code in a special function called drawEvent(), as well as start and stop the painting by calling the QPainter::begin() and QPainter::end() functions. Listing 9.1 provides a simple example.

LISTING 9.1   Drawing a Simple Rectangle

```
 1: #include <qapplication.h>
 2: #include <qwidget.h>
 3: #include <qpainter.h>
 4:
 5: class MyMainWindow : public QWidget
 6: {
 7: public:
 8:         MyMainWindow();
 9: private:
10:         void paintEvent( QPaintEvent* );
11:         QPainter *paint;
12: };
13:
14: //Here is our implementation of paintEvent():
15: void MyMainWindow::paintEvent( QPaintEvent* )
16: {
17:         paint = new QPainter;
18:         //Start the painting:
19:         paint->begin( this );
20:         //Draw a rectangle:
21:         paint->drawRect( 20, 20, 160, 160 );
22:         //End the painting:
23:         paint->end();
24: }
25:
26: MyMainWindow::MyMainWindow()
27: {
28:         setGeometry( 100, 100, 200, 200 );
29: }
30:
31: void main( int argc, char **argv )
```

```
32: {
33:        QApplication a(argc, argv);
34:        MyMainWindow w;
35:        a.setMainWidget( &w );
36:        w.show();
37:        a.exec();
38: }
```

9

First, the `QPainter` object is created on line 17. Then, the painting is started on line 19 with the call to `QPainter::begin()`. On line 21, the rectangle is painted. This is done with the `QPainter::drawRect()` function. This function takes three arguments. The first two define the position of the rectangle's upper-left corner (relative to the window) and the last two define the width and height of the rectangle. Finally, the drawing is ended on line 23 with a call to `QPainter::end()`. This program will create a 200×200 pixel window with a 160×160 black, unfilled rectangle in it (see Figure 9.1).

FIGURE 9.1

A program with a rectangle in it.

As you see, the result of Listing 9.1 is a simple black rectangle. This example is not fancy at all, but it has introduced you to the `QPainter` class, and that was the meaning of this section.

Setting the Drawing Style

Before you start the actual drawing process, you need to select how you want `QPainter` to draw the lines, rectangles, and so on. This is done via a few `QPainter` member functions.

Selecting a Pen

By calling the `QPainter::setPen()` function with the appropriate arguments, you can select the style of the pen you want to use. You'll now try this out by changing the program in Listing 9.1 to use a 4-pixel–wide blue pen that draws dashed lines. Just add the following line of code between the calls to `begin()` (line 19 of Listing 9.1) and `end()` (line 23 of Listing 9.1):

```
paint->setPen( QPen( blue, 4, QPen::DashLine ) );
```

The result of this is shown in Figure 9.2.

FIGURE 9.2
Changing the pen type with the `QPainter::setPen()` *function.*

As you see, you can change the drawing style quite dramatically with one single line of code.

Selecting Fill Style

You can choose to fill your rectangle with a pattern or a solid color. This is done with the "brush." For example, if you want to fill the rectangle from Listing 9.1 with a solid red color, add the following line of code between the calls to `begin()` (line 19 of Listing 9.1) and `end()` (line 23 of Listing 9.1):

```
paint->setBrush( QBrush( red, SolidPattern ) );
```

The result of this function call is shown in Figure 9.3.

FIGURE 9.3
Setting the fill style to a solid red color.

However, by changing `SolidPattern`, you can fill the rectangle in other ways. For example, if you change it to `Dense6Pattern`, the fill style will be changed from 100% (`SolidPattern`) to 12% (`Dense6Pattern`). Figure 9.4 shows an example of this.

FIGURE 9.4
Changing the fill style from 100% to 12%.

A complete description of the different fill styles can be found in Table 9.1.

TABLE 9.1 Fill Styles

Fill Style	Description
SolidPattern	A solid fill pattern (refer to Figure 9.3).
Dense1Pattern	A 94% fill pattern.
Dense2Pattern	An 88% fill pattern.
Dense3Pattern	A 63% fill pattern.
Dense4Pattern	A 50% fill pattern.
Dense5Pattern	A 37% fill pattern.
Dense6Pattern	A 12% fill pattern (refer to Figure 9.4).
Dense7Pattern	A 6% fill pattern.
HorPattern	Fills the figure with horizontal lines.
VerPattern	Fills the figure with vertical lines.
CrossPattern	Fills the figure with lines crossing each other (a grid pattern).
BDiagPattern	A fill style of diagonal lines, pointing to the upper-right corner.
FDiagPattern	Diagonal lines pointing to the upper-left corner.
DiagCrossPattern	Diagonal lines crossing each other.
CustomPattern	This fill style should be used when you use a pixmap pattern.

Changing the Font

You can also draw text with QPainter. When you do, it's quite possible that you'll want to change the font. This is very simple—just call the setFont() function. Listing 9.2 shows a sample program that works with text.

LISTING 9.2 Drawing Text with a Custom Font

```
 1: #include <qapplication.h>
 2: #include <qwidget.h>
 3: #include <qpainter.h>
 4: #include <qfont.h>
 5:
 6: class MyMainWindow : public QWidget
 7: {
 8: public:
 9:         MyMainWindow();
10: private:
11:         void paintEvent( QPaintEvent* );
```

continues

LISTING 9.2   continued

```
12:          QPainter *paint;
13: };
14:
15: void MyMainWindow::paintEvent( QPaintEvent* )
16: {
17:          paint = new QPainter;
18:          paint->begin( this );
19:          //Set the font, size and style:
20:          paint->setFont( QFont( "Arial", 16, QFont::Bold ) );
21:          //Draw the text:
22:          paint->drawText( 20, 20, 260, 60, AlignCenter,
23:                          "Font: Arial, Size: 16, Style: Bold" );
24:          paint->end();
25: }
26:
27: MyMainWindow::MyMainWindow()
28: {
29:          setGeometry( 100, 100, 300, 100 );
30: }
31:
32: void main( int argc, char **argv )
33: {
34:          QApplication a(argc, argv);
35:          MyMainWindow w;
36:          a.setMainWidget( &w );
37:          w.show();
38:          a.exec();
39: }
```

Here, you see the definition of `paintEvent()` on lines 15 through 25. This definition starts by creating a QPainter object (line 17). Then, the drawing starts on line 18. On line 19, the font and style are set by calling the `QPainter::setFont()` function. On lines 22 and 23, text is drawn by the `QPainter::drawText()` function. Six arguments are given to this function. The first two define the upper-left corner of the rectangle on which the text will be drawn. The following two arguments represent the width and height of the rectangle. With the fifth argument, you set the alignment of the text. The last argument represents (of course) the text you want to draw. This program creates a window and then draws the following text in the center of it:

```
Font: Arial, Size: 16, Style: Bold
```

Figure 9.5 shows this program in action.

FIGURE 9.5

Text drawn using QPainter.

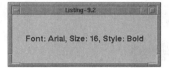

You could also achieve this easily with a label. However, this lesson is about graphics, and you need to learn the text functions provided by QPainter as well.

You have the same alignment options when working with QPainter as with QLabel.

Getting to Know the QPainter Drawing Functions

QPainter provides many more functions for drawing text and rectangles. In this section, some other interesting drawing functions are covered (although not all of them). See the QPainter section of the Qt Reference Documentation for complete coverage of QPainter's member functions.

Remember that the code examples in the following sections will always be inserted between the function calls to begin() and end() in the paintEvent() function.

Drawing Circles and Ellipses

For drawing circles and ellipses with QPainter, you should use the drawEllipse() function. It takes four integer arguments. The first and second arguments represent the number of pixels between the circle/ellipse and the left and upper sides of the window. The third and fourth arguments represent the width and height of the circle/ellipse. Take a look at the following example:

```
paint->setPen( QPen( blue, 4, QPen::SolidLine ) );
paint->drawEllipse( 20, 20, 210, 160 );
```

The result of this code is shown in Figure 9.6.

FIGURE 9.6

*An ellipse drawn with
a solid blue line.*

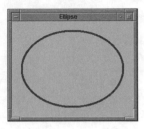

FIGURE 9.6

*An ellipse drawn with
a solid blue line.*

Drawing a Rounded Rectangle

To draw a rectangle with rounded corners, you use the QPainter::drawRoundRect()
function. See the following code snippet and Figure 9.7 for an example:

```
paint->setPen( QPen( red, 4, QPen::SolidLine ) );
paint->drawRoundRect( 20, 20, 210, 160, 50, 50 );
```

The last two arguments determine the level of roundness for the corners. This can be any
value between 0 and 99 (99 represents maximum roundness).

FIGURE 9.7

*A rectangle with
rounded corners.*

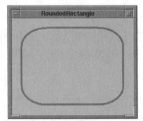

Drawing a Slice of a Circle

To draw just a piece of a circle, you should use the QPainter::drawPie() function.
Here's an example:

```
paint->setPen( QPen( green, 4, QPen::SolidLine ) );
paint->drawPie( 20, 20, 210, 160, 0, 500 );
```

The first four arguments define the circle (just as with drawEllipse()). The last two
arguments define the style of the circle. 0 is the starting angle (actually one-sixteenth of
a degree) and 500 (also one-sixteenth of a degree) is the arc length of the pie slice. If
you're not familiar with trigonometry, you might find this hard to understand. If so, you
should test a few different values. Before long, you'll understand how it works. Figure
9.8 shows this program.

FIGURE 9.8

A green slice of a circle.

 Neither of the last two arguments represents a whole degree; instead, each represents one-sixteenth of a degree. Therefore, in this case, a whole circle is represented by 5760 (16×360).

Drawing a Chord of a Circle

To get a chord of a circle, draw a straight line inside a circle. This line is the chord. However, it is the piece of the circle that is *outside* the line that will be drawn by QPainter. You need to use the QPainter::drawChord() function:

```
paint->setPen( QPen( green, 4, QPen::SolidLine ) );
paint->drawChord( 20, 20, 210, 160, 500, 1000 );
```

The arguments for the drawChord() function are exactly the same as for drawPie(). Figure 9.9 shows the result of this code.

FIGURE 9.9

A green chord of a circle.

Drawing an Arc

Drawing an arc with QPainter is easy—just use the QPainter::drawArc() function. The arguments for the function are the same as for drawPie() and drawChord(). An example follows:

```
paint->setPen( QPen( green, 4, QPen::SolidLine ) );
paint->drawArc( 20, 20, 210, 160, 500, 1000 );
```

See Figure 9.10 for the result of this code.

FIGURE **9.10**

A green arc of a circle.

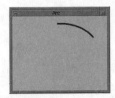

Drawing a Bèzier Curve

To draw a Bèzier curve (a curve described by four points), you should use the
QPainter::drawQuadBezier() function. A simple example follows:

```
paint->setPen( QPen( green, 4, QPen::SolidLine ) );
paint->drawQuadBezier( QPointArray( QRect(20, 20, 210, 160) ) );
```

The only argument given to this function represents the rectangle in which you want to
create the curve (the other arguments are predefined and can be left out). Figure 9.11
provides an example of a Bèzier curve.

FIGURE **9.11**

A green Bèzier curve.

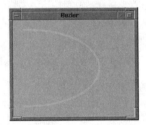

You've now learned a few QPainter drawing functions. However, there are still a few
more, such as QPainter::drawPixmap() (for drawing a pixmap) and
QPainter::drawPolygon() (for drawing a polygon). You should look in the Reference
Documentation for information about these functions.

Working with Colors

To make your applications look good, you need to know how to manage the colors you
want them to use. Because of all the different types of hardware out there, managing colors can be tricky. However, Qt makes this task a bit easier for you.

Managing Colors

When choosing colors for your applications, keep in mind that there will probably be
many users of your applications who can't access more than 256 colors at a time (8-bit

color depth). Therefore, you should try not to allocate too many custom colors and also try to use colors already allocated by other applications. By doing this, you leave more color cells free (each color takes one color cell).

Of course, it's impossible for you to know which colors are already in use and which are not. However, you should make it a practice to use the Qt predefined colors—`black`, `white`, `red`, `green`, `blue`, `cyan`, `yellow`, `magenta`, `gray`, `darkGray`, `lighGray`, `darkRed`, `darkGreen`, `darkBlue`, `darkCyan`, `darkMagenta`, `darkYellow`, `color0`, and `color1`. These colors are most likely already in use.

> `color0` and `color1` are special colors for drawing in two-color bitmaps; they're guaranteed to contrast well.

One other thing you can do to avoid taking up too many colors is to use a color pattern (a given set of colors). You can set a color pattern with the `QApplication::setColorSpec()` function. Here are a few standard arguments you can pass to this function:

- `QApplication::Normal`. This is the default. You should use this if your application uses mainly standard colors.

- `QApplication::ManyColors`. This should be used if your application will use a lot of colors. A special method (which makes your application more color friendly for other applications) is used to determine which color will actually be allocated. This option only applies to UNIX systems.

- `QApplication::CustomColors`. This applies only to Microsoft Windows systems. It's a function that gives more colors to the active application and fewer colors to the applications in the background. If you've ever used Windows set to 256 colors, you've probably seen how applications tend to get strange colors when they're inactive. That's caused by this method.

> You must call the `QApplication::setColorSpec()` function before you create the `QApplication` object!

Specifying Colors

You have three ways of specifying a color in Qt: using the RGB (Red/Green/Blue) model, the HSV (Hue/Saturation/Value) model, or named colors.

The RGB Model

RGB is the most common method for specifying colors, and you've most likely heard about it before. With RGB, you specify colors with three integer values—one for each of the colors red, green, and blue. The higher value you specify for one of the three colors, the more the result will be dominated by that color. The value for each color must be an integer between 0 and 255. For example, (0, 0, 0) represents black, and (255, 255, 255) represents white.

To allocate a color using RGB with Qt, you create a QColor object and pass the three RGB values as arguments to its constructor. Here's an example:

```
QColor myBlack( 0, 0, 0 );
```

This makes the QColor object black. If you want a pure red color, use this:

```
QColor myRed( 255, 0, 0 );
```

The HSV Model

The HSV (Hue Saturation Value) model is another way of defining a color. HSV splits a color into its hue, saturation, and value. Which values you can specify differs a bit. However, in Qt, the hue can be any integer between -1 and 360, and the saturation and value can be any integer from 0 to 255.

You can use HSV with QColor as well. Just add the argument QColor::Hsv to the QColor constructor. Here's an example:

```
QColor hsvColor( 150, 73, 213, QColor::Hsv );
```

Using Named Colors

All X11 (UNIX) systems have a database that maps color names to RGB values. By using these named colors, the chance of picking a color already in use is much greater, and you'll probably save some color cells as well. Named colors can also be used with QColor. Here's an example:

```
QColor lBlue( "SteelBlue" );
```

Qt also provides this color database on Windows systems.

Changing the Standard Palette

If you don't like the standard color palette, you can define a custom one. A palette consists of three color groups: active (used when the application has focus), disabled (used when the application is not available to the user), and normal (used for all other purposes). Each color group consists of a number of colors that should be used for a certain part of the application.

Therefore, if you want to create a color palette of your own, you need to create three color groups. You do this with the QColorGroup class, and you pass the colors as arguments to the QColorGroup constructor. (See the Reference Documentation for a description of these arguments.) Next, you create a QPalette object and pass the three color groups as arguments to the QPalette constructor. Again, see the Reference Documentation for more information about this.

Printing Graphics with Qt

Printing graphics from Qt is an easy task. The QPrinter class is used for printing and, because this is a subclass of QPaintDevice (like QWidget), you can draw with QPainter "on" the QPrinter object. Everything you draw will then be printed! The only thing you actually have to control is when a new page is needed. You do this by calling the QPrinter::newPage() function.

However, you might want to let the user change the print settings. The Print dialog appears if you call the QPrinter::getPrinter() function. This dialog is shown in Figure 9.12.

FIGURE 9.12

The Qt Print dialog.

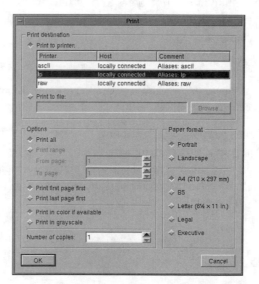

If you're on the Windows platform, the look of the Print dialog will depend on which type of printer you have.

The `QPrinter::setup()` function returns `true` if you click the OK button. Therefore, if the function returns `true`, the printing will proceed. If it does not returns `true`, the printing will be aborted. Here's an example of how to do this:

```
QPrinter print;
int proceed = print.setup()
if( proceed == true )
{
    //Start printing
    //(e.g. Start drawing to the
    //QPrinter object)
}
else
{
    //Abort
}
```

It's as simple as that! Of course, you can also set the different printing options programmatically. You can set the orientation with the `QPrinter::setOrientation()` function (by passing either `QPrinter::Portrait` or `QPrinter::Landscape` to it). You can also set the maximum and minimum number of pages to be printed with the `QPrinter::setMinMax()` function.

Summary

Qt comes with a lot of functions for drawing, and they're not all covered in this lesson. The remaining ones will be covered in Lesson 15, "Learning More About Graphics."

In the last section of this lesson, you learned how to implement a function for printing graphics in your Qt program. However, although Qt provides a few great features for printing, you should keep in mind that this is a very platform-dependent task. Therefore, you need to make sure you have the appropriate drivers set up on your system; otherwise, the printing won't work.

Q&A

Q **When I add some drawing code to my class constructor, my graphics just don't appear onscreen. What's wrong?**

A As stated earlier, you need to place the drawing code in a special function called `paintEvent()`. This keeps your code from interfering with Qt's internal drawing code. However, you can put the drawing code in some other functions as well, just not in the constructor.

Q **When I'm drawing text with `QPainter`, I get an error message about a missing font. What's wrong?**

A Actually, you've already found what's wrong. You simply don't have the font you've chosen or you've misspelled it.

Q **Why doesn't anything happen when I try to print graphics?**

A Make sure you have a printer correctly installed. This is a very common problem. Check your graphics code that outputs to the printer for errors. Also, make sure you've called the `begin()` function with the `QPrinter` object as an argument.

9

Workshop

You're encouraged to work through the following questions and exercises to help you retain what you've learned in this lesson. By completing these questions and exercises, you'll ensure that you understand how to work with graphics in your programs.

Quiz

1. What class is used for creating graphics?
2. What does the `setPen()` function do?
3. What is the brush used for?
4. Is there more than one fill style to select from?
5. Why should you use `QPainter` to show text?
6. What is RGB?
7. What is a palette?
8. What would you do to print a circle on a piece of paper?

Exercises

1. Create a program that draws a circle (not an ellipse). The outline should be red, dashed, and 5 pixels wide. Fill the circle with a solid blue color.

2. Pretend it's your birthday. Your mom has made a real nice cake for you, and you're cutting a big slice of it. Draw a slice of that cake.

3. Write a program with a print function. Create a button labeled "Print." When you click this button, the Print dialog should appear. Then, when you click OK, the program should print out the slice you created in the previous exercise. Also, add the text "This slice comes from a really nice cake!" under it.

HOUR 10

Understanding Qt Dialogs

If you want to interact with your users in some way—for example, you want them to select a file to open in a text editor—you need to implement a *dialog* to let them do it.

Qt comes with a few predefined dialogs for the most common tasks, such as selecting files. In many cases, these predefined dialogs will do the job for you, and you'll save yourself a lot of work by using them. In fact, it's sufficient in most cases to use just one line of code to implement one of the predefined dialogs.

Of course, if you're in need of a very special dialog, you'll have to create it yourself. However, with the tools Qt provides for creating dialogs, this shouldn't be too hard for you.

In this lesson, you'll learn how to use the predefined dialogs as well as create your own.

Using Predefined Dialogs

Qt comes with a few predefined dialogs. They are QColorDialog, QFileDialog, QFontDialog, QMessageBox, and QProgressDialog. These classes can be used to create the most usual dialogs, like for choosing files, fonts, or colors, but also for asking users yes/no questions and informing them about what's happening in the application. The last dialog class, QProgressDialog, can be used to create a progress dialog that informs users about the application's current state. These dialogs are the most common ones, and are therefore predefined in the Qt library. This section goes through these dialogs one by one.

Using the Color Dialog

QColorDialog provides you with a dialog for selecting colors. The class's only member function, getColor(), should be called to make the dialog appear. This function returns the selected color (actually, a QColor object representing that color). Listing 10.1 provides an example.

LISTING 10.1   A Color Dialog

```
 1: #include <qapplication.h>
 2: #include <qwidget.h>
 3: #include <qcolordialog.h>
 4: #include <qcolor.h>
 5:
 6: class MyMainWindow : public QWidget
 7: {
 8: public:
 9:         MyMainWindow();
10: private:
11:         QColorDialog *cdialog;
12:         QColor myColor;
13: };
14:
15: MyMainWindow::MyMainWindow()
16: {
17:         setGeometry( 100, 100, 200, 50 );
18:
19:         //Select a color and store it
20:         //in myColor for further use:
```

```
21:         myColor = cdialog->getColor( QColor( 0, 0, 0 ) );
22: }
23:
24: void main( int argc, char **argv )
25: {
26:         QApplication a(argc, argv);
27:         MyMainWindow w;
28:         a.setMainWidget( &w );
29:         w.show();
30:         a.exec();
31: }
```

Here, the return value of QColorDialog::getColor() is stored in myColor. By doing this, you can easily use this color for something useful. For example, you could set this color to be the color of the pen in a drawing program. The argument given to the getColor() function is preselected color. Figure 10.1 shows the color dialog.

FIGURE 10.1

The color dialog provided by Qt.

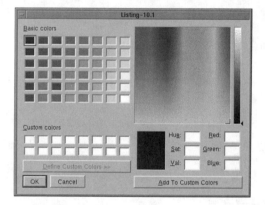

However, there's still one other task you need to perform. You see, if a user clicks the Cancel button in the color dialog, the getColor() function will return an invalid color, and myColor won't represent an actual color. However, you can easily check whether this is the case, as shown in the following example:

```
if( myColor.isValid() == TRUE )
{
    //myColor is okay and ready
    //to be used.
}
if( myColor.isValid() == FALSE )
{
    //myColor is not valid and
    //we must therefore abort.
}
```

As you can see, the `QColor::isValid()` function is used to determine whether `myColor` is valid. The first if-statement checks if the selected color is valid. If that is true, the program can go on and use this color. The second if-statement (which could simply be an else-statement, but an if-statement is used for clarity) checks if the selected color is invalid. If that is the case, the program must abort the operation. This is a simple way of avoiding problems. If an invalid color is selected, the program will not be able to use it, and in the worst case, the program will crash.

Using the File Dialog

The class `QFileDialog` provides a nice dialog for selecting a file. Like `QColorDialog`, it's very easy to use and can be implemented by a single line of code. See Listing 10.2 for an example.

LISTING 10.2   A File Dialog

```
 1: #include <qapplication.h>
 2: #include <qwidget.h>
 3: #include <qfiledialog.h>
 4: #include <qstring.h>
 5:
 6: class MyMainWindow : public QWidget
 7: {
 8: public:
 9:         MyMainWindow();
10: private:
11:         QFileDialog *fdialog;
12:         QString file;
13: };
14:
15: MyMainWindow::MyMainWindow()
16: {
17:         setGeometry( 100, 100, 200, 50 );
18:         //Select a file and store it in
19:         //file for further use:
20:         file = fdialog->getOpenFileName( "/", "*.txt" );
21: }
22:
23: void main( int argc, char **argv )
24: {
25:         QApplication a(argc, argv);
26:         MyMainWindow w;
27:         a.setMainWidget( &w );
28:         w.show();
29:         a.exec();
30: }
```

Here, memory is allocated for the QFileDialog object on line 11. Then, the dialog is executed on line 20 (this is where the dialog will be shown on screen). The filename selected in the file dialog (with its full search path) is stored in the QString object file (created on line 12). Also, two arguments are passed to the QFileDialog::getOpenFileName() function (line 20). The first argument represents the starting point in the file system (Windows users should change this to something like c:\), and the second is the filter that will be used. In this case, you'll only see files that end with .txt (text files). Figure 10.2 shows the file dialog.

FIGURE 10.2

The file dialog provided by Qt.

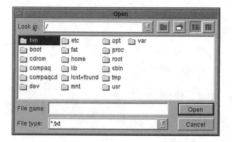

10

Again, the user has the ability to cancel the file section by clicking the Cancel button (just as with the color dialog). Therefore, you need some code that that takes care of this:

```
if( file.isNull() == FALSE )
{
    //A file name was found and
    //we can proceed.
}
if( file.isNull() == TRUE )
{
    //The file name is NULL
    //and we must abort.
}
```

Here, the QString::isNull() function is used to determine whether a file is selected.

QFileDialog includes a couple other interesting functions. QFileDialog::getExistingDirectory() lets the user select a directory, and QFileDialog::getOpenFileNames() lets the user select multiple files. See the Reference Documentation for more information about these functions.

Using the Font Dialog

In Qt, the QFontDialog class should be used to implement a font dialog. The function QFontDialog::getFont() is used to make the dialog appear. This function then returns a QFont object that represents the newly selected font. Listing 10.3 provides an example.

LISTING 10.3   A Font Dialog

```
 1: #include <qapplication.h>
 2: #include <qwidget.h>
 3: #include <qfontdialog.h>
 4: #include <qfont.h>
 5:
 6: class MyMainWindow : public QWidget
 7: {
 8: public:
 9:         MyMainWindow();
10: private:
11:         QFontDialog *fdialog;
12:         QFont myFont;
13: };
14:
15: MyMainWindow::MyMainWindow()
16: {
17:         setGeometry( 100, 100, 200, 50 );
18:
19:         //ok will be TRUE if the user
20:         //selected a font:
21:         bool ok;
22:
23:         //Select a file and store it in
24:         //file for further use:
25:         myFont = fdialog->getFont( &ok );
26: }
27:
28: void main( int argc, char **argv )
29: {
30:         QApplication a(argc, argv);
31:         MyMainWindow w;
32:         a.setMainWidget( &w );
33:         w.show();
34:         a.exec();
35: }
```

On lines 11 and 12, memory is allocated for one QFontDialog and one QFont object. On line 21, a bool variable is created. This variable is then used on line 25, where the QFontDialog::getFont() is called bring up the font dialog. On line 25, the selected font (returned by QFontDialog::getFont()) is also stored in the QFont object myFont. The font dialog is shown in Figure 10.3.

To determine whether the user has selected a font, you need to create a boolean variable (as done in Listing 10.3) and then pass the memory address of this variable to the QFontDialog::getFont() function. This variable (ok, in this case) will then be TRUE if the user selects a new font and FALSE of he or she clicks the Cancel button. Here's an example of how this can be done:

```
if( ok == TRUE )
{
    //A new font was selected,
    //we can proceed.
}
if( ok == FALSE )
{
    //The user clicked the cancel
    //button, we better abort.
}
```

If the user selects a new font, you then have that font stored in myFont, and you can use it for anything you like. For example, to define the font in a QLabel object.

FIGURE 10.3

The font dialog provided by Qt.

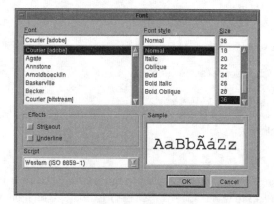

Using the Message Box

The message box, provided by the QMessageBox class, is the simplest of the predefined Qt dialogs. It can be used to show some short information (as demonstrated in an earlier lesson) or to ask the user whether he or she wants to proceed. The message box can show an icon and up to three buttons. Listing 10.4 provides an example.

LISTING 10.4 A Message Box

```
1: #include <qapplication.h>
2: #include <qwidget.h>
3: #include <qmessagebox.h>
4:
5: class MyMainWindow : public QWidget
```

continues

LISTING **10.4**   continued

```
 6: {
 7: public:
 8:         MyMainWindow();
 9: private:
10:         QMessageBox *mbox;
11: };
12:
13: MyMainWindow::MyMainWindow()
14: {
15:         setGeometry( 100, 100, 200, 50 );
16:         mbox = new QMessageBox( "Proceed?", "Do you want to proceed?",
17:                             QMessageBox::Critical,
18:                             QMessageBox::Ok | QMessageBox::Default,
19:                             QMessageBox::Cancel | QMessageBox::Escape,
20:                             0 );
21:         mbox->show();
22: }
23:
24: void main( int argc, char **argv )
25: {
26:         QApplication a(argc, argv);
27:         MyMainWindow w;
28:         a.setMainWidget( &w );
29:         w.show();
30:         a.exec();
31: }
```

Here, the QMessageBox constructor is used to create the message box (line 16 through 20). On line 21, a call to QMessageBox::show() is made, which causes the message box appear onscreen. As you see, quite a few arguments are passed to the QMessageBox constructor. The first argument (line 16) represents the text string that will be shown at the top of the window (also known as the window *caption*). The second argument (line 16) is the text string that will be shown in the message box (the actual message). The third argument (line 17) is the icon you want to be shown in the message box. Here you have four options:

- QMessageBox::NoIcon will not show any icon at all.
- QMessageBox::Information shows in information icon.
- QMessageBox::Warning shows an icon suitable for a warning message.
- QMessageBox::Critical should be used if you want to show some critical information or you want the user to make a critical selection.

In this case, the QMessageBox::Critical icon is used (line 17). The fourth argument (line 18) defines the first icon. In this case, the QMessageBox::Ok icon is used. This is combined with QMessageBox::Default to make it the default icon (it will be "clicked" if the user presses Enter or Return). The fifth argument (line 19) defines the second button. In this case, the Cancel button is chosen. This button is also combined with QMessageBox::Escape. By doing this, the button will be "clicked" if the user hits the Escape button.

You're not required at all to combine any of the buttons with QMessageBox::Default or QMessageBox::Escape.

The last argument defines the third button. However, this example only uses two buttons, so 0 is entered here. The result of this code is shown in Figure 10.4.

FIGURE 10.4

A message box with two buttons, a short question and an icon.

Of course, you have more to choose from than the OK and Cancel buttons. The others choices are QMessageBox::Yes, QMessageBox::No, QMessageBox::Abort, QMessageBox::Retry, and QMessageBox::Ignore.

Using the Progress Dialog

The progress dialog is used to inform the user about the application's current state (just like the progress bar). What makes a progress dialog different from a progress bar is that a progress dialog can interact with the user (that is, the user can abort the current task of he or she wants to). See Listing 10.5 for an example.

LISTING 10.5 A Progress Dialog

```
1: #include <qapplication.h>
2: #include <qwidget.h>
3: #include <qprogressdialog.h>
4:
5: class MyMainWindow : public QWidget
6: {
```

continues

10

LISTING **10.5** continued

```
 7: public:
 8:     MyMainWindow();
 9: private:
10:     QProgressDialog *pdialog;
11: };
12:
13: MyMainWindow::MyMainWindow()
14: {
15:     setGeometry( 100, 100, 200, 50 );
16:
17:     pdialog = new QProgressDialog( "Doing something...",
18:                     "Abort Operation", 100,
19:                         this, "pdialog", TRUE );
20:     pdialog->show();
21:
22:     int x = 0;
23:     int i = 0;
24:     while( x <= 100 )
25:     {
26:         for( i = 0; i < 1000000; i++ );
27:         pdialog->setProgress(x);
28:         x++;
29:     }
30: }
31:
32: void main( int argc, char **argv )
33: {
34:     QApplication a(argc, argv);
35:     MyMainWindow w;
36:     a.setMainWidget( &w );
37:     w.show();
38:     a.exec();
39: }
```

A total of six arguments are passed to the QProgressDialog constructor (lines 17, 18, and 19). The first argument (line 17) represents the text at the top of the progress dialog (not the caption). This should inform the user about what's happening. The second argument (line 18) represents the text on the "cancel" button. The third argument (line 18) is the total number of steps. In this case, the progress bar will reach 100 percent when QProgressDialog::setProgress(100) is called. The last three arguments have predefined values and can, in fact, be left out. However, if you want the progress dialog to be redrawn while it's working, you need to set the sixth argument to TRUE, and to do that, you also need to define the fourth and fifth arguments. If you don't set the sixth argument to TRUE, the label for the cancel button will never be visible.

To show how to use a progress dialog, I've created a loop that calls setProgress() with a higher value each time. This is definitely not what you would call a *real-life* example. However, it does show you how it works (see Figure 10.5).

FIGURE 10.5

Here, the progress bar is active and currently at 57 percent.

Creating Custom Dialogs

When the predefined dialogs aren't enough for you, you need to create custom ones—dialogs that are especially designed to meet your needs. Qt comes with a couple classes that make the creation of custom dialogs easier: QDialog (the base class for all dialogs) and QTabDialog (for creating tab dialogs).

Creating Custom Dialogs with QDialog

QDialog is the base dialog class—all other dialog classes are based on it. It provides you with a few basic functions for creating dialogs.

When creating dialogs, you have two types to select from: modal dialogs and modeless dialogs. A *modal dialog* starts its own event loop, and by doing this it blocks the rest of the program until the dialog is closed. A *modeless dialog*, on the other hand, doesn't block the rest of the application. You control whether your dialog should be modal or modeless by passing a boolean value as the third argument to the QDialog constructor. TRUE mean modal, and FALSE mean modeless.

Now, you'll look at a few important functions for working with QDialog. The QDialog::setCaption() function is used to set the caption of the dialog window. The functions QDialog::accept(), QDialog::reject, and QDialog::done() all destroy the dialog and return a value. Accept() returns the constant QDialog::Accepted (1), and Reject() returns the constant QDialog::Rejected (0). You can also define your own return value by passing the value (an integer) as an argument to the done() function. In fact, you can make calls to done(1) and done(0) instead of using accept() and reject(); you get the same result.

Another interesting feature of QDialog is that you don't have to use setGeometry() or resize() to define the size for the window. If you just place your widgets in the dialog, QDialog will automatically resize the window so that the child widgets fit. Listing 10.6 shows a simple example of how you can use QDialog to create a custom dialog.

10

LISTING 10.6   A Custom Dialog Created with `QDialog`

```
 1: #include <qapplication.h>
 2: #include <qdialog.h>
 3: #include <qlabel.h>
 4: #include <qpushbutton.h>
 5:
 6: class Question : public QDialog
 7: {
 8: public:
 9:     Question();
10: private:
11:     QLabel *label;
12:     QPushButton *big;
13:     QPushButton *small;
14: };
15:
16: //Here we define the dialog window. We pass three
17: //arguments to the QDialog constructor. The first
18: //two (parent and name) are set to 0. The third
19: //makes this dialog modal.
20: Question::Question() : QDialog( 0, 0, TRUE )
21: {
22:     setCaption( "Big or small?" );
23:
24:     label = new QLabel( this );
25:     label->setText( "Do you want to see a big
26:             or a small window?" );
27:     label->setGeometry( 10, 10, 300, 100 );
28:     label->setFont( QFont( "Arial", 18, QFont::Bold ) );
29:     label->setAlignment( AlignCenter );
30:
31:     big = new QPushButton( "BIG!", this );
32:     big->setGeometry( 50, 120, 90, 30 );
33:     big->setFont( QFont( "Arial", 14, QFont::Bold ) );
34:
35:     small = new QPushButton( "small!", this );
36:     small->setGeometry( 180, 120, 90, 30 );
37:     small->setFont( QFont( "Arial", 14, QFont::Bold ) );
38:
39:     connect( big, SIGNAL( clicked() ), this, SLOT( accept() ) );
40:     connect( small, SIGNAL( clicked() ), this, SLOT( reject() ) );
41: }
42:
43: class MyProgram : public QWidget
44: {
45: public:
46:         MyProgram();
47: private:
48:         Question *q;
```

```
49: };
50:
51: MyProgram::MyProgram()
52: {
53:     q = new Question();
54:     //Because Question is a modal dialog,
55:     //we call exec() instead of show():
56:     int i = q->exec();
57:
58:     //If the user clicks the button
59:     //labeled "BIG!", show a big window:
60:     if( i == QDialog::Accepted )
61:     {
62:         resize( 500, 500 );
63:     }
64:
65:     //If the user clicks the button
66:     //labeled "small!", show a small window:
67:     if( i == QDialog::Rejected )
68:     {
69:         resize( 50, 50 );
70:     }
71: }
72:
73: void main( int argc, char **argv )
74: {
75:     QApplication a(argc, argv);
76:     MyProgram w;
77:     a.setMainWidget( &w );
78:     w.show();
79:     a.exec();
80: }
```

10

As you can see, this program consist of two classes: one based on QDialog (lines 6 through 41), and one based on QWidget (lines 43 through 71). In the Question constructor, the dialog is set up with a label (lines 24 through 29) and two buttons (lines 31 through 37). On lines 39 and 40, the two buttons' clicked() signals are connected to the accept() and reject() slots of QDialog. This makes sure that the dialog will return the correct constant (that is stored in i at line 56). The class based on QWidget (MyProgram) is the main widget, and from this an object of the Question class is created (lines 48, 53, and 56). The value returned by the Question object (q) is then checked on lines 60 through 70, and the window size is set accordingly. You shouldn't have any problem understanding this program if you've studied and understood the preceding lessons. The comments in the code give you some further explanation. When you run the program, the first thing you'll see is the dialog shown in Figure 10.6.

FIGURE 10.6

The dialog created by the class Question *from Listing 10.6.*

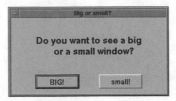

Now, if you click the "BIG!" button, a fairly large window will appear. On the other hand, if you click on the "small!" button, a little window will appear. These windows are shown in Figures 10.7 and 10.8, respectively.

FIGURE 10.7

The window that appears when you click the BIG! button.

FIGURE 10.8

The window that appears when you click the small! button.

You should now have a good understanding of how QDialog can be used. The example in Listing 10.6 could have been created with QMessageBox as well. But, now that you know how to use QDialog, you'll find it easy to create dialogs that are suited to your particular needs. You should, however, as often as you can, use the predefined dialogs to save time and work. But, when those dialogs can't do the job for you, you must do it yourself with QDialog.

Using the Tab Dialog

The other Qt class you can use to create custom dialogs is `QTabDialog`. With this, you can create so-called *tab dialogs*. A tab dialog is a widget that consist of several *pages*. You've probably seen this type of dialog in many applications. A tab dialog is good to use when you have a lot of widgets and you feel it would be confusing to have them all on one page. By using a tab dialog, you can split them up into categories, creating a page in the tab dialog for each category. This makes your application look much neater and easier to follow.

Listing 10.7 demonstrates how a tab dialog looks in its original state (when no tabs have been added to it).

LISTING 10.7   A `QTabDialog` Object in Its Original Form

```
 1: #include <qapplication.h>
 2: #include <qwidget.h>
 3: #include <qtabdialog.h>
 4:
 5: class MyMainWindow : public QWidget
 6: {
 7: public:
 8:         MyMainWindow();
 9: private:
10:         QTabDialog *tdialog;
11: };
12:
13: MyMainWindow::MyMainWindow()
14: {
15:         setGeometry( 100, 100, 200, 50 );
16:
17:         tdialog = new QTabDialog();
18:         tdialog->resize( 300, 250 );
19:         tdialog->show();
20: }
21:
22: void main( int argc, char **argv )
23: {
24:         QApplication a(argc, argv);
25:         MyMainWindow w;
26:         a.setMainWidget( &w );
27:         w.show();
28:         a.exec();
29: }
```

Figure 10.9 shows this empty tab dialog.

10

FIGURE 10.9

An empty tab dialog created by QTabDialog. *If you click the OK button, the tab dialog closes.*

If you want to add widgets to the tab dialog, you must create a few QWidget objects with child widgets *on* them, and then add the QWidget objects to the tab dialog with the QTabDialog::insertTab() function. You'll find an example of this in Listing 10.8.

LISTING 10.8   A Tab Dialog with Three Pages

```
 1: #include <qapplication.h>
 2: #include <qwidget.h>
 3: #include <qtabdialog.h>
 4: #include <qlabel.h>
 5:
 6: class MyMainWindow : public QWidget
 7: {
 8: public:
 9:     MyMainWindow();
10: private:
11:     QTabDialog *tdialog;
12:     QWidget *page1;
13:     QWidget *page2;
14:     QWidget *page3;
15:     QLabel *label;
16: };
17:
18: MyMainWindow::MyMainWindow()
19: {
20:     setGeometry( 100, 100, 200, 50 );
21:
22:     tdialog = new QTabDialog();
23:     tdialog->resize( 300, 250 );
24:
25:     page1 = new QWidget();
26:     page1->resize( 280, 180 );
27:     label = new QLabel( "This is Page 1.", page1 );
28:     label->setGeometry( 20, 20, 240, 140 );
29:     label->setAlignment( AlignCenter );
30:
31:     page2 = new QWidget();
```

```
32:        page2->resize( 280, 180 );
33:        label = new QLabel( "This is Page 2.", page2 );
34:        label->setGeometry( 20, 20, 240, 140 );
35:        label->setAlignment( AlignCenter );
36:
37:        page3 = new QWidget();
38:        page3->resize( 280, 180 );
39:        label = new QLabel( "This is Page 3.", page3 );
40:        label->setGeometry( 20, 20, 240, 140 );
41:        label->setAlignment( AlignCenter );
42:
43:        tdialog->insertTab( page1, "Page 1" );
44:        tdialog->insertTab( page2, "Page 2" );
45:        tdialog->insertTab( page3, "Page 3" );
46:        tdialog->show();
47: }
48:
49: void main( int argc, char **argv )
50: {
51:        QApplication a(argc, argv);
52:        MyMainWindow w;
53:        a.setMainWidget( &w );
54:        w.show();
55:        a.exec();
56: }
```

10

Here, the tab dialog is created on lines 22 and 23. Three QWidget objects that will represent each tab in the tab dialog are created on lines 25 through 41. One label is added to each QWidget object. Then, on lines 43, 44, and 45, the QWidget objects are added to the tab dialog with the QTabDialog::insertTab() function. On line 46, the QTabDialog::show() function is called to make the tab dialog visible. Figure 10.10 shows this program.

FIGURE 10.10

A tab dialog with three pages. Each page has a label on it.

That's all there is to it. You just create widgets as usual and then insert them using the QTabDialog::insertTab() function.

When you're inserting pages with the insertTab() function, you can add an ampersand sign (&) to the beginning (or in front of any character you want the shortcut to be associated to) of the label to automatically create a keyboard shortcut. For example, look at the following line:

tdialog->insertTab(page1, "&Options");

In this case, you can access the Options page by pressing Ctrl+O on the keyboard. This feature works with many other Qt widgets as well (such as menus, for example).

Summary

Dialogs play an important role in every serious application. Don't be surprised if you need to create 30 or more dialogs for a medium-sized application, and maybe over hundred for a large project.

Often you'll find that the predefined dialogs will be all you need. However, when they aren't, Qt's classes for building custom dialogs can be used. What's more, they do much of the work for you.

In this lesson, you have learnt to work with QT's predefined dialogs as well as creating custom ones. With the knowledge, you should be able to use Qt to create any kind of dialog for your program, no matter if it's a commonly used dialog or a personal creation.

Q&A

Q The widgets at the bottom of my tab dialog are only partly visible. What's wrong?

A As you can see, the tab dialog doesn't take up the entire window. There is free space all around it. If you expected the page to be the same size as the window, some of your widgets might not be visible or only partly visible.

Q I can't see the label or the cancel button on my progress dialog. What's wrong?

A You need to make your dialog modal. This is done by passing the boolean value TRUE as the sixth argument to the QProgressBar constructor.

Q Do I have to have three buttons in my message box? I just want one or two!

A No, you don't have to have three buttons. Just give the QMessageBox constructor the value 0 at the place where you would normally define the third button.

Workshop

The questions and exercises in this section of this lesson will help you retain what you've learned about dialogs.

Quiz

1. What is a dialog?

2. Does Qt provide any dialog for choosing a file?

3. Is it possible to select multiple files?

4. Why would you want to let the user select a color?

5. What class should be used to create a font dialog?

6. Which dialog should you use if you want to ask the user a simple question?

7. If you were about to open 50 files, what should you set the maximum progress value to?

8. Can you use the base class `QDialog` to create your own tab dialog?

Exercises

1. Create a program that uses the font dialog to let the user select a font. When this is done, show some text using this font.

2. Implement a color dialog in the program from Exercise 1. Let the user select both a color and a font; then use `QPainter` to show some text using the selected color and font.

3. Create a custom dialog that asks the user for his or her name. The user should be able to enter his or her name in a text-entry field and then push an OK button (or a similar button) to submit the response. After this, the program should respond by showing a new window with the message `Hello <name>, how are you today?`.

4. Create tab dialog. Add a few pages to it and then add some radio buttons, check buttons, and other widgets to these pages. If you have some other program that uses a tab dialog, try to copy the look of that tab dialog using Qt widgets. (A good example is the Options dialog in Microsoft Word.)

10

PART III

Learning More About Qt

Hour

HOUR 11

Using Layout Managers

Until now, you've placed your Qt objects by giving the absolute coordinates to the `QWidget::resize` and `QWidget::setGeometry` functions. The problem with this method is that if you resize the parent window, it will either be too small or too big for its child widgets to fit in. Your program will simply not look good anymore. This is where layout managers come in.

Layout managers are a set of Qt classes that control how and when the main window is resized. By registering your widgets with a layout manager and not giving the widgets absolute positions, the layout manager will resize or move the child widgets as needed when you (the user) resize the parent window. This makes your application easier to use and gives it a much better look.

Layout managers are also a great help when you need to place many widgets. This process is often very time consuming. With layout managers, you can do it much faster.

Understanding Layout Managers

To give you a better understanding of the layout manager concept (also known as *geometry management* or *layout management*), we'll now go through a real-life example (although a very basic one) of when layout managers can be useful.

Figure 11.1 shows a window with two QPushButton widgets on it.

FIGURE 11.1

A window with two QPushButton *widgets on it. It's not connected to any layout manager, so what will happen if it's resized?*

Let's say you want to make this window bigger; the result will then be something like what is shown in Figure 11.2.

FIGURE 11.2

What happens if you resize an image that doesn't use layout managers. In most cases, you want the widgets (buttons, in this case) to be resized and/or moved to suit the main window.

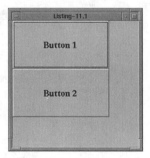

On the other hand, if you use a layout manager in the example shown in Figure 11.1, the result of resizing the window would look like what's shown in Figure 11.3.

FIGURE 11.3

A layout manager is used to control the position of the buttons. When you resize the window, the buttons' positions are changed to suit the new window size.

As mentioned earlier, you can also use layout managers when you need to place many widgets. For example, if you want to place ten `QPushButton` widgets, it would be very time consuming to enter the absolute position for every single button. Instead, you can create the buttons, not enter any absolute positions for them, and then register each one with a layout manager.

Using Layout Managers

Now you know what layout managers are and how they can be used. Therefore, let's go through what you should do to implement them in your program.

First of all, you need to know what layout managers are included in Qt and what you have to choose from. Table 11.1 lists the layout managers included in Qt 2.0 and describes what they do.

TABLE 11.1   Qt's Layout Managers

Layout Manager	Description
QLayout	This is the layout manager base class. All the other layout managers inherit this class. If you want to create a custom layout manager, it should be based in QLayout.
QGridLayout	This layout manager should be used when you want to arrange your widgets in a grid.
QBoxLayout	This is the base class for QHBoxLayout and QVBoxLayout. It should only be used if you, at compile time, can't decide whether the widgets should be placed in rows or columns.
QHBoxLayout	This is used when you want to arrange widgets in a row.
QVBoxLayout	This is used when you want to arrange widgets in a column.

The first class listed in the above table is the base class for the other four. You will rarely need to use this class, since you can solve most (not to say all) layout problems by mixing `QGridLayout`, `QBoxLayout`, `QHBoxLayout`, and `QVBoxLayout` (an example of how these layout managers can be mixed to achieve more complex layouts can be found in Listing 11.5).

Arranging Widgets in Rows and Columns

In the examples from the "Understanding Layout Managers" section, the two `QPushButton` widgets were arranged in a column. In the first example, the buttons were placed by hand. In the second example, the `QVBoxLayout` layout manager was used. The source code for Figure 11.1 is shown in Listing 11.1.

LISTING 11.1   Placing Widgets by Hand

```
 1: #include <qapplication.h>
 2: #include <qwidget.h>
 3: #include <qpushbutton.h>
 4: #include <qfont.h>
 5:
 6: class MyWidget : public QWidget
 7: {
 8: public:
 9:     MyWidget();
10: };
11:
12: MyWidget::MyWidget()
13: {
14:     setMinimumSize( 200, 200 );
15:
16:     QPushButton *b1 = new QPushButton( "Button 1", this );
17:     b1->setGeometry( 0, 0, 200, 100 );
18:     b1->setFont( QFont( "Times", 18, QFont::Bold ) );
19:
20:     QPushButton *b2 = new QPushButton( "Button 2", this );
21:     b2->setGeometry( 0, 100, 200, 100 );
22:     b2->setFont( QFont( "Times", 18, QFont::Bold ) );
23: }
24:
25: int main( int argc, char **argv )
26: {
27:     QApplication a( argc, argv );
28:     MyWidget w;
29:     w.setGeometry( 100, 100, 200, 200 );
30:     a.setMainWidget( &w );
31:     w.show();
32:     return a.exec();
33: }
```

As you can see, Listing 11.1 doesn't present anything new to you. But to make sure you understand the code, let's go through what basically happens. First, a new class is created, MyWidget, that inherits the QWidget base class. Then two buttons are created in MyWidget's only constructor. Finally, MyWidget's minimum size is set to 200 times 200 pixels. It's as simple as that! However, as stated earlier, the problem with this example is that the two buttons, b1 and b2, won't be resized/moved if you resize their parent widget (MyWidget). In Listing 11.2 (shown visually in Figure 11.3), this problem is solved.

LISTING 11.2 Layout Out Widgets with `QVBoxLayout`

```
 1: #include <qapplication.h>
 2: #include <qwidget.h>
 3: #include <qpushbutton.h>
 4: #include <qfont.h>
 5: #include <qlayout.h>
 6:
 7: class MyWidget : public QWidget
 8: {
 9: public:
10:     MyWidget();
11: };
12:
13: MyWidget::MyWidget()
14: {
15:     setMinimumSize( 200, 200 );
16:
17:     QPushButton *b1 = new QPushButton( "Button 1", this );
18:     b1->setMinimumSize( 200, 100 );
19:     b1->setFont( QFont( "Times", 18, QFont::Bold ) );
20:
21:     QPushButton *b2 = new QPushButton( "Button 2", this );
22:     b2->setMinimumSize( 200, 100 );
23:     b2->setFont( QFont( "Times", 18, QFont::Bold ) );
24:
25:     QVBoxLayout *vbox = new QVBoxLayout( this );
26:     vbox->addWidget( b1 );
27:     vbox->addWidget( b2 );
28: }
29: int main( int argc, char **argv )
30: {
31:     QApplication a( argc, argv );
32:     MyWidget w;
33:     w.setGeometry( 100, 100, 200, 200 );
34:     a.setMainWidget( &w );
35:     w.show();
36:     return a.exec();
37: }
```

11

This version of the program uses a layout manager (vbox, based on `QVBoxLayout`), and therefore looks slightly different. Let's go through the differences one by one:

- To begin with, a new header file from the Qt header library is included, called `qlayout.h`. This file holds the definitions for the layout manager's classes. In this case, `qlayout.h` is included to get access to the `QVBoxLayout` class.

- The second difference you'll notice is that `QWidget::setGeometry()` isn't used to change the size and position of the buttons. Instead, `QWidget::setMinimumsize()` is used to set the smallest size the buttons can have (200 times 100 pixels, in both cases). The buttons will appear with this size when you first launch the program, but this size is not absolute.

- Finally, a whole new object is added to the program. It's an object of the `QVBoxLayout` class, called vbox. This is the actual layout manager in the program. To make vbox know about the buttons (b1 an b2) and tell it to take care of their layout, the buttons have to be registered with the layout manager. This is done on line 26 and 27 with the `QVBoxLayout::addWidget()` function. When you're using layout managers, all widgets have to be registered like this.

 It's not only `QPushButton` widgets that can be registered and controlled by a layout manager. You can, in fact, use a layout manager to control the layout of any Qt widget.

That wasn't hard, was it? If you want to arrange your widgets in a row instead, simply use `QHBoxLayout` instead of `QVBoxLayout`.

Using `QGridLayout`

If you want to lay out your widgets in a grid, you should use the `QGridLayout` class (you could use `QHBoxLayout` and `QVBoxLayout` as well to create each row and column, but it's easier to use `QGridLayout`). Let's look at a simple example that uses `QGridLayout` to place six `QPushButton` objects in three rows and two columns. The source code for the example is shown in Listing 11.3.

LISTING 11.3   Placing Out Widgets with `QGridLayout`

```
 1: #include <qapplication.h>
 2: #include <qwidget.h>
 3: #include <qpushbutton.h>
 4: #include <qfont.h>
 5: #include <qlayout.h>
 6:
 7: class MyWidget : public QWidget
 8: {
 9: public:
10:     MyWidget();
11: };
```

```
12:
13: MyWidget::MyWidget()
14: {
15:     setMinimumSize( 200, 200 );
16:
17:     QPushButton *b1 = new QPushButton( "Button 1", this );
18:     b1->setMinimumSize( 200, 100 );
19:     b1->setFont( QFont( "Times", 18, QFont::Bold ) );
20:
21:     QPushButton *b2 = new QPushButton( "Button 2", this );
22:     b2->setMinimumSize( 200, 100 );
23:     b2->setFont( QFont( "Times", 18, QFont::Bold ) );
24:
25:     QPushButton *b3 = new QPushButton( "Button 3", this );
26:     b3->setMinimumSize( 200, 100 );
27:     b3->setFont( QFont( "Times", 18, QFont::Bold ) );
28:
29:     QPushButton *b4 = new QPushButton( "Button 4", this );
30:     b4->setMinimumSize( 200, 100 );
31:     b4->setFont( QFont( "Times", 18, QFont::Bold ) );
32:
33:     QPushButton *b5 = new QPushButton( "Button 5", this );
34:     b5->setMinimumSize( 200, 100 );
35:     b5->setFont( QFont( "Times", 18, QFont::Bold ) );
36:
37:     QPushButton *b6 = new QPushButton( "Button 6", this );
38:     b6->setMinimumSize( 200, 100 );
39:     b6->setFont( QFont( "Times", 18, QFont::Bold ) );
40:
41:     QGridLayout *grid = new QGridLayout( this, 3, 2 );
42:     grid->addWidget( b1, 0, 0 );
43:     grid->addWidget( b2, 1, 0 );
44:     grid->addWidget( b3, 2, 0 );
45:     grid->addWidget( b4, 0, 1 );
46:     grid->addWidget( b5, 1, 1 );
47:     grid->addWidget( b6, 2, 1 );
48: }
49:
50: int main( int argc, char **argv )
51: {
52:     QApplication a( argc, argv );
53:     MyWidget w;
54:     w.setGeometry( 100, 100, 200, 200 );
55:     a.setMainWidget( &w );
56:     w.show();
57:     return a.exec();
58: }
```

11

This example is shown in Figure 11.4.

FIGURE 11.4

QGridLayout *is used to place out six buttons in a grid.*

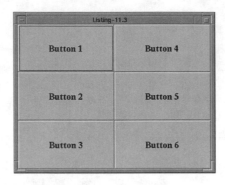

Now, the QGridLayout class is used to control the buttons. The syntax for creating and using this class is slightly different from QHBoxLayout and QVBoxLayout. To begin with, three arguments are given to the QGridLayout constructor instead of one. This is done on this line:

```
QGridLayout *grid = new QGridLayout( this, 3, 2 );
```

The first argument, this, is as usual a pointer to the uncreated MyWidget object. However, the second and third arguments are new to you. The second argument, 3, indicates how many rows the grid should have. The third argument, 2, indicates how many columns the grid should have. In this case, there should be three rows and two columns.

Then, just as with QVBoxLayout and QHBoxLayout, the QLayout::addWidget() function is used to add the widgets (buttons, in this case) to the layout manager (grid). As you can see though, two arguments are also added here. In addition to the this pointer being given as the first argument, QLayout::addWidget() is told in which row and column to insert the button. Take a look at the following line:

```
grid->addWidget( b1, 0, 0 );
```

Here, an object (b1) is inserted into the first row in the first column of the grid. This represents the upper-left button in Figure 11.4. Therefore, in the example from Listing 11.3, (0, 1) represents button 4, (2, 1) represents button 6, and so on. Figure 11.5 gives you a better view of this.

Now you know how to create grids of widgets with QGridLayout. For more information about this, see the Qt Reference Documentation, in the section earlier in this hour, "Understanding Layout Managers."

FIGURE 11.5

How the cells in a grid are identified.

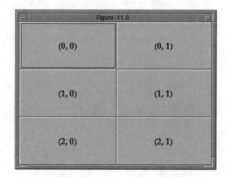

Understanding Nested Layout Managers

If you're familiar with C programming (or any other programming language, for that matter), you may have used nesting on the existing features of the language to achieve some other feature. For example, nested `if` statements are very usual in C. Basically, you put `if` statements inside other `if` statements, and in this way you get much better control over the program. Nesting can also be useful when working with layout managers.

For example, suppose you want to change the program in Listing 11.3 so that the left column has three rows but the right column only two. By using nested layout managers, it's quite easy to achieve this.

> Of course, you could also easily do this by placing the widgets by hand. But then you wouldn't get the layout manager features.

Listing 11.4 shows a solution to this problem, and Figure 11.6 shows the graphical result.

LISTING 11.4 Layout Out Widgets with Nested Layout Managers

```
1: #include <qapplication.h>
2: #include <qwidget.h>
3: #include <qpushbutton.h>
4: #include <qfont.h>
5: #include <qlayout.h>
6:
7: class MyWidget : public QWidget
8: {
```

continues

LISTING 11.4   continued

```
 9: public:
10:     MyWidget();
11: };
12:
13: MyWidget::MyWidget()
14: {
15:     setMinimumSize( 200, 200 );
16:
17:     QPushButton *b1 = new QPushButton( "Button 1", this );
18:     b1->setMinimumSize( 200, 100 );
19:     b1->setFont( QFont( "Times", 18, QFont::Bold ) );
20:
21:     QPushButton *b2 = new QPushButton( "Button 2", this );
22:     b2->setMinimumSize( 200, 100 );
23:     b2->setFont( QFont( "Times", 18, QFont::Bold ) );
24:
25:     QPushButton *b3 = new QPushButton( "Button 3", this );
26:     b3->setMinimumSize( 200, 100 );
27:     b3->setFont( QFont( "Times", 18, QFont::Bold ) );
28:
29:     QPushButton *b4 = new QPushButton( "Button 4", this );
30:     b4->setMinimumSize( 200, 100 );
31:     b4->setFont( QFont( "Times", 18, QFont::Bold ) );
32:
33:     QPushButton *b5 = new QPushButton( "Button 5", this );
34:     b5->setMinimumSize( 200, 100 );
35:     b5->setFont( QFont( "Times", 18, QFont::Bold ) );
36:
37:     QHBoxLayout *hbox = new QHBoxLayout( this );
38:     QVBoxLayout *vbox1 = new QVBoxLayout();
39:     QVBoxLayout *vbox2 = new QVBoxLayout();
40:
41:     hbox->addLayout( vbox1 );
42:     hbox->addLayout( vbox2 );
43:
44:     vbox1->addWidget( b1 );
45:     vbox1->addWidget( b2 );
46:     vbox1->addWidget( b3 );
47:
48:     vbox2->addWidget( b4 );
49:     vbox2->addWidget( b5 );
50: }
51:
52: int main( int argc, char **argv )
53: {
54:     QApplication a( argc, argv );
55:     MyWidget w;
```

```
56:     w.setGeometry( 100, 100, 200, 200 );
57:     a.setMainWidget( &w );
58:     w.show();
59:     return a.exec();
60: }
```

FIGURE 11.6

The buttons are put in place using nested layout managers.

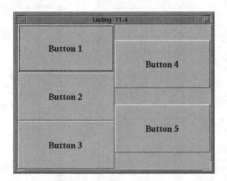

Some of the code in Listing 11.4 probably looks new to you. However, this new code is not hard to understand. On lines 37, 38, and 39, three layout managers are created—two QVBoxLayout (vbox1 and vbox2) and one QHBoxLayout (hbox). For the two QVBoxLayout objects, no parent widgets are entered (lines 41 and 42 explain this). On these lines, the two QVBoxLayout objects are inserted in the QHBoxLayout layout manager; this makes vbox1 and vbox2 child widgets of hbox. Note that the QLayout::addWidget() function isn't used to do this. Instead, the function QLayout::addLayout() takes care of this. On lines 44 through 49, the five QPushButton objects are inserted in vbox1 and vbox2.

There are some really useful functions available that let you place widgets dynamically, depending on the screen size and the window size:

- Call QApplication::desktop()->width() and QApplication::desktop()->height() to get the height and width of the screen that the program is currently running on.

- From your class's constructor, call this->height() and this->width() to get the width and height of your widget (most likely the main window).

Figure 11.7 shows a graphical explanation of the program in Listing 11.4.

FIGURE 11.7

*How the layout man-
agers are organized in
Listing 11.4.*

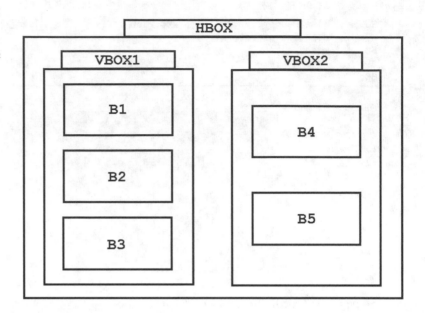

A Real-life Example

The preceding examples of using QPushButton objects are good to get you started with
layout managers. However, your programs will most likely contain more than just a few
buttons; they'll probably include other widgets as well. We'll now look at a more realistic sample program. The source code for this program is shown in Listing 11.5.

LISTING 11.5   A Real-Life Example of How Layout Managers Can Be Used

```
 1: #include <qapplication.h>
 2: #include <qlabel.h>
 3: #include <qcolor.h>
 4: #include <qpushbutton.h>
 5: #include <qlayout.h>
 6: #include <qlineedit.h>
 7: #include <qmultilineedit.h>
 8: #include <qmenubar.h>
 9: #include <qpopupmenu.h>
10:
11: class RLExample : public QWidget
12: {
13: public:
14:     RLExample();
15:     ~RLExample();
16: };
17:
```

```
18: RLExample::RLExample()
19: {
20:     QVBoxLayout *topLayout = new QVBoxLayout( this, 5 );
21:
22:     QMenuBar *menubar = new QMenuBar( this );
23:     menubar->setSeparator( QMenuBar::InWindowsStyle );
24:     QPopupMenu* popup;
25:     popup = new QPopupMenu;
26:     popup->insertItem( "&Quit", qApp, SLOT(quit()) );
27:     menubar->insertItem( "&File", popup );
28:
29:     topLayout->setMenuBar( menubar );
30:
31:     QHBoxLayout *buttons = new QHBoxLayout( topLayout );
32:     int i;
33:
34:     for ( i = 1; i <= 4; i++ )
35:     {
36:     QPushButton *but = new QPushButton( this );
37:     QString s;
38:     s.sprintf( "Button %d", i );
39:     but->setText( s );
40:
41:     buttons->addWidget( but, 10 ); used
42:     }
43:
44:     QHBoxLayout *buttons2 = new QHBoxLayout( topLayout );
45:     QPushButton *but = new QPushButton( "Button five", this );
46:     buttons2->addWidget( but );
47:     but = new QPushButton( "Button 6", this );
48:     buttons2->addWidget( but );
49:     buttons2->addStretch( 10 );
50:
51:     QMultiLineEdit *bigWidget = new QMultiLineEdit( this );
52:     bigWidget->setText( "This widget will get all the remaining space" );
53:     bigWidget->setFrameStyle( QFrame::Panel | QFrame::Plain );
54:     topLayout->addWidget( bigWidget );
55:
56:     const int numRows = 3;
57:     const int labelCol = 0;
58:     const int linedCol = 1;
59:     const int multiCol = 2;
60:
61:     QGridLayout *grid = new QGridLayout( topLayout, 0, 0, 10 );
62:     int row;
63:
64:     for ( row = 0; row < numRows; row++ )
65:     {
66:     QLineEdit *ed = new QLineEdit( this );
```

continues

11

LISTING 11.5   continued

```
67:        grid->addWidget( ed, row, linedCol );
68:
69:        QLabel *label = new QLabel( this );
70:        QString s;
71:        s.sprintf( "Line &%d", row+1 );
72:        label->setText( s );
73:        grid->addWidget( label, row, labelCol );
74:        label->setBuddy( ed );
75:        }
76:
77:        QMultiLineEdit *med = new QMultiLineEdit( this );
78:        grid->addMultiCellWidget( med, 0, -1, multiCol, multiCol );
79:        grid->setColStretch( linedCol, 10 );
80:        grid->setColStretch( multiCol, 20 );
81:
82:        QLabel *sb = new QLabel( this );
83:        sb->setText("Let's pretend this is a status bar");
84:        sb->setFrameStyle( QFrame::Panel | QFrame::Sunken );
85:        sb->setFixedHeight( sb->sizeHint().height() );
86:        sb->setAlignment( AlignVCenter | AlignLeft ); used
87:
88:        topLayout->addWidget( sb );
89: }
90:
91: RLExample::~RLExample()
92: {
93:        // All child widgets are deleted by Qt.
94: }
95:
96: int main( int argc, char **argv )
97: {
98:        QApplication a( argc, argv );
99:        RLExample *w = new RLExample;
100:        a.setMainWidget(w);
101:        w->show();
102:        return a.exec();
103: }
```

I recommend you study this code in depth and don't hesitate to use the Qt Reference Documentation whenever you find something new to you. Note that the widgets in this example don't all have the same "stretch" factor. This means that they're resized differently depending on what stretch factor they have. For example, the QMultiLineEdit widget bigwidget gets all new vertical space, whereas all widgets share new horizontal space. You'll find a visual explanation of the program in Listing 11.5 in Figure 11.8, and a screenshot of the compiled result in Figure 11.9 used.

FIGURE 11.8

A visual explanation of how the layout managers are organized in Listing 11.5.

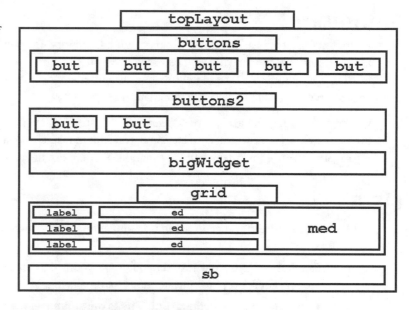

FIGURE 11.9

This is the result of Listing 11.5. As you can see, layout managers can do a lot more than laying out simple buttons.

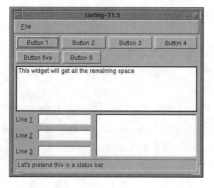

That's about it. Now you know how nested layout managers work. There's an unlimited number of ways you can mix the different layout managers to make them do what you want them to.

In some cases, even nested layout managers can't do the job for you. Then you have two choices: You can create a manual layout (described in the section "Creating Manual Layouts" of this lesson) or you can create your own custom layout manager. This is described in the Qt Reference Documentation in the file customlayout.html used.

Summary

Layout managers are a very important part of the Qt library. In many cases, using layout managers instead of manual layout can save you hours of work. You may think it's easier to stick with your usual (and more time-consuming) methods of placing widgets, but you should give the layout managers a fair chance.

Of course, this lesson hasn't covered every single aspect of layout managers. However, the Qt Reference Documentation does, and you should take a look, too, for additional information. You'll find many helping functions that are not mentioned in this lesson.

Q&A

Q Is there any difference in using a layout manager with Qt 2.x as opposed to Qt 1.4x?

A In fact there is. In the old 1.4*x* version of Qt, you had to make a call to `QLayout::Activate()` to activate the layout manager.

Q I'm making a very special layout. The layout managers simply can't do what I want them to. What should I do?

A You have two options: You can either create your own layout manager by creating a new class based on the `QLayout` class or you can reimplement the `QWidget::ResizeEvent()` function. Both these tasks are described in the Qt Reference Documentation.

Q Which Qt widgets can be controlled by layout managers?

A All Qt widgets can be controlled by layout managers. `QPushButton` widgets have mainly been used in this lesson for clarity reasons. Just remember to use the right function when you insert the widget in the layout manager.

Workshop

You're encouraged to work through the following questions and exercises to help you retain what you've learned in this lesson. Completing these questions will help you make sure you understand how layout managers work.

Quiz

1. What is a layout manager?

2. How can layout managers help you in your work?

3. How does `QVBoxLayout` organize its child widgets?

4. How does `QHBoxLayout` organize its child widgets?

5. How does `QGridLayout` organize its child widgets?

6. Which two numbers represent the upper-left widget in a `QGridLayout` layout manager?

7. When do you need to use nested layout managers?

8. When do you have to call the `QLayout::Activate()` function?

Exercises

1. Change the program in Listing 11.2 so that it organizes the two buttons in a row instead of a column. (You're not allowed to change more than two letters.)

2. Write a program that uses `QGridLayout` to organize six buttons in two rows and three columns.

3. Write a program that uses nested layout managers. It should place five buttons in three rows and two columns. The first and third rows hold two buttons, whereas the second (middle) row only holds one.

11

Hour 12

Working with Files and Directories

Have you ever thought about the importance that files and directories actually have in a computer? Without these two elements, you wouldn't be able to store anything on your computer, and it wouldn't be half as useful as it is today. Maybe this sounds silly, but there actually was a time when computers didn't have seemingly unlimited storing space (as many of today's computers do). At that time, storing information when the computer was turned off was always a problem, which people tried hard to overcome.

Luckily, this isn't where technology stands today. Therefore, it's probably safe to assume that you have at least a few bytes free to play with on your hard drive.

In this lesson, you'll learn how to use the hard drive (also known as *secondary memory*) to store and read information. In other words, you'll learn how to work with files and directories. This is an important issue that will come into play whenever you don't want your information to disappear after you exit your application and/or turn off your computer.

It's possible that you've worked with files and directories from within a C program before, and if you have, you've most likely used the file and directory functions specific for your operating system. However, if you do this, your program won't be portable at all; it will be hard to use on platforms other than yours. On the other hand, if you use Qt classes, your program will work on all other Qt platforms. What's more, even if portability is not (and never is going to be) an important issue for you, using Qt classes will make working with files and directories easier.

Reading Files Using Qt Classes

Maybe the simplest file system operation you can perform is to read a file. For example, if you want to show a help file to the user, it's more convenient to store this help text in a file rather than implementing the entire text in the program.

You'll now look at an example of how this can be done. You'll use Qt classes to open the file README that comes with the Qt distribution, create a text stream to it, and then show it in a QMultiLineEdit object. Listing 12.1 shows an example of how this can be done.

LISTING 12.1   Reading a Text File and Showing It Onscreen

```
 1: #include <qapplication.h>
 2: #include <qwidget.h>
 3: #include <qfile.h>
 4: #include <qtextstream.h>
 5: #include <qstring.h>
 6: #include <qmultilineedit.h>
 7:
 8: class MyMainWindow : public QWidget
 9: {
10: public:
11:     MyMainWindow();
12: private:
13:     QMultiLineEdit *medit;
14: };
15:
16: MyMainWindow::MyMainWindow()
17: {
18:     setGeometry( 100, 100, 480, 400 );
19:
```

```
20:      //Create the QMultiLineEdit object in
21:      //which we will show the text file:
22:      medit = new QMultiLineEdit( this );
23:      medit->setGeometry( 10, 10, 460, 380 );
24:      medit->setReadOnly( TRUE );
25:
26:      //Here, we assign the object file myFile
27:      //to the Qt README file.
28:      QFile myFile( "/usr/local/qt/README" );
29:
30:      //Set the mode to read-only:
31:      myFile.open( IO_ReadOnly );
32:
33:      //Create a text stream for the QFile object:
34:      QTextStream myStream( &myFile );
35:
36:      //Create a QString object and use the text
37:      //stream to read the file contents into it:
38:      QString myString;
39:
40:      //Until we have reached the end of the
41:      //file, read one line at a time:
42:      while( myStream.atEnd() == 0 )
43:      {
44:          //Read one line from the file:
45:          myString = myStream.readLine();
46:
47:          //Insert that line to the
48:          //QMultiLineEdit object:
49:          medit->insertLine( myString );
50:      }
51:
52:      //Close the connection to the file:
53:      myFile.close();
54: }
55:
56: void main( int argc, char **argv )
57: {
58:      QApplication a(argc, argv);
59:      MyMainWindow w;
60:      a.setMainWidget( &w );
61:      w.show();
62:      a.exec();
63: }
```

12

Here, the standard pattern for reading files is followed. First, a QFile object is created (line 28) to represent the file. Then, the mode of the QFile object (in this case, read-only) is set (line 31). A QTextStream object is then created (myStream) (line 34). This object will read the text from the file. The while loop then starts (line 42), reads one line at a time from the file, and outputs it to the `QMultiLineEdit` object. When the end of the file is reached, the `while` loop will stop. Finally, the connection to the file is closed via a call to the `QFile::close()` function (line 53).

> If you ever have problems opening a file, you might be trying to open it in a mode you don't have permissions for. In the preceding example, if you don't set the mode to read-only, the file will most likely not open because the default opening mode gives you more permissions than you actually have on the system.
>
> However, this problem shouldn't occur often in Windows 95 and 98 because it doesn't have the same strict file permissions.

> In this example, a text file is opened. However, it's possible that you'll need to open binary file at some point. In that case, you should use the `QDataStream` class instead of `QTextStream`.
>
> If you use `QDataStream` to write binary files, these files will become portable across all Qt platforms!

Figure 12.1 shows this program in action.

FIGURE 12.1

A `QMultiLineEdit` object showing a text file.

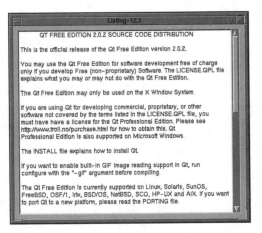

As stated, you often need to set the mode in which the file will be opened. You'll find a description of all modes in Table 12.1.

TABLE 12.1   File-Opening Modes

Mode	Explanation
IO_Raw	Opens the file in raw mode (no buffer will be used). This is probably not a mode you'll have to worry about.
IO_ReadOnly	This is the mode used in Listing 12.1. In this mode, you can only read the file, not write to it.
IO_WriteOnly	In this mode, you can only write to the file, not read it.
IO_ReadWrite	This opens the file on read-write mode. By using this mode, you can both read and write to the file (same as IO_ReadOnly | IO_WriteOnly).
IO_Append	This mode sets the file index to the end of the file. This means that when you write something to the file, it will be added at the end of it. This is often very useful when you want to add text to a file without deleting its current contents.
IO_Truncate	With this mode set, the file will be truncated if it exists.
IO_Translate	This mode turns on carriage return/linefeed translation in MS-DOS, Windows, and OS/2 systems.

You should also know that QTextStream includes definitions for the usual C++ streaming operators (<< and >>). Therefore, if you're more comfortable with those operators, you can use them instead to read and write to files.

Other interesting QTextStream functions include QTextStream::read() and QTextStream::setEncoding(). Instead of reading just one line, like QTextStream::readLine(), QTextStream::read() reads the entire stream. With QTextStream::setEncoding(), you can set the text encoding.

QFile also has some functions you might find useful. For example, QFile::exists() returns the boolean value TRUE if the file exists and the boolean value FALSE if it doesn't. QFile::remove() removes the file currently set. This function returns TRUE if the deletion was successful and FALSE of it wasn't. With QFile::setName(), you can set the name of a file. You can also get the name set by QFile::setName() by calling the QFile::name() function. See the Reference Documentation for a complete list of functions.

Reading Directories Using Qt Classes

In this section, you'll learn how to use the QDir class. You'll read the contents of a directory and output it to a QMultiLineEdit object. As you can see in Listing 12.2, this is very easy to do if you use Qt classes—you don't need to write more than a few lines of code!

12

LISTING 12.2   Reading the Contents of a Directory

```
 1: #include <qapplication.h>
 2: #include <qwidget.h>
 3: #include <qmultilineedit.h>
 4: #include <qdir.h>
 5:
 6: class MyMainWindow : public QWidget
 7: {
 8: public:
 9:     MyMainWindow();
10: private:
11:     QMultiLineEdit *medit;
12: };
13:
14: MyMainWindow::MyMainWindow()
15: {
16:     resize( 170, 400 );
17:
18:     //Create the QMultiLineEdit object which
19:     //will display the files:
20:     medit = new QMultiLineEdit( this );
21:     medit->setGeometry( 10, 10, 150, 380 );
22:     medit->setReadOnly( TRUE );
23:
24:     //Create a QDir object for the /etc
25:     //directory:
26:     QDir myDir( "/etc" );
27:
28:     //Write each file name to the QMultiLineEdit
29:     //object on a line of its own:
30:     for( int i = 0; i < myDir.count(); i++ )
31:     {
32:         medit->insertLine( myDir[i] );
33:     }
34: }
35:
36: void main( int argc, char **argv )
37: {
38:     QApplication a(argc, argv);
39:     MyMainWindow w;
40:     a.setMainWidget( &w );
41:     w.show();
42:     a.exec();
43: }
```

The concept here is quite different from reading files. You see, when you create the QDir object (line 26), you don't just create an object describing that directory; instead, you actually read the contents of the whole directory and can easily access the contents by using the index operator [ ] on the QDir object. In the preceding listing, the for loop is used to read all the directory contents, one by one (line 32). Note how the QDir::count() function is used (line 30) to get the number of items in the directory. Figure 12.2 shows this program.

FIGURE 12.2

A QMultiLineEdit object showing the contents of a directory (in this case, the /etc directory of a Linux file system).

In fact, QDir comes with a bunch of member functions that let you do all kinds of different directory operations. Table 12.2 describes some of the most popular ones.

TABLE 12.2 QDir Member Functions

Function	Description
QDir::setPath()	With this function, you can set the path to the directory you want to work with. In Listing 12.2, the path is defined through the constructor instead.
QDir::path()	Returns the path to the directory currently selected.
QDir::absPath()	Returns the absolute path—that is, a path that starts with / (the root directory).
QDir::canonicalPath()	Returns the path without any symbolic links (that is, the *real* path).
QDir::dirName()	Returns just the name of the directory (not the entire path to the directory).
QDir::filePath()	Returns the path to the file you enter as an argument.
QDir::absFilePath()	Returns the absolute path to the file you define as an argument.
QDir::cd()	Works just like the cd command. You enter the name of the directory you want to change to by entering it as an argument of this function.

continues

12

TABLE 12.2 continued

Function	Description
QDir::cdUp()	Moves up one level in the directory tree.
QDir::setFilter()	If you just want to see one or more particular types of items in the directory, you can set a filter with this function. You can then access this filtered list through the QDir::entryList() function. See the Qt Reference Documentation for more information.
QDir::mkdir()	Creates a directory with the name you give as an argument.
QDir::rmdir()	Removes the directory you give as an argument.
QDir::exists()	Returns TRUE if the directory exists; otherwise, it returns FALSE. If you enter a filename as an argument, the function will check whether that file exists instead.
QDir::remove()	This function removes the file you enter as an argument.
QDir::rename()	With this function, you can rename a file. The first argument is the name of the file, and the second argument is the *new* name of the file.

Another thing you should have in mind when working with QDir is that you don't have to convert the directory paths from UNIX to Windows style. If you just use / (UNIX style) to separate the directory names, Qt will take care of the conversion if the program is compiled under Windows.

QDir is a very useful class. Personally, I've used this class many times in programs other than actual Qt programs, just because it's so powerful. Although the standard C++ classes can do all the things QDir can, the fact that QDir is so much easier to use makes it superior to everything else (at least everything I've tested). A good example of this is how the [] operator can be used to traverse a whole directory. This is much harder to do with C++'s standard functions, although it's fully possible to use them for traversing a directory as well.

Getting File Information with Qt Classes

If you think of files in terms of human qualities, the file *attributes* would be the file's personality. Attributes describe how a file looks, what it can and can't do, and so on. It's very possible you'll need to know the attributes of a certain file to know how it should be handled. For example, an employer doesn't decide which employee to hire before he knows what every employee can do and whether the potential employee will fit in with the team. In the same way, you often need to know the size of a file, and whether it's readable, writable, and executable.

For this, you need to use the Qt class QFileInfo. With this class, you can easily get the file information you need. Just create a QFileInfo object and pass a string to it with the name of the file you want information about (it's also possible to pass a QFile object to it). After you've done that, you can find out the file's attributes by calling various QFileInfo member functions. All these functions return TRUE if the item (a file, a directory, or a symbolic link) has the attribute the function name applies Otherwise, FALSE is returned. Listing 12.3 shows an example of how QFileInfo can be used.

LISTING 12.3   Reading the Attributes of the Items in a Directory

```
 1: #include <qapplication.h>
 2: #include <qwidget.h>
 3: #include <qmultilineedit.h>
 4: #include <qdir.h>
 5: #include <qfileinfo.h>
 6:
 7: class MyMainWindow : public QWidget
 8: {
 9: public:
10:    MyMainWindow();
11: private:
12:    QMultiLineEdit *medit;
13:    QFileInfo *finfo;
14: };
15:
16: MyMainWindow::MyMainWindow()
17: {
18:    resize( 180, 400 );
19:
20:    //Create the QMultiLineEdit object which
21:    //will display the files:
22:    medit = new QMultiLineEdit( this );
23:    medit->setGeometry( 10, 10, 160, 380 );
24:    medit->setReadOnly( TRUE );
25:
26:    QDir myDir( "/" );
27:
28:    //We create an int variable to control
29:    //on which line in the QMultiLineEdit
30:    //object we are inserting:
31:    int line;
32:
33:    //This for-loop will investigate each item
```

12

continues

LISTING 12.3   continued

```
34:    //in the directory myDir. Each item will be
35:    //processed through the if-statements to
36:    //determine which attributes the item has.
37:    for( int i = 0; i < myDir.count(); i++ )
38:      {
39:        finfo = new QFileInfo( myDir[i] );
40:
41:        medit->insertLine( finfo->filePath(), line );
42:        line++;
43:
44:        if( finfo->isFile() == TRUE )
45:      {
46:        medit->insertLine( "is a file.", line );
47:        line++;
48:      }
49:
50:        if( finfo->isDir() == TRUE )
51:      {
52:        medit->insertLine( "is a directory.", line );
53:        line++;
54:      }
55:
56:        if( finfo->isSymLink() == TRUE )
57:      {
58:        medit->insertLine( "is a symbolic link.", line );
59:        line++;
60:      }
61:
62:        if( finfo->isReadable() == TRUE )
63:      {
64:        medit->insertLine( "is readable.", line );
65:        line++;
66:      }
67:        else
68:      {
69:        medit->insertLine( "is not readable.", line );
70:        line++;
71:      }
72:
73:        if( finfo->isWritable() == TRUE )
74:      {
75:        medit->insertLine( "is writable.", line );
76:        line++;
77:      }
78:        else
79:      {
```

```
80:          medit->insertLine( "is not writable.", line );
81:          line++;
82:       }
83:
84:          if( finfo->isExecutable() == TRUE )
85:       {
86:          medit->insertLine( "is executable.", line );
87:          line++;
88:       }
89:          else
90:       {
91:          medit->insertLine( "is not executable", line );
92:          line++;
93:       }
94:
95:          medit->insertLine( " " );
96:          line++;
97:       }
98: }
99:
100: void main( int argc, char **argv )
101: {
102:      QApplication a(argc, argv);
103:      MyMainWindow w;
104:      a.setMainWidget( &w );
105:      w.show();
106:      a.exec();
107: }
```

12

On lines 22, 23, and 24, a QMultiLineEdit object is created. This object will be used to present the results of the file-investigation. On lines 26, a QDir object is created for the / directory (which will be converted to C:\ if the program is compiled under Windows). Then, a for-loop starts on line 37. Inside this loop, a QFileInfo object (finfo) is referred to the current item. After this, a few if and else-statements are used to determine the attributes of the item. For this, the QFileInfo member functions are used. What will be written to the QMultiLineEdit object depends on what is returned by thos function.

So, the conclusion is that this program investigates each item in the / directory. Each item in the directory is processed by the for loop, and a few if statements determine which attributes the current item has. Figure 12.3 shows this program in action.

Other functions you might find useful when working with QFileInfo can be found in Table 12.3. Note, however, that some of the functions in this table aren't of much use on platforms other than UNIX/Linux.

FIGURE 12.3

The directory-investigation program from Listing 12.3. As you see, the first two items it finds are (.) and (. .).

TABLE 12.3   Useful `QFileInfo` Member Functions

Function	Description
`QFileInfo::readLink()`	Returns the name of the item a symbolic link is pointing at.
`QFileInfo::owner()`	Returns the owner of the item.
`QFileInfo::ownerID()`	Returns the ID of the owner of the item.
`QFileInfo::group()`	Returns the name of the group that the item belongs to.
`QFileInfo::groupId()`	Returns the ID of the group.
`QFileInfo::permission()`	With this function, you can test whether an item has a specific attribute. For example, `QFileInfo::permission( QFileInfo::WriteUser )` would test whether the item is writable by the owner (the user). If this is the case, `QFileInfo::permission()` will return `TRUE`. (See the Reference Documentation for more information.)
`QFileInfo::size()`	Returns the size of the item (most likely a file) .
`QFileInfo::lastModified()`	Returns a `QDateTime` object with the date and time the item was last modified.
`QFileInfo::lastRead()`	Returns a `QDateTime` object with the date and time the item was last read.

`QFileInfo` is a great invention; it can get you any information you want about a file, like its size and it's permissions, when it was last read, its owner and so on. What's more, like all other Qt classes, it's ridiculously easy to use.

Summary

As mentioned earlier in this chapter, quite often I choose to use Qt's classes for working with files and directories when I'm developing programs using some other library. I've even used these classes in text-based programs. Although my programming habits might not be of interest to you, they show you just how powerful these classes really are.

Perhaps you've used the standard C++ classes (or even the C functions and structures) when working with your file system, and you feel very comfortable with them. Maybe you have no plans at all to make your programs available on platforms other than you own. If so, you can continue using the methods you're already familiar with without problems. You should, however, keep one point in mind: Qt's classes for working with files and directories are great. Once you've learned to use them (which not will take long), you'll never want to use anything else.

Q&A

Q I use Windows and I don't understand all this talk about users, groups, file permissions, and so on. What are you talking about?

A These terms don't apply to the Windows platform; instead, they apply to UNIX. Your programs will work just fine anyway, without using the UNIX-specific functions.

Q I just can't open this file I'm trying to work with. I can't understand what's wrong!

A Make sure you have the permissions to open the file. The most usual cause of this problem is a lack of permissions.

Q In Listing 12.3, at the end of the `for` loop, I see the line
`medit->insertLine( " " );`
Why do you use this? Wouldn't it be easier to just increase `line` by two instead of one?

A Actually, you can't do that in this case. You see, the `QMultiLineEdit::insertLine()` function works such that if you give it a line number that's higher than the current number of lines, the text will be added to the line just after the last line anyway. Therefore, here an empty line is added to make some space between the item descriptions.

12

Workshop

It's time to work through the Quiz and Exercise sections in order to solidify your understanding of working with files and directories in Qt.

Quiz

1. Which class represents a file in Qt?

2. What is the QTextStream class used for?

3. What does the QDir class do?

4. How would you get the name of the fifth item in a directory?

5. When would you need to use the QFileInfo class?

Exercises

1. Use QDir to traverse a directory. Then use QFileInfo to get the size of each file in the directory. Finally, print out each filename and its size on screen (choose a good Qt widget for showing this information).

2. Write a simple program that uses Qt classes to save some text to a file. If you want, you can use a QMultiLineEdit object to let the user write the text and then save that text in a file. Note that you need to study the Qt Reference Documentation for this because the process of saving files was not covered in this lesson.

3. Write a simple program that creates a directory with QDir and then creates some files in that directory.

4. Write a program that deletes the files and directories created by the program in Exercise 3. Of course, you should use Qt classes to do this as well.

HOUR 13

Processing Text and Understanding Regular Expressions

If you want to retrieve some kind of information from a user, such as the user's name or email address, you need some kind of function to validate the input. This function should make sure the user enters appropriate information. For example, it's not desirable that the user enter his or her full name when you actually want is his or her email address.

You need something that can validate the submitted text and ensure it's the information that the program needs. Qt provides the QValidator class for doing this. It's an abstract class you can base new classes on and exactly define what's valid information and what's not. Validators can be used with QLineEdit, QSpinBox, and QComboBox.

To make it easier to define what should be valid information, Qt includes a number of definitions for regular expressions in the QRegExp class. A *regular expression* provides a way of defining an unknown character or an unknown number of characters. By using regular expressions, the process of creating a new validator class becomes much easier.

In this lesson, you'll learn to create validator functions using QValidator and QRegExp.

Understanding Regular Expressions

You'll start this lesson by going through the regular expressions included in the QRegExp class. This comes rather natural because the creation of validator classes more or less depends on regular expressions. If you've worked with regular expressions before with some other programming language, such as Perl, you probably won't find much new in this section. However, for those of you who are totally new to regular expressions, this section will be very useful.

As stated, a regular expression is a character that represents one or more other characters. You have probably seen the regular expression * that represents any character. A common use of this is to define file types. For example *.txt means all the files end with .txt (text files). By using all the different regular expressions that come with Qt, it's simple to create a validator that defines which strings are of interest to you and which are not.

Actually, there are two types of regular expression in Qt. First, there is the *meta* characters that represent one or more literal characters (depending on which meta character you're talking about). The other type of regular expression is the *excape sequence*. In contrast to the meta character, escape sequences represent one particular character.

Understanding the Meta Characters

This discussion will begin with *meta characters*. You'll likely find this type of regular expressions most useful. Table 13.1 lists and explains all the meta characters.

TABLE 13.1   The Meta Characters

Regular Expression	Explanation
.	Matches any single character. For example, 1.3 could be 1, followed by any character, followed by 3.
^	Matches the start of a string. For example, ^12 could be 123 but not 312.
$	Matches the end of the string. For example, 12$ could be 312 but not 123.

Regular Expression	Explanation
[ ]	Matches any of the characters you enter between the brackets. For example, [123] could be 1, 2, or 3.
*	Matches any number of the preceding character. For example, 1*2 could be any number of 1's (even none), followed by a 2.
+	Matches at least one character of the preceding type. For example, 1+2 must be one or more 1's followed by a 2.
?	Matches one or none of the characters of the preceding type. For example, 1?2 could be 12 or 2.

The meta character can also be set to *wildcard mode* by making a call to QRegExp::setWildcard(TRUE). When in wildcard mode, only three of the meta characters can be used, and their functions change a bit. This is described in Table 13.2.

TABLE 13.2 Meta Characters in Wildcard Mode

Regular Expression	Explanation
?	Matches any single character. For example, 1?2 could be a 1 followed by any single character, followed by a 2.
*	Matches any sequence of characters. For example, 1*2 could be a 1 followed by any number of characters, followed by a 2.
[ ]	Matches a defined set of characters. For example, [a-zA-z\.] matches any character (upper or lowercase) from a to z, and dot. [^a] matches everything but lowercase a.

If you've ever worked with regular expressions at a Linux/UNIX prompt, you're probably more familiar with the meta characters in wildcard mode. Which mode you select to work in is a matter of taste and what you're needing to do.

Understanding the Escape Sequences

The other type of regular expressions is called the *escape sequences*. These regular expressions are used to represent those characters that cannot be entered as usual, such as * and ?. A description of these expressions can be found in Table 13.3.

13

TABLE 13.3 The Escape Sequences

Regular Expression	Explanation
\.	Matches "."
\^	Matches "^"
\$	Matches "$"
\[	Matches "["
\]	Matches "]"
*	Matches "*"
\+	Matches "+"
\?	Matches "?"
\b	Represents the bell character (makes your computer beep)
\t	Represents a tab
\n	The newline character
\r	Represents the return character
\s	Represents any white space
\xnn	Matches the character with the hexadecimal value nn
\0nn	Matches the character with the octal value nn

As can you see, these expressions all start with a backslash (\). This is also how C++ represents certain characters. For example, the \ character should be typed as \\ in a C++ program. Therefore, to use one of the escape sequences defined in QRegExp, you need to add another \ to tell the program you actually want "\" to be printed. Therefore, to match ".", you actually need to enter "\\.".

Using the Predefined Validator Classes

In this section, you'll learn how to use the predefined validator classes QDoubleValidator and QIntValidator. You can use these two classes to validate double and int values. You'll go though two examples to see how to do this.

Using the QDoubleValidator Class

The QDoubleValidator class can be used to verify floating-point numbers. For example, if you want the user to input a floating-point number between 1 and 2, you can use QDoubleValidator to make sure the number really is between 1 and 2, and nothing else. QDoubleValidator is very easy to use. See Listing 13.1 for an example.

LISTING 13.1   An Example of How `QDoubleValidator` Can Be Used

```
 1: #include <qapplication.h>
 2: #include <qwidget.h>
 3: #include <qlineedit.h>
 4: #include <qvalidator.h>
 5: #include <qmessagebox.h>
 6:
 7: class MyMainWindow : public QWidget
 8: {
 9:     Q_OBJECT
10: public:
11:     MyMainWindow();
12: private:
13:     QDoubleValidator *dvalid;
14:     QLineEdit *edit;
15: public slots:
16:     void slotReturnPressed();
17: };
18:
19: //Define the slot which will be called
20: //when the user has entered a valid string
21: //and then presses Enter:
22: void MyMainWindow::slotReturnPressed()
23: {
24:     QMessageBox *mbox = new QMessageBox( "Validation Results",
25:                  "If you see this message, the string
26:                  you entered in the QLineEdit object is
27:                  acceptable.", QMessageBox::Information,
28:                  QMessageBox::Ok, 0, 0 );
29:     mbox->show();
30: }
31:
32: MyMainWindow::MyMainWindow()
33: {
34:     setGeometry( 100, 100, 200, 50 );
35:
36:     //We make the validator accept values from 0
37:     //to 10, with one decimal:
38:     dvalid = new QDoubleValidator( 0.0, 10.0, 1, this );
39:
40:     edit = new QLineEdit( this );
41:     edit->setGeometry( 10, 10, 180, 30 );
42:     edit->setValidator( dvalid );
43:
44:     //We connect the signal returnPressed() of
45:     //our QLineEdit object to our custom slot
46:     //slotReturnPressed()
```

13

continues

LISTING 13.1   continued

```
47:     connect( edit, SIGNAL( returnPressed() ),
48:          this, SLOT( slotReturnPressed() ) );
49: }
50:
51: void main( int argc, char **argv )
52: {
53:     QApplication a(argc, argv);
54:     MyMainWindow w;
55:     a.setMainWidget( &w );
56:     w.show();
57:     a.exec();
58: }
```

You probably understand most of this listing. However, there are a couple of new items that need some further explanation.

To begin with, you need to know what the arguments given to the QDoubleValidator class stand for. It's a very simple concept: The first argument represents the lowest value that the validator will accept, the second argument represents the highest value, and the third argument represents the maximum number of decimal places the validator should accept. In this case, the constructor will accept all values between 0.0 and 10.0, with one decimal place at most.

Also, the QLineEdit object (edit) is told to use the validator dvalid as its validator. This is done with the following line of code:

```
edit->setValidator( dvalid );
```

This procedure is exactly the same with QComboBox and QSpinBox objects as well; they also have the setValidator() function.

Now, compile and run the program. See Figure 13.1 for the result of this code.

FIGURE 13.1

A simple QLineEdit
*object that's connected
to a validator, which,
of course, you cannot
see at this point.*

If you now try to enter some text in the line edit, you'll discover that it's simply not accepted; no characters will appear. On the other hand, the line edit accepts digits, so they will appear onscreen. However, you've defined the validator only to accept numbers between 0.0 and 10.0 (with one decimal at most). You can test this by entering an unacceptable number and then hitting Enter. For example, try 123. Because you enter a number that the validator does not accept, nothing will happen. However, if you enter a valid number, such as 3.4, the slotReturnPressed() slot will be called and the window in Figure 13.2 will appear on your screen.

FIGURE 13.2

The message box that will appear after you've entered a valid number and then pressed Enter.

If you want to test more numbers, just click the OK button and then enter another number. This simple example illustrates well the validator concept: Wanted numbers (or characters) are accepted and unwanted numbers (or character) are ignored. As in this example, you can be sure to get the numbers you want, and don't have to worry about numbers that are out-of-range.

Using the QIntValidator Class

The other predefined validator that comes with Qt is the QIntValidator class. As mentioned previously, this class should be used to validate integers, in contrast to QDoubleValidator, which is used for validating floating-point numbers. You use QIntValidator almost exactly like QDoubleValidator. The only difference is that you leave out the constructor argument representing the maximum number of decimal places. After all, QIntValidator only works with integers.

You can change Listing 13.1 to use a QIntValidator object instead by just changing all QDoubleValidator instances to QIntValidator. Then, you simply delete the third argument to the QIntValidator constructor and change first and second arguments from double values to int values. Doing this will transform Listing 13.1 into a validator for integers instead of floating-point numbers.

13

Creating a Custom Validator

While the predefined validator classes are great for validating floating-point numbers and integers, you will most likely need to validate other things as well (such as characters or mixtures of characters and numbers). For example, for validating an email address. This is what you'll learn in this section.

You can create a custom validator class by using QValidator as its base class. In Listing 13.2, you'll learn how to create a class for validating an email address. With your new knowledge about regular expressions, this will not be a difficult task.

LISTING 13.2   An Email Validator

```
 1: #include <qapplication.h>
 2: #include <qwidget.h>
 3: #include <qstring.h>
 4: #include <qlineedit.h>
 5: #include <qvalidator.h>
 6: #include <qmessagebox.h>
 7: #include <qregexp.h>
 8:
 9: // ----- Start definition of custom validator -----
10: class EMailValidator : public QValidator
11: {
12: public:
13:     EMailValidator();
14:     QValidator::State validate( QString&, int& ) const;
15: };
16:
17: //We don't need to do anything in the constructor:
18: EMailValidator::EMailValidator() : QValidator(0)
19: {
20: }
21:
22: QValidator::State EMailValidator::validate( QString &text, int &pos ) const
23: {
24:     //Create a regular expression that matches any
25:     //e-mail address with a top-domain of three characters:
26:     QRegExp regexp( "*@*.???", FALSE, TRUE );
27:
28:     //Store the result of the query in result:
29:     int result = regexp.match( text );
30:
31:     //If the string matches the query, return Acceptable:
32:     if( result != -1 )
33:     {
34:         return QValidator::Acceptable;
35:     }
36:     //If it doesn't match, return Invalid:
37:     else
38:     {
39:         return QValidator::Invalid;
40:     }
41: }
42: //----- End definition of custom validator -----
43:
```

```
44: //----- Start Definition of MyMainWindow -----
45:
46: //Remember to make a .moc file of this class
47: //declaration and then include that file instead:
48: class MyMainWindow : public QWidget
49: {
50:     Q_OBJECT
51: public:
52:     MyMainWindow();
53: private:
54:     EMailValidator *evalid;
55:     QLineEdit *edit;
56: public slots:
57:     void slotReturnPressed();
58: };
59:
60: void MyMainWindow::slotReturnPressed()
61: {
62:     QMessageBox *mbox = new QMessageBox( "Validation Results",
63:                 "If you see this message, the string
64:                 you entered in the QLineEdit object is
65:                 acceptable.", QMessageBox::Information,
66:                 QMessageBox::Ok, 0, 0 );
67:     mbox->show();
68: }
69:
70: MyMainWindow::MyMainWindow()
71: {
72:     setGeometry( 100, 100, 200, 50 );
73:
74:     evalid = new EMailValidator();
75:
76:     edit = new QLineEdit( this );
77:     edit->setGeometry( 10, 10, 180, 30 );
78:     edit->setValidator( evalid );
79:
80:     connect( edit, SIGNAL( returnPressed() ),
81:         this, SLOT( slotReturnPressed() ) );
82: }
83: //----- End definition of MyMainWindow -----
84:
85: void main( int argc, char **argv )
86: {
87:     QApplication a(argc, argv);
88:     MyMainWindow w;
89:     a.setMainWidget( &w );
90:     w.show();
91:     a.exec();
92: }
```

13

When `QDoubleValidator` and `QIntValidator` were used in the previous examples, the predefined `validate()` function was used to determine whether the entered string was acceptable. However, here you need to define your own version of `validate()` (lines 22 through 41), because that's a virtual function of `QValidator`. In `EMailValidator::validate()`, you create a regular expression with `QRegExp` (line 26) and then check whether the entered string matches this expression with `QRegExp::match()`. If it does, you tell the validator to accept the string by returning `QValidator::Acceptable` (lines 32 through 35). If it doesn't match, `QValidator::Invalid` is returned (lines 37 through 40).

This new validator class is then used in the `MyMainWindow` class. Here, a `QLineEdit` object is created (lines 76, 77, and 78) and the `EmailValidator` class is used to validate the input to this object (line 78). A slot, `slotReturnPressed()` is also created (lines 60 through 68). This slot uses `QMessageBox` to show a message to the user. `slotReturnPressed()` is connected to the `QLineEdit::returnPressed()` signal (line 80 and 81), which is emitted when the user presses Return or Enter.

The result of this is that if you type an email address that matches `<anything>@<anything>.<three characters>`, the message box will appear. If you type something else, nothing will happen.

As you may have noticed, this validator doesn't accept all email addresses. This is because the top-level domain is defined to always consist of three characters. If the top-level domain of your email address only has two characters, the address will not be accepted. However, this is easy to fix.

The concept used in this example should be used to create any custom validator. And, with the powerful regular expressions provided by `QRegExp`, writing validators get really easy.

Using the `fixup()` Function

If you've looked up `QValidator` in the Reference Documentation, you've probably noticed that this class has another virtual function: `fixup()`. You can use this function for fixing strings that are not acceptable but not invalid either. Actually, `QValidator` includes a special type for this state: `QValidator::Valid`. If you find that the entered string is not acceptable, but it could be made acceptable, you should return `QValidator::Valid`, and the validator will then call the `fixup()` function, which should include the necessary code to make the string acceptable.

For example, if you only want to accept email addresses with the `.org` top-level domain, you could check this in `validate()`:

```
if( text[pos-3] != 'o' || text[pos-2] != 'r' || text[pos-1] = 'g' )
{
    return QValidator::Valid
}
```

Now, if the top-level domain isn't `.org`, `QValidator::Valid` will be returned and the `fixup()` function will be called. Here's an example of how you can use the `fixup()` function in this case:

```
void EMailValidator::fixup( QString &text )
{
    int pos = text.length();
    text[pos-3] = 'o';
    text[pos-2] = 'r';
    text[pos-1] = 'g';
}
```

This code makes sure the address ends with the three characters o, r, and g. This function can be helpful to correct small mistakes by users, as in the previous example. Or, to convert an entered string into the correct format. For example, of you want the user to enter his or her name and phone number, starting with the name. At this point, it's possible that users misunderstands this and enters the phone number first. By using the `fixup()` function, it's easy correct this.

Summary

Validators should be implemented whenever you feel there's a risk that the user will not enter fully correct information.

Many times, the actual validation (the code you write in `validate()`) can be done in many different ways. For example, you can choose to use wildcard mode. However, as mentioned earlier, this is a matter of taste and requirements.

As a final recommendation, you should avoid making the validation too strict; in other words, it's better to let an almost-acceptable string through than not to accept one that possibly should have been.

13

Q&A

Q I've worked a lot with MS-DOS; therefore, I think using the regular expressions in wildcard mode would suit me best. However, they don't seem to work exactly like what I'm used to. Is this correct?

A Yes, as you can see in Table 13.2, the meta characters in wildcard mode work as regular expressions in UNIX. Therefore, they don't work exactly like they do in MS-DOS.

Q The escape sequences don't work for me! What can be wrong?

A Remember that in C++ you need to type two backslashes (\\) to achieve one backslash. Therefore, you also need to use two backslashes with the escape sequences defined in QRegExp.

Q What about the escape sequence \b? What should it be used for?

A Test the following line of code:

```
cout << "\b";
```

If your computer is able to play beeps (it has a so-called *PC speaker*), you'll hear a beep from your computer when you run the code.

Workshop

Take a look at this section. You'll find some questions and exercises that will help you retain what you've learned about text processing and regular expressions.

Quiz

1. Why do you think QValidator is such an abstract class?

2. Are there any predefined validator classes at all?

3. If you answered Yes in the previous question, can you tell what this validator (or these validators) can be used for?

4. Which Qt classes can use a validator?

5. Which function do you need to call to tell an object to use a validator?

6. When creating your own validator classes, which virtual function do you insert the actual validation code in?

7. There's one certain virtual function that you can use to fix strings that are almost acceptable. What function is it?

Exercises

1. Rewrite Listing 13.2 so that it accepts addresses with top-level domains that consist of two characters as well.

2. Use `QIntValidator` to create a validator that verifies the temperature. Make it only accept reasonable values for your geographical area.

3. Write a custom validator for International Standard Book Numbers (ISBNs). These numbers use the form X-XXXXX-XXXX. (The form of ISBNs can actually vary a bit. However, just stick with one form here for the sake of simplicity.) The validator should make sure the entered string is in the correct form.

13

HOUR 14

Learning to Use Container Classes

In this hour, you'll learn one of the more technical aspects of Qt: the use of
container classes. You can use these classes to store other elements (such as
objects of other classes). Qt comes with a few container classes that,
together, make a full container class library that should be enough for any
task.

Before you begin, you should be aware that some parts of this hour might be
quite difficult to understand if you have no experience with C++ memory-
management techniques. However, just take it easy, step by step, and everything will be just fine.

Getting to Know Qt's Container Classes

As stated, container classes are used to store other elements (often objects of other classes). However, there are a few different methods you can use to store and access objects in a container class. Therefore, Qt comes with a few different container classes, and although some of them work very similarly, they all have different purposes.

An overview of Qt's container classes can be found in Table 14.1. This table illustrates the different uses of Qt's container classes. Take a look at it to get an overview of what the different container classes can be used for.

TABLE 14.1 Qt's Container Classes

Class	Description
QArray	This is a very simple class that can only store very simple elements. It can't store any other objects than the built-in ones and its elements mustn't have any constructors, destructors, or virtual functions.
QBitArray	This is a class derived from QArray. However, it can only store bits. It can be useful when you want to collect flags in a program.
QPointArray	This is another class derived from QArray. It can be used to store QPoint objects.
QDict	This class stores its elements in a hash table. A *hash table* is a table where elements are accessed via strings. For example, you can store pairs of strings in a QDict object and then access one of the strings through the other.
QIntDict	Works like QDict but uses long values instead of char*.
QPtrDict	Same as QDict but can use data other than char* for the keys (the strings that represent the elements in the hash table).
QCache	QCache works just like QDict. However, you can control the number of elements on a QCache object so that the list doesn't get too big.
QIntCache	Works like QCache but uses long values instead of char*.
QList	This class provides a doubly linked list, which is a common element in C++ programming. This is a very powerful kind of list that lets you insert and access elements in all kinds of ways. See the Reference Documentation for more information.
QStrList	This is a class derived from QList for storing lists of strings.
QStrIList	Same as QStrList, but this one use case-sensitive compare operations.
QStack	This class should be used when you want to create a list and then access the elements in reverse order (last in, first out).
QQueue	Use this if you want to create a list and then access the elements in the same order you inserted them (first in, first out).

These classes make a complete set of containers for storing any kind of data, from single bits to complete class objects. The most trivial container class, QBitArray, can store only bits (1s and 0s), in contrast to, for example, QList, which provides a double-linked list of any Qt class object.

By learning to use these classes, you will be able to create any kind of list with any kind of elements. The use of these classes will be discussed in more detail in the following sections.

Using Stacks and Queues

A *stack* is a well-known structure among programmers. It is used when you want to insert elements (of any kind) into a list and then retrieve them in the opposite order (last in, first out).

A *queue* is the opposite of a stack. With this kind of list, you retrieve the elements in the same order as they were inserted (first in, first out).

In Qt, stacks and queues are created with the classes QStack and QQueue. Working with these classes differs a bit from the other container classes. Therefore, they will be discussed separately in the following sections. The first section starts by looking at how QStack can be used.

Creating a Stack with the QStack Class

As stated, a stack should be used when you need to create a list of objects and then retrieve them in reverse order. This can be useful in many programming situations. Imagine, for example, that you are creating a Qt widget that the user can add icons to. However, you don't want the widget to hold more than ten icons at a time. If an icon is added when the widget is already full, the last inserted one should be removed to make room for the new one. By using a stack, this would be very easy to achieve.

Listing 14.1 provides an example of how QStack can be used. Here, a stack that can store strings (char) is created. Three elements are inserted into the stack. Finally, the elements are retrieved (and at the same time removed) and shown in a QMultiLineEdit object.

LISTING 14.1   Creating a Stack with QStack

```
1: #include <qapplication.h>
2: #include <qapplication.h>
3: #include <qwidget.h>
```

14

continues

LISTING 14.1   continued

```
 4: #include <qmultilineedit.h>
 5: #include <qstack.h>
 6:
 7: void main( int argc, char **argv )
 8: {
 9:     QApplication a(argc, argv);
10:     QWidget w;
11:     w.resize( 150, 150 );
12:     a.setMainWidget( &w );
13:
14:     QMultiLineEdit edit( &w );
15:     edit.setGeometry( 10, 10, 130, 130 );
16:
17:     //Create a stack for the char elements:
18:     typedef QStack<char> StringStack;
19:     //Create an object of this stack:
20:     StringStack stringstack;
21:     //Insert a few elements to the stack:
22:     stringstack.push( "Element 1" );
23:     stringstack.push( "Element 2" );
24:     stringstack.push( "Element 3" );
25:
26:     //While there's any element left in the stack,
27:     //get it and output it the QMultiLineEdit
28:     //object. Note that the pop() function also
29:     //removes one object from the stack.
30:     while( stringstack.current() )
31:     {
32:         edit.insertLine( stringstack.pop() );
33:     }
34:
35:     w.show();
36:     a.exec();
37: }
```

Almost everything in this example is very straightforward. However, line 18 might look new to you.

```
typedef QStack<char> StringStack;
```

This line creates a special type of stack that handles char elements; this stack is called StringStack. If, for example, you want to create a stack for int elements, the line would look something like this:

```
typedef QStack<int> IntStack;
```

As you can see, you just change the type between the angle brackets (< >). The name of the stack was also changed, but this, of course, is not required—you can call it whatever you like.

> It's very possible that you haven't even seen this use of angle brackets before. However, there's nothing mysterious about it; it's just C++'s way of defining what type a container class should store. However, if you have worked with the STL (Standard Template Library), this is nothing new to you.

> Note that the stack will handle its elements as pointers by default. You don't need to enter this:
>
> typedef QStack<char*> StringStack
>
> The stack will store pointers anyway. If you use this line, pointers to pointers will be stored instead. This applies to all container classes except QArray and QBitArray.

Just as with other classes, you can create an object of this class using the following line:

StringStack stringstack;

Then you use the class's member functions to insert elements into and retrieve elements from the stack. QStack::push() should be used to insert an item; QStack::pop() to retrieve an item (QStack::pop() also removes the item it retrieves from the list); and QStack::current() to get the current item without removing it. To remove an item from the stack without retrieving it, use the QStack::remove() function. Figure 14.1 shows the program created in Listing 14.1.

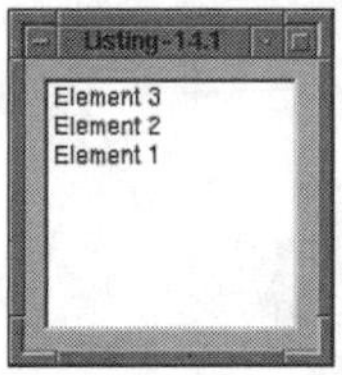

FIGURE 14.1

A QMultiLineEdit *object that has retrieved three items from a stack.*

As you can see, the items are retrieved in reverse order, with Element 3 first. As discussed earlier, this is because QStack retrieves elements from the same side as they were inserted. If a queue (QQueue) had been used, the elements would have been inserted in the QMultiLineEdit object in reverse order, starting with Element 1.

14

Creating a Queue with the `QQueue` Class

In contrast to a stack, a *queue* inserts its elements on one side and retrieves them on the other. This way, you can retrieve the elements from the queue in the same order as you inserted them.

So, if you decide to change the icon-widget example from the last section so that it removes the first item instead of the last when it needs to make room for a new one, you just need to change it to use `QQueue` instead of `QStack`. This would make the list work as a real queue: first in also gets out first.

Listing 14.2 is very similar to Listing 14.1, it just uses `QQueue` instead of `QStack`. The result of this is that the elements will be presented in the right order (as they were inserted).

LISTING 14.2   Creating a Queue with `QQueue`

```
 1: #include <qapplication.h>
 2: #include <qwidget.h>
 3: #include <qmultilineedit.h>
 4: #include <qqueue.h>
 5:
 6: void main( int argc, char **argv )
 7: {
 8:     QApplication a(argc, argv);
 9:     QWidget w;
10:     w.resize( 150, 150 );
11:     a.setMainWidget( &w );
12:
13:     QMultiLineEdit edit( &w );
14:     edit.setGeometry( 10, 10, 130, 130 );
15:
16:     typedef QQueue<char> StringQueue;
17:     StringQueue stringqueue;
18:     stringqueue.enqueue( "Element 1" );
19:     stringqueue.enqueue( "Element 2" );
20:     stringqueue.enqueue( "Element 3" );
21:
22:     while( stringqueue.current() )
23:     {
24:         edit.insertLine( stringqueue.dequeue() );
25:     }
26:
27:     w.show();
28:     a.exec();
29: }
```

As you can see, QQueue works pretty much the same as QStack. However, QQueue uses enqueue() and dequeue() to insert and remove elements instead of push() and pop(). Figure 14.2 shows the program created in Listing 14.2 in action.

FIGURE 14.2

A QMultiLineEdit object that has retrieved three items from a queue.

As stated, because a queue is being used this time, the items are retrieved in the order in which they were inserted, starting with Element 1.

There's no rule that tells you exactly when you should use a queue instead of a stack. This totally relies on how your program is organized and what your current needs are. However, as stated, queues should always be used when you want to retrieve elements in the same order as they were inserted, and stacks should be used when you want to retrieve the elements in reverse order. Note that the elements could be virtually anything, from single bits to Qt widgets.

Using Hash Tables

A *hash table* is a list from which you can retrieve objects through string keys. This can be useful in many cases. For example, if you're creating an email program and want to implement a contact list, you could easily create a hash table out of the names and email addresses. One particular email address could then be retrieved by the referring name. Or, on the other hand, a name could be retrieved by the referring email address. Listing 14.3 provides an example of how a hash table can be used.

LISTING 14.3   Creating a Hash Table with QDict

```
1: #include <qapplication.h>
2: #include <qwidget.h>
3: #include <qmultilineedit.h>
4: #include <qdict.h>
5:
6: void main( int argc, char **argv )
7: {
8:     QApplication a(argc, argv);
9:     QWidget w;
```

14

continues

LISTING 14.3 continued

```
10:        w.resize( 150, 150 );
11:        a.setMainWidget( &w );
12:
13:        QMultiLineEdit edit( &w );
14:        edit.setGeometry( 10, 10, 130, 130 );
15:
16:        typedef QDict<char> StringDict;
17:        StringDict stringdict;
18:        stringdict.insert( "Sweden", "Stockholm" );
19:        stringdict.insert( "Germany", "Berlin" );
20:        stringdict.insert( "France", "Paris" );
21:        stringdict.insert( "England", "London" );
22:
23:        edit.insertLine( stringdict["England"] );
24:        edit.insertLine( stringdict["France"] );
25:        edit.insertLine( stringdict["Germany"] );
26:        edit.insertLine( stringdict["Sweden"] );
27:
28:        w.show();
29:        a.exec();
30: }
```

This example was quite easy, wasn't it? First, a hash table for strings is created in lines 16 and 17. Then, four items are inserted to the hash table at lines 18 through 21. And finally, they are retrieved and inserted into the QMultiLineEdit object on lines 23 through 26. Note that the [] operator is used to access the strings. Figure 14.3 shows what this program looks like.

FIGURE 14.3

A QMultiLineEdit *object that has retrieved four strings from a hash table.*

As you can see in Listing 14.3, the strings have to be printed out, one by one—you can't use a while loop or something similar. Instead, you have to use an iterator to traverse a hash table. Iterators will be addressed later in this chapter.

QDict has a few other functions you might find useful, like QDict::clear() (which clears the whole hash table) and QDict::isEmpty() (to check whether the hash table is empty or not). See the Reference Documentation for information about those.

Note that the second argument given to the insert() function is the actual element. The first argument is the string key. Because strings are used as elements in this example, this can be hard to see.

Don't forget the other dictionary function: QIntDict. It can be used to store int values. If you can use QDict, you can use QIntDict as well.

Understanding Data Caching

The classes QCache and QIntCache can be used to create hash tables with a size limit. This means that you set a maximum size that the container can become, and if this size is reached, the least recently used element will be deleted. This could be useful if you want to pick up an exact amount of information, or you just want to control how many elements a hash table can have to reduce memory consumption. Listing 14.4 provides an example.

LISTING 14.4 Creating a Size-Limited Hash Table with QCache

```
 1: #include <qapplication.h>
 2: #include <qwidget.h>
 3: #include <qmultilineedit.h>
 4: #include <qcache.h>
 5:
 6: void main( int argc, char **argv )
 7: {
 8:     QApplication a(argc, argv);
 9:     QWidget w;
10:     w.resize( 150, 150 );
11:     a.setMainWidget( &w );
12:
13:     QMultiLineEdit edit( &w );
14:     edit.setGeometry( 10, 10, 130, 130 );
15:
16:     typedef QCache<char> StringCache;
17:     StringCache stringcache;
18:     //We set the maximum total cost to 6:
19:     stringcache.setMaxCost( 6 );
20:     //We let the cost for each element be 2
21:     //(default is 1):
22:     stringcache.insert( "Sweden", "Stockholm", 2 );
```

continues

14

LISTING 14.4   continued

```
23:     stringcache.insert( "Germany", "Berlin", 2 );
24:     stringcache.insert( "France", "Paris", 2 );
25:
26:     //Here, the total cost has already reached 6,
27:     //so what will happen?
28:     stringcache.insert( "England", "London", 2 );
29:
30:     edit.insertLine( stringcache["England"] );
31:     edit.insertLine( stringcache["France"] );
32:     edit.insertLine( stringcache["Germany"] );
33:     edit.insertLine( stringcache["Sweden"] );
34:
35:     w.show();
36:     a.exec();
37: }
```

Here, the cache is created on lines 16 and 17. On line 19, the maximum *cost* (explained below) is created for the hash table. On lines 22 through 28, four elements are inserted into the table. Each element is set to the cost of 2. On lines 30 through 33, the elements are retrieved and inserted into the QMultiLineEdit object. You can see the result of this program in Figure 14.4.

FIGURE 14.4

A QMultiLineEdit *object that has received three strings from a* QCache *object. But where is Stockholm?*

As you can see, only three strings have been received from the cache. Where is Stockholm? (Now, if you're silently thinking, *Hmmm...somewhere in Sweden*, you should know that your humor is not what it should be!) The simple explanation is that the maximum total cost was reached before the last element was added to the cache. Therefore, the cache simply removed the element that had been untouched for the longest time. Because none of the elements had been touched yet, the one inserted first was deleted.

Using QCache is very similar to using QDict. However, note how the maximum total cost was set with the setMaxCost() function and that each element's cost was defined by adding a third argument to the insert() function. If you don't define a cost for an item, the cost will default to 1.

QIntCache works just like QCache, but it should be used to store integers instead of strings. But, could it really be useful to refer one integer to another? Actually, it could. If you have a few integers that need to be organized in some way, you can add them to a QIntCache to number them, starting at 1, 2, 3, and so on. This way, you can easily retrieve the integer through its referring number.

Working with Iterators

For traversing a container class, it's best to use an *iterator*. An iterator is a special kind of class that is created for this special purpose; traversing a container. Although it's fully possible to use a while loop or something similar (as shown in Listings 14.1 and 14.2), it's better (since the traversing is safer) to use an iterator. For example, iterators can work with containers that change during the traverse. Also, you're required to use iterators for traversing the dictionary classes.

There's one type of iterator for each type of container class: QDictIterator, QCacheIterator, QIntCacheIterator, QIntIterator, QListIterator, and QPtrIterator.

All iterators include a few functions for traversing through a container. toFirst() can be used to get the first element in the container, and toLast() can be used to get the last element in the container. You can also use the ++ and -- operators with iterators to move forward and backward in the container. current() can be used to get the current element.

Listing 14.5 alters Listing 14.3 a bit so that it uses an iterator to traverse through the elements.

LISTING 14.5   Reversing a QDict Object with an Iterator

```
1: #include <qapplication.h>
2: #include <qwidget.h>
3: #include <qmultilineedit.h>
4: #include <qdict.h>
5:
6: void main( int argc, char **argv )
7: {
8:     QApplication a(argc, argv);
9:     QWidget w;
10:    w.resize( 150, 150 );
11:    a.setMainWidget( &w );
12:
```

14

continues

LISTING 14.5   continued

```
13:       QMultiLineEdit edit( &w );
14:       edit.setGeometry( 10, 10, 130, 130 );
15:
16:       typedef QDict<char> StringDict;
17:       StringDict stringdict;
18:       stringdict.insert( "Sweden", "Stockholm" );
19:       stringdict.insert( "Germany", "Berlin" );
20:       stringdict.insert( "France", "Paris" );
21:       stringdict.insert( "England", "London" );
22:
23:       //Create an iterator for our stringdict object:
24:       typedef QDictIterator<char> StringDictIterator;
25:       StringDictIterator stringdictiterator( stringdict );
26:       //Print out the elements to the QMultiLineEdit object,
27:       //one by one:
28:       for( stringdictiterator.toFirst(); stringdictiterator.current();
29:           ++stringdictiterator )
30:       {
31:           edit.insertLine( stringdictiterator.current() );
32:       }
33:
34:       w.show();
35:       a.exec();
36: }
```

Here, a QDict container is created on lines 16 and 17. A few elements are inserted at lines 18 through 21. On lines 24 and 25, an iterator is created. Then, lines 28 through 32 retrieves and inserts the elements into the QMultiLineEdit object. This is done by using a for loop and the iterator.

As you can see in Figure 14.5, the result of this listing is exactly the same as the result of Listing 14.3, but in a slightly different order.

FIGURE 14.5

A QMultiLineEdit object that has received four strings from an iterator.

Of course, you use the other iterators just like you use QDictIterator. Just make sure you use the right iterator for the right container.

By using iterators instead of loops to traverse a container, your program gets much safer and you are less likely to end up with a memory error. Since iterators are specifically designed to handle container traversing, they are capable of fixing most problems that might occur when you're stepping through a container (for example, when an element is added to the container during the traverse). A simple `for` or `while` loop would get confused about this and the program would most likely exit. So, you are encouraged to use iterators whenever you can to avoid bugs and other problems.

Summary

Using containers can be tough in the beginning. However, the Qt container classes make this whole concept easier. To be more precise, Qt container classes make the concept look easier, since the internal functions are still the same. If you've ever tried to create any of the functions provided by Qt's container classes by hand, such as a linked list, you understand. This is rather complicated stuff, so take the time to learn how to use the container classes.

Q&A

Q I'm trying to use the ++ operator with iterators, but I get a warning that this operator doesn't exist and another one will be tried instead. What's wrong?

A Make sure you've added the ++ operator before the iterator object, not after.

Q Can I have elements with different costs in the same cache?

A Yes. Just define the cost you want the elements to have when you insert them with `insert()`.

Q Can I store a class that I've created myself in a container class?

A Yes, you can. Just make sure you enter the name of your class between the angle brackets (< >) when you define the container (the line that starts with `typedef`).

Workshop

The following questions and exercises will test your knowledge of the material covered in this hour.

Quiz

1. When should you use the `QStack` container class?
2. When should you use the `QQueue` container class?
3. What is a hash table?
4. Which class would you use if you want to create a hash table with integer keys instead of string keys?

14

5. What is the QCache used for?

6. What happens when the maximum total cost value is reached in a cache?

7. When are you required to use an iterator?

Exercises

1. Create a queue with the QQueue class. Then, write a little loop that counts the number of elements in the queue and then prints out this number to some Qt widget that's suitable for this task.

2. Create a hash table with QIntDict. Add a few elements to it and then print out all the elements in reverse order using an iterator.

3. Create a cache with QCache and set the maximum total cost to 20. Add a few elements to the cache (they don't need to have the same cost). Make sure the total cost is 19 before you add the last element. Now, when you add the last element, what happens?

HOUR 15

Learning More About Graphics

In Hour 9, "Creating Simple Graphics," you learned the basics of Qt's painting functions. You saw how to make simple drawings with the `QPainter` class, how to change colors, and how to print out the graphics you created. This hour continues that discussion.

You'll look at a few other interesting graphic functions in this hour. Initially, you'll see how you can use the `QMovie` class to show animation in a program using the Graphics Interchange Format (GIF). You'll also learn how to load and save images to disk in addition to some other interesting techniques that can be used with `QPainter`.

Working with Animation

Qt provides you with a class called QMovie for showing animation (movies) in your programs. Currently, QMovie can only handle the GIF image/animation format. However, it's expected that other formats (such as AVI) will be added in the future. For now, you have to live with this limitation.

Creating a QMovie object, assigning it an animation, and then showing it onscreen is very simple, as shown in Listing 15.1.

LISTING 15.1   Animation in a QLabel Object

```
 1: #include <qapplication.h>
 2: #include <qwidget.h>
 3: #include <qlabel.h>
 4: #include <qmovie.h>
 5:
 6: class MyMainWindow : public QWidget
 7: {
 8: public:
 9:     MyMainWindow();
10: private:
11:     QLabel *label;
12: };
13:
14: MyMainWindow::MyMainWindow()
15: {
16:     setGeometry( 100, 100, 140, 80 );
17:
18:     //Create a QMovie object and tell it the
19:     //the animation we want to use can be found
20:     //in the file trolltech.gif. We make this
21:     //object a constant reference, otherwise
22:     //QLabel::setMovie won't accept it.
23:     const QMovie &movie( "trolltech.gif" );
24:
25:     label = new QLabel( this );
26:     label->setGeometry( 10, 10, 120, 60 ); ·
27:     //Tell label to use movie:
28:     label->setMovie( movie );
29: }
30:
31: void main( int argc, char **argv )
32: {
33:     QApplication a(argc, argv);
34:     MyMainWindow w;
35:     a.setMainWidget( &w );
36:     w.show();
37:     a.exec();
38: }
```

15

In this example, you use the animation `trolltech.gif`, which can be found in the `examples/movies/` directory of your Qt distribution. A `QMovie` object is created (line 23) for this animation (movie) and a `QLabel` object is used to show the animation (lines 25, 26, and 28). The `QLabel::setMovie()` function is used to tell the label about the movie (line 28). Also note that the `QMovie` object is a constant reference. This is simply because `QLabel::setMovie()` won't accept anything else. Figure 15.1 shows this program.

FIGURE 15.1

A window showing the `trolltech.gif` *animation.*

If you just see an empty window when running Listing 15.1, you probably didn't include GIF support when you compiled Qt (as mentioned in Hour 1, "Introduction to Qt"). You do this by adding the `-gif` option when running the `configure` script. Therefore, if you didn't include GIF support, you must recompile Qt as follows:

```
cd /usr/local/qt
./configure -gif
make
```

Then, recompile and run Listing 15.1 again.

When you start an animation, as in Listing 15.1, it will continue looping (starting over and over again) until you terminate the window that holds the animation. However, a few functions are available that you can use to control the animation. These are described in Table 15.1.

TABLE 15.1 Functions for Controlling Animation

Function	Description
`QMovie::pause()`	Call this function to pause the animation.
`QMovie::unpause()`	Call this function to turn on the animation again after you've paused it.
`QMovie::step()`	After you've paused an animation, you can make it step forward one frame by calling this function. After this is done, the animation is paused again. Actually, another version of this function exists that takes an `int` argument (it's overloaded so it's also named `QMovie::step()`; it just has a different argument list). This argument represents the number of frames that will be shown before the animation is paused again.

continues

TABLE 15.1   continued

Function	Description
QMovie::restart()	Rewinds the animation and, if it has not been paused, starts the animation over again.
QMovie::setSpeed()	With this function, you can set the speed of the animation. Just give the speed (as a percentage) as an argument to the function. The default, of course, is 100%.

> If you don't understand the difference between stepping and running a movie, here's an explanation: When you run a movie, the frames are changing all the time, and the objects are moving smoothly. On the other hand, if you call the QMovie::step() function, the movie will only change one frame and then stop again (as if it were a picture). You could say that running a movie is the same thing as calling QMovie::step() an unlimited number of times.

QMovie also includes a few functions for determining the current state of an animation. These functions are described in Table 15.2.

TABLE 15.2   Functions for Determining the State of an Animation

Function	Description
QMovie::steps()	After you've called step() to advance the animation a given number of steps, you can use this function to get the number of remaining steps. 0 is returned if the animation is paused.
QMovie::paused()	This function returns TRUE if the animation is currently paused.
QMovie::finished()	This function returns TRUE if the animation is stopped and finished (that is, all loops of all frames are complete).
QMovie::running()	Returns TRUE if the animation is running. Note that if an animation is single-stepping, it's not considered "running."
QMovie::speed()	Returns the current speed as a percentage.

By using the functions described in Table 15.1 and Table 15.2, you have full control over any GIF animation from within your Qt program. One or two animations can make any boring program look much more exciting. A good example of this is the little Netscape movie running at the upper-right corner of all Netscape windows.

15

 If you're looking for animated GIFs or tools to build GIF animation with, here's a good place to start:

http://dir.yahoo.com/Arts/Visual_Arts/Animation
/Computer_Animation/Animated_GIFs/

Loading and Saving Images

It's possible that you'll want to save the images you've created to a file. When doing this, you must first decide which image format to use. Qt comes with support for the most common image formats—PNG, BMP, XPM, XBM, and all the various PNM formats. As mentioned earlier, the GIF format is also supported. However, you can only view (load) GIF images, not save them. This is due to GIF patent restrictions. Qt also has its own platform-independent image format (that, on the other hand, only can be handled by Qt).

Working with Qt's Own Image Format

By using the QPicture class to record the operations you perform with the QPainter class, you can save your work done with QPainter to a file using Qt's own image format. Listing 15.2 shows an example.

LISTING 15.2   Saving QPainter Operations to a File

```
 1: #include <qapplication.h>
 2: #include <qwidget.h>
 3: #include <qlabel.h>
 4: #include <qpainter.h>
 5: #include <qpicture.h>
 6:
 7: class MyMainWindow : public QWidget
 8: {
 9: public:
10:         MyMainWindow();
11: private:
12:     void paintEvent( QPaintEvent* );
13:     QPainter *paint;
14:     QLabel *label;
15:     QPicture pic;
16: };
17:
18: MyMainWindow::MyMainWindow()
19: {
20:         resize( 200, 200 );
21:
```

continues

LISTING 15.2   continued

```
22:        paint = new QPainter();
23:        //Instead of painting in the window,
24:        //we choose to output to the QPicture
25:        //object:
26:        paint->begin( &pic );
27:        //We draw a rectangle. Not to the screen,
28:        //but to the QPicture object:
29:        paint->drawRect( 20, 20, 160, 160 );
30:        paint->end();
31:
32:        //Save what has been drawn to the QPicture
33:        //object to a file, called file.pic. When
34:        //you have run this program, a file with this
35:        //name will be created (in the directory which
36:        //this program is located in).
37:        pic.save( "file.pic" );
38: }
39:
40: //Of course, we also want to see the image
41: //on screen. This is taken care of by the
42: //paintEvent() function:
43: void MyMainWindow::paintEvent( QPaintEvent* )
44: {
45:        paint = new QPainter();
46:        //This time, we want to draw in the
47:        //window, so we let the this-pointer
48:        //define our drawing-area:
49:        paint->begin( this );
50:        //We use the drawPicture() function
51:        //to draw QPicture object:
52:        paint->drawPicture( pic );
53:        paint->end();
54: }
55:
56: void main( int argc, char **argv )
57: {
58:        QApplication a(argc, argv);
59:        MyMainWindow w;
60:        a.setMainWidget( &w );
61:        w.show();
62:        a.exec();
63: }
```

Here, a simple rectangle is saved to the file file.pic at line 36. By doing this, you can open the file at any time and show its contents onscreen. A paintEvent() function is also implemented (lines 42 through 53) to show the rectangle in the window. If you skip

15

this, the window appears empty, and only the output from QPainter will be saved to the file (see Figure 15.2).

FIGURE 15.2

A window with a simple black rectangle in it. What you don't see is that this rectangle has also been saved to a file.

As stated, you can now load the file.pic file at any time and show it onscreen. To do this, you need to use the QPicture::load() function:

```
QPicture pic;
pic.load( "file.pic" );
QPainter paint;
paint.begin( this );
paint.drawPicture( pic );
paint.end();
```

These few lines do it all for you: They load the file and show it in the widget you defined. You could easily implement these lines in the paintEvent() function of your program.

Working with Images of the Supported Formats

Loading and showing an image of one of the supported formats (that is, a format that you don't need any extra library to use) is not hard. You just create a QPixmap object for the image and then paint it with the QPainter::drawImage() function. Listing 15.3 shows an example.

LISTING 15.3 Opening and Showing an Image

```
 1: #include <qapplication.h>
 2: #include <qwidget.h>
 3: #include <qpainter.h>
 4: #include <qpixmap.h>
 5:
 6: class MyMainWindow : public QWidget
 7: {
 8: public:
 9:     MyMainWindow();
10: private:
```

continues

LISTING 15.3   continued

```
11:     void paintEvent( QPaintEvent* );
12: };
13:
14: MyMainWindow::MyMainWindow()
15: {
16:     resize( 150, 120 );
17: }
18:
19: void MyMainWindow::paintEvent( QPaintEvent* )
20: {
21:     //Create a QPixmap object for the
22:     //trolltech.bmp image:
23:     QPixmap image( "trolltech.bmp" );
24:
25:     QPainter paint;
26:     paint.begin( this );
27:     //Paint the image with its top-left
28:     //corner at horizontal position 11 and
29:     //vertical position 13:
30:     paint.drawPixmap( 11, 13, image );
31:     paint.end();
32: }
33:
34: void main( int argc, char **argv )
35: {
36:     QApplication a(argc, argv);
37:     MyMainWindow w;
38:     a.setMainWidget( &w );
39:     w.show();
40:     a.exec();
41: }
```

As you can see (line 23), you don't need to specify which format you want to load here. The QPixmap class takes care of this for you; it reads a small bit at the beginning of the file and, by this, can decide what format is used. Therefore, you don't have to bother with which format you're actually working with. Instead, you just have to know the name of the file (line 23).

In this example, a BMP image file, called trolltech.bmp, is used (line 23). You'll find this in the examples/widgets/ directory of your Qt distribution. Figure 15.3 shows what this image looks like.

FIGURE 15.3

A BMP image shown by the QPixmap *and* QPainter *classes.*

15

If your program will include functions that change the loaded images in some way, you'll most likely want to save any changes. Luckily, this is also a very simple task. You just use the QPixmap::save() function. This function takes two arguments: The first is a string representing the filename you want to save to, and the second argument is a string representing the image format you want to use. However, it's easiest to use the QPixmap::imageFormat() function for the second argument. This function returns the image format of the image that this QPixmap object represents. So, if you wanted to save an image to the file /home/user/image.bmp using the file format used by the image represented by the QPixmap object pixmap, you should make the following function call:

```
pixmap->save( "/home/user/image.bmp", pixmap->imageFormat() );
```

Support for the JPG format is not included in the Qt library. However, it's possible to use this format anyway. To do this, you need to include the qimageio.h header file, make a call to the qInitJpegIO() function, and then link your program with a JPG library. On Linux/UNIX systems, you link with the JPG library by adding the -ljpeg argument to your compiler (of course, you must have the JPG library installed to do this). See the section of the Qt Reference Documentation for more information about this.

Using QPainter's Transformation Functions

QPainter comes with many useful functions that can be used to transform your images in all kinds of ways. These functions are quite straightforward to use. Therefore, this section won't include any complete examples but rather just single lines of code.

Scaling Images

The QPainter::scale() function lets you rescale an image. It takes two double arguments. The first represents the horizontal scaling factor, and the second represents the vertical scaling factor. Figure 15.4 shows a small rectangle, and Figure 15.5 shows the same rectangle after scale(1.2, 1.2) (makes the rectangle 0.2 times bigger) has been called.

FIGURE 15.4
*The rectangle before
the scaling.*

FIGURE 15.5
*The rectangle after the
scaling.*

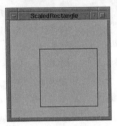

As you can see, the whole image is scaled, not just the rectangle. Therefore, it looks like the rectangle has moved toward the bottom-right corner of the window.

Shearing Images

With the `QPainter::shear()` function, you can shear an image. Figure 15.6 shows what happens with the rectangle in Figure 15.4 when `shear( 1.2, 1.2 )` is called.

FIGURE 15.6
*The rectangle from
Figure 15.4 after*
`shear( 1.2, 1.2 )` *is
called.*

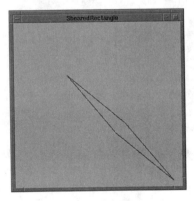

The two double arguments represent the coordinate system you want to shear.

Rotating Images

With the QPainter::rotate() function, you can rotate an image. Just enter the number of degrees you want to rotate the image as the argument. Figure 15.7 shows what happens to the rectangle from Figure 15.4 when rotate(30) is called.

FIGURE 15.7

The rectangle from Figure 15.4 after rotate(30) *is called.*

Keep in mind that the whole image is rotated, not just the rectangle.

Translating Images

You can translate (move the coordinate system of) an image with the QPainter::translate() function. It takes two arguments: The first argument represents the number of horizontal pixels that should be translated, and the second argument represents the number of vertical pixels that should be translated. In Figure 15.8, a call to translate(-20, -30) has been implemented for the image shown in Figure 15.4.

FIGURE 15.8

The rectangle from Figure 15.4 after translate(-20, -30) *is called.*

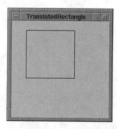

As you can see, the rectangle has moved 20 pixels to the left and 30 pixels up.

Changing the Viewport

With the QPainter::setViewport() function, you can set the size (in pixels) of the rectangle in which you want to paint. This way, you only paint in a given area of the paint device. By default, this rectangle is set to the size of your paint device (usually a window). Figure 15.9 shows what happens when you implement the line setViewport(10, 10, 40, 40) for the image shown in Figure 15.4.

FIGURE **15.9**

The rectangle from Figure 15.4 after setViewport(10, 10, 40, 40) *is called.*

This function can be useful when you've drawn borders around an area and want to continue drawing inside that area without touching the borders.

Setting the Window Size

With the QPainter::setWindow() function, you can set the size of the paint device. This function takes four integer arguments that define the rectangle representing the paint device. The first two define the upper-left corner of the rectangle and the following two define the bottom-right corner of the rectangle. Figure 15.10 shows what happens when you implement a call to setWindow(30, 30, 140, 140) for the sample image.

FIGURE **15.10**

Here, the size of the paint device is made smaller. Therefore, the rectangle appears to be larger than before.

As you see in Figure 15.10, making the paint device smaller gives you the same result as if you zoomed in on the area. On the other hand, if you make the paint device bigger, the rectangle will appear to be smaller than before. In Figure 15.11, a call to setWindow(-20, -20, 240, 240) has been made.

FIGURE **15.11**

Here, the size of the paint device is larger. Therefore, the rectangle appears to be smaller than before.

15

Summary

`QPainter` is very powerful. However, when it comes to programming, powerful often means *complicated*. This is also true of `QPainter`. It's a big class with many members and many options for each member. Fortunately, what you've learned in this hour and in Hour 9 should be enough in most cases. When it's not, the Qt Reference Documentation can help you find what you're looking for.

However, to find the right function with the Reference Documentation, you'll at least need to have a clue what the operation you're looking for is called. If you've worked with any graphics program, such as The Gimp or Photoshop, this shouldn't be any problem. If not, your task becomes harder, and your only choice is to simply test various functions to see what happens. Keep in mind, though, that empirical learning is the best way of learning, and testing can be really fun!

Q&A

Q Recompiling Qt is really time consuming! Isn't there any way I can speed up this process?

A You can't speed up the actual compilation. If you're short on space, you can leave the `.o` files on your hard drive after you've compiled Qt the first time. Then, if you need to recompile Qt (to add GIF support, for example), this process will be much faster. The `.o` files are deleted when you run `make clean`. So, if you have enough space, just skip this.

Q I'm trying to run a GIF animation that changes size during the animation. How can I make the `QLabel` object resize as the animation resizes?

A This is easy. First, create a slot that resizes the label:

```
void MyMainWindow::resizeLabel( const QSize &size)
{
    label->resize( size );
}
```

Then, tell the animation about this slot with the following function call:

```
movie->connectResize( this, SLOT( resizeLabel( const QSize& ) ) );
```

Now, the label will resize whenever the animation resizes.

Q After I've made a few transformations with `QPainter`'s transformation function, I want be able to undo these transformations so that the image looks as it did from the start. Is there an easy way of doing this?

A Yes, there is. Just make a call to `QPainter::resetXForm()`, and all your transformation operations will be undone.

Q Can't I just use a `QPixmap` object to open a GIF animation just as I would with any other GIF image?

A Well, actually you can. But you would just see the first frame of the animation. Therefore, the animation wouldn't be an animation but rather an image.

Workshop

You're encouraged to work through the following questions and exercises to help you retain what you learned in this hour about graphics.

Quiz

1. What's the first thing you need to do before you can show a GIF animation?
2. Is there any way you can speed up an animation?
3. Is there any way you can get the current speed of an animation?
4. Does Qt have its own image format?
5. Why should you use Qt's own image format?
6. Is it possible to use JPG images with Qt?

Exercises

1. Change the `paintEvent()` function in Listing 15.2 so that it reads the image file from disk instead of using the `QPicture` object directly.

2. Find a GIF animation that changes size (if you don't have any animation of this kind, a good place to look is `http://dir.yahoo.com/Arts/Visual_Arts/ Animation/Computer_Animation/Animated_GIFs/`). Implement a function in your program that makes the `QLabel` object resize as the animation resizes (as described in the "Q&A" section).

3. Make a program that draws a circle (a circle, not an ellipse). Use the `QPainter::rotate()` function to rotate the image. Rotating a circle won't make any visual difference. If there is a difference, find out why.

HOUR 16

Making Your Programs Communicate

By implementing functions for communication between objects in a program, or between separate programs, you can make the programs a lot easier to use.

The communication feature called the *Clipboard* is a memory area where you can temporarily store different kinds of data that you work with in your application (usually text). The Clipboard makes it very simple to move or copy data within a program or between programs.

The drag-and-drop feature provides an even more user-friendly way of moving or copying data. By using drag and drop, you can just grab an object with your mouse, drag it into another program (or another part of the same program), and drop it there.

Qt provides you with an easy way of implementing both Clipboard and drag-and-drop features. These are features you'll find in most modern GUI applications, so they're definitely something you should consider using in your application as well. This lesson will teach you how to do this.

Using the Clipboard

You can very easily implement Clipboard functionality in your Qt application. Actually, some Qt classes come with predefined Clipboard functions that are ready to use.

Using the Clipboard for Text

In most cases, the Clipboard is used to move or copy text. Fortunately, the QLineEdit and QMultiLineEdit classes include this functionality by default; the Clipboard function is activated when you create an object of one of these classes. You can copy or move text between QLineEdit and/or QMultiLineEdit objects with the key combinations Ctrl+C for copy, Ctrl+X for cut or move, and Ctrl+V for paste. These key combinations are standard for many GUI applications on both UNIX and Windows, so you're probably already familiar with them.

However, it's very possible that you'll want to let the users use buttons or menus for working with the Clipboard. For this, you need to connect the buttons or menus to the appropriate slots. See Listing 16.1 for an example of how this can be done.

LISTING 16.1   Working with the Clipboard Through Buttons

```
 1: #include <qapplication.h>
 2: #include <qwidget.h>
 3: #include <qmultilineedit.h>
 4: #include <qpushbutton.h>
 5:
 6: class MyMainWindow : public QWidget
 7: {
 8: public:
 9:     MyMainWindow();
10: private:
11:     QMultiLineEdit *medit1;
12:     QMultiLineEdit *medit2;
13:     QPushButton *copy1, *cut1, *paste1;
14:     QPushButton *copy2, *cut2, *paste2;
15: };
16:
17: MyMainWindow::MyMainWindow()
18: {
```

```
19:     resize( 300, 300 );
20:
21:     //Create the Copy, Cut, and Paste buttons
22:     //for the left QMultiLineEdit object:
23:     copy1 = new QPushButton( "Copy", this );
24:     copy1->setGeometry( 10, 5, 40, 40 );
25:     cut1 = new QPushButton( "Cut", this );
26:     cut1->setGeometry( 55, 5, 40, 40 );
27:     paste1 = new QPushButton( "Paste", this );
28:     paste1->setGeometry( 100, 5, 40, 40 );
29:
30:     //Create the Copy, Cut, and Paste buttons
31:     //for the right QMultiLineEdit object:
32:     copy2 = new QPushButton( "Copy", this );
33:     copy2->setGeometry( 160, 5, 40, 40 );
34:     cut2 = new QPushButton( "Cut", this );
35:     cut2->setGeometry( 205, 5, 40, 40 );
36:     paste2 = new QPushButton( "Paste", this );
37:     paste2->setGeometry( 250, 5, 40, 40 );
38:
39:     //Create the left QMultiLineEdit object:
40:     medit1 = new QMultiLineEdit( this );
41:     medit1->setGeometry( 5, 50, 140, 245 );
42:
43:     //Create the right QMultiLineEdit object:
44:     medit2 = new QMultiLineEdit( this );
45:     medit2->setGeometry( 155, 50, 140, 245 );
46:
47:     //Connect the left buttons to the appropriate slots:
48:     connect( copy1, SIGNAL( clicked() ), medit1, SLOT( copy() ) );
49:     connect( cut1, SIGNAL( clicked() ), medit1, SLOT( cut() ) );
50:     connect( paste1, SIGNAL( clicked() ), medit1, SLOT( paste() ) );
51:
52:     //Connect the right buttons to the appropriate slots:
53:     connect( copy2, SIGNAL( clicked() ), medit2, SLOT( copy() ) );
54:     connect( cut2, SIGNAL( clicked() ), medit2, SLOT( cut() ) );
55:     connect( paste2, SIGNAL( clicked() ), medit2, SLOT( paste() ) );
56: }
57:
58: void main( int argc, char **argv )
59: {
60:     QApplication a(argc, argv);
61:     MyMainWindow w;
62:     a.setMainWidget( &w );
63:     w.show();
64:     a.exec();
65: }
```

16

Here, you create two QMultiLineEdit objects (lines 40, 41, 44, and 45) and three buttons for each QMultiLineEdit object for controlling the Cut, Copy, and Paste functions.

The buttons for the left QMultiLineEdit object are created on lines 23 through 28, and the buttons for the right QMultiLineEdit object is created on lines 32 through 37. Then, on lines 48, 49, and 50, and on lines 53, 54, and 55, the buttons' clicked() signals are connected to the appropriate slots on the respective QMultiLineEdit objects (copy(), cut(), and paste()). The result of this is that you can copy, cut, and paste text between the two QMultiLineEdit objects through the six buttons. Figure 16.1 shows this program in action.

FIGURE 16.1

Text was entered in the left QMultiLineEdit *object (medit1) and then copied to the right* QMultiLineEdit *object (medit2).*

You can now copy or move text between medit1 and medit2 by using the buttons or the keyboard combinations for accessing the Clipboard.

Using the Clipboard for Pixmaps

The QClipboard class (which handles the Clipboard functions in Qt) also supports pixmaps. However, there are no defined functions for copying, cutting, and pasting pixmaps, so you have to do that yourself. Actually, this is much easier than it sounds. Listing 16.2 shows an example of how this can be done.

LISTING 16.2   Using Pixmaps on the Clipboard

```
 1: #include <qapplication.h>
 2: #include <qwidget.h>
 3: #include <qpixmap.h>
 4: #include <qlistbox.h>
 5: #include <qpushbutton.h>
 6: #include <qclipboard.h>
 7:
 8: #include "clipboard.moc"
 9:
10: //Since this class includes custom slots,
11: //remember to put the class definition in
12: //a file of its own and then use the MOC
13: //on it.
```

```
14: class MyMainWindow : public QWidget
15: {
16:     Q_OBJECT
17: public:
18:     MyMainWindow();
19: private:
20:     QListBox *left;
21:     QListBox *right;
22:     QPushButton *copy;
23:     QPushButton *cut;
24:     QPushButton *paste;
25: public slots:
26:     //We define one slot for each of the
27:     //clipboard functions:
28:     void copyXPM();
29:     void cutXPM();
30:     void pasteXPM();
31: };
32:
33: //The copyXPM() function will take the currently
34: //selected pixmap from the left QListBox object
35: //and copy it to the clipboard:
36: void MyMainWindow::copyXPM()
37: {
38:     const QPixmap temp( *(left->pixmap( left->currentItem())) );
39:     QApplication::clipboard()->setPixmap( temp );
40: }
41:
42: //The cutXPM() function works just like copyXPM().
43: //However, it also removed the item you selected
44: //to cut:
45: void MyMainWindow::cutXPM()
46: {
47:     const QPixmap temp( *(left->pixmap( left->currentItem())) );
48:     QApplication::clipboard()->setPixmap( temp);
49:     left->removeItem( left->currentItem() );
50: }
51:
52: //The pasteXPM() function inserts the pixmap
53: //currently in the clipboard into the right
54: //QListBox object:
55: void MyMainWindow::pasteXPM()
56: {
57:     right->insertItem( QApplication::clipboard()->pixmap() );
58: }
59:
60: MyMainWindow::MyMainWindow()
61: {
62:     resize( 200, 180 );
63:
```

continues

LISTING 16.2 continued

```
64:        QPixmap pixmap( "home.xpm" );
65:
66:        left = new QListBox( this );
67:        left->setGeometry( 10, 40, 85, 130 );
68:        left->insertItem( pixmap );
69:
70:        right = new QListBox( this );
71:        right->setGeometry( 105, 40, 85, 130 );
72:
73:        copy = new QPushButton( "Copy", this );
74:        copy->setGeometry( 10, 10, 35, 20 );
75:
76:        cut = new QPushButton( "Cut", this );
77:        cut->setGeometry( 55, 10, 35, 20 );
78:
79:        paste = new QPushButton( "Paste", this );
80:        paste->setGeometry( 115, 10, 75, 20 );
81:
82:        //Connect the buttons to the slots we just created:
83:        connect( copy, SIGNAL( clicked() ), this, SLOT( copyXPM() ) );
84:        connect( cut, SIGNAL( clicked() ), this, SLOT( cutXPM() ) );
85:        connect( paste, SIGNAL( clicked() ), this, SLOT( pasteXPM() ) );
86: }
87:
88: void main( int argc, char **argv )
89: {
90:        QApplication a(argc, argv);
91:        MyMainWindow w;
92:        a.setMainWidget( &w );
93:        w.show();
94:        a.exec();
95: }
```

In this program, you explicitly call the QClipboard member functions to insert and retrieve pixmaps between two QListBox objects. For this, three slots are created: copyXPM(), cutXPM(), and pasteXPM(). The copyXPM() slot, defined in lines 26 through 40, takes the currently selected item from the left QListBox object and copies it into the Clipboard with the QClipboard::setPixmap() function (lines 38 and 39). The cutXPM() slot, defined in lines 45 through 50, looks pretty much like copyXPM() but with the difference that it also removes the selected item with the QListBox::removeItem() function (line 49). The last custom slot in this listing is pasteXPM() (lines 55 through 58). This includes one single line of code (line 57) that takes the pixmap currently in the Clipboard (by using the QClipboard::pixmap() function) and inserts it into the right QListBox object with the QListBox::insertItem() function. Then, in the MyMainWindow contructor, three buttons, `copy`, `cut`, and `paste`, are created (lines 73 through 80). The `clicked()` signals of the buttons are connected to the appropriate slots on lines 83, 84, and 85. The result of this is that you can copy or cut the pixmap (created and inserted at lines 64 and 68) in the left `QListBox` object to the right `QListBox` object. See Figures 16.2, 16.3, and 16.4 for how the program works.

FIGURE 16.2

The program in its initial state (as it first appears onscreen).

FIGURE 16.3

The Copy button has been clicked once and the Paste button has been clicked three times.

FIGURE 16.4

Starting from the program's initial state, the Cut button has been clicked once and the Paste button has been clicked five times.

If you want to work with images instead of pixmaps, use the `QClipboard::setImage()` and `QClipboard::image()` functions instead of `QClipboard::setPixmap()` and `QClipboard::pixmap()`.

Note that you don't create any `QClipboard` objects. Actually, because the `QClipboard` constructor and destructor are private, you can't create any objects of this class. Instead, `QClipboard` objects are created automatically by `QApplication`, and you can access them through the function `QApplication::clipboard()`.

You can use this program to copy any number of pixmaps from the left side to the right side. You can also use the cut feature to move the pixmap from the left to the right side. However, this example is quite weak, because you can just use the Clipboard in one direction (left to right). Implementing functions for copying and moving in the other direction wouldn't be hard at all.

> Actually, there are two QClipboard functions that let you use the Clipboard for other types of data as well. These are QClipboard::setData() (for copying data to the Clipboard) and QClipboard::data() (for retrieving data from the Clipboard). Both these functions can only deal with objects of the QMimeSource class and its subclasses. Therefore, you must let the class you want to use with the Clipboard inherit from the QMimeSource class. However, see the "Drag and Drop" section of the Qt Reference Documentation for more information about that.

Implementing Drag-and-Drop Features

As stated earlier, the drag-and-drop feature is considered to be more user friendly than the Clipboard. However, drag and drop also has a downside: It's complicated to implement. Fortunately, implementing drag and drop isn't all that hard with Qt.

In fact, the QMultiLineEdit class comes with drag-and-drop features by default. You can test this with Listing 16.1. Enter some text in one of the fields, highlight the text with your left mouse button, and then click and hold down the left mouse button while you drag the text over to the right field. Just release the left mouse button and the text will be copied from the left to the right field. It's as simple as that!

However, unless you're satisfied with the drag-and-drop features already provided, you need to learn how to implement custom drag-and-drop functions. Therefore, pretend that the drag-and-drop features provided with the QMultiLineEdit class don't exist (as was the case in Qt 1.4x) and you need to implement these functions yourselves. Listing 16.3 shows you how to implement this functionality. When you fully understand Listing 16.3, you will have no problems implementing other (more complex) drag-and-drop features.

LISTING 16.3 Implementing the Drag-and-Drop Feature

```
1: #include <qapplication.h>
2: #include <qwidget.h>
3: #include <qmultilineedit.h>
4: #include <qdragobject.h>
5:
```

```
 6: // ***** Start Definition Of Class MyDragSite *****
 7: //The following class is our drag site. We can drag
 8: //objects from this class to the drop site:
 9: class MyDragSite : public QMultiLineEdit
10: {
11: public:
12:         MyDragSite( QWidget *parent );
13: protected:
14:     //We need two functions for controlling
15:     //the drag:
16:         void mousePressEvent( QMouseEvent *event );
17:         void mouseMoveEvent( QMouseEvent *event );
18: };
19:
20: //This is a virtual function that is called when the
21: //mouse is pressed. You should add the code
22: //you want to be executed when the mouse is pressed
23: //into this function.
24: void MyDragSite::mousePressEvent( QMouseEvent *event )
25: {
26:         QMultiLineEdit::mousePressEvent( event );
27: }
28:
29: //This is a virtual function that is called when a
30: //drag is started.
31: void MyDragSite::mouseMoveEvent( QMouseEvent *event )
32: {
33:     //Here, a QTextDrag object os created. This is
34:     //our dragging object. We insert the text into
35:     //it (first argument) and set the dragging object
36:     //(the object we are dragging from) to this object.
37:     QTextDrag *drag = new QTextDrag( text(), this );
38:     //Start the dragging. By using dragCopy() instead
39:     //of dragMove(), the text will be copied, not moved.
40:     drag->dragCopy();
41:     QMultiLineEdit::mouseMoveEvent( event );
42: }
43:
44: MyDragSite::MyDragSite( QWidget *parent ) : QMultiLineEdit( parent )
45: {
46:     //We don't need anything in the constructor.
47: }
48: //***** End Definition Of Class MyDragSite
49:
50:
51: //***** Start Definition Of Class MyDropSite *****
52: //This is our drop class. We can drop things into
53: //objects of this class.
54: class MyDropSite : public QMultiLineEdit
55: {
```

16

continues

LISTING 16.3   continued

```
56: public:
57:     MyDropSite( QWidget *parent );
58: protected:
59:     //Two functions are needed to control the drop:
60:     void dragEnterEvent( QDragEnterEvent *event );
61:     void dropEvent( QDropEvent *event );
62: };
63:
64: //dragEnterEvent should be implemented if the whole object
65: //shall accept drops. If just a part of the object shall
66: //accept drops, use the dragMoveEvent() instead. However,
67: //these functions are called when the object you are dragging
68: //is somewhere over this object. dragEnterEvent and
69: //dragMoveEvent() should be used to control if the dragging
70: //data can be received or not. In this case, we can only
71: //receive text.
72: void MyDropSite::dragEnterEvent( QDragEnterEvent *event )
73: {
74:     //The canDecode() function is used to check
75:     //whether the data can be decoded or not.
76:     //If the data is text, it can be decoded and
77:     //canDecode() returns TRUE.
78:     if( QTextDrag::canDecode( event ) )
79:     {
80:         if( QTextDrag::canDecode( event ) )
81:         {
82:             event->accept();
83:         }
84:     }
85: }
86:
87: //This virtual function is called when the data
88: //is accepted and it is dropped over the receiving
89: //object. In this case, we use the QTextDrag::decode()
90: //function to decode the QDropEvent object event into
91: //a QString object. This object is then inserted at the
92: //current position.
93: void MyDropSite::dropEvent( QDropEvent *event )
94: {
95:     QString text;
96:
97:     if( QTextDrag::decode( event, text ) )
98:     {
99:         int row, col;
100:        getCursorPosition( &row, &col );
101:        insertAt( text, row, col );
102:    }
103: }
104:
```

```
105: MyDropSite::MyDropSite( QWidget *parent ) : QMultiLineEdit( parent )
106: {
107:     //We don't need anything to be done in the constructor.
108: }
109: //***** End Definition Of Class MyDropSite *****
110:
111: void main( int argc, char **argv )
112: {
113:         QApplication a(argc, argv);
114:         QWidget w;
115:     w.resize( 200, 200 );
116:
117:     //Create an object of the MyDragSite class:
118:     MyDragSite dragsite( &w );
119:     dragsite.setGeometry( 10, 10, 85, 180 );
120:
121:     //Create an object of the MyDropSite class:
122:     MyDropSite dropsite( &w );
123:     dropsite.setGeometry( 105, 10, 85, 180 );
124:
125:         a.setMainWidget( &w );
126:         w.show();
127:         a.exec();
128: }
```

16

This listing is very well commented. In addition, here's the basic breakdown of what's happening:

- When the left mouse button is pressed over an object, the mousePressEvent() (lines 24 through 27) function is called. If you want anything to happen when the user presses the mouse, you should add that code to this function.

- When the user starts to move the mouse (with the left mouse button pressed), the mouseMoveEvent() (lines 31 through 42) function is called. If you want anything to happen at this point, just add the appropriate code to this function.

- When the cursor is located over the receiving object, that object's dragEnterEvent() (lines 72 through 85) function is called (of course, only if this object has this function). You should add code to this function that determines whether the data can be decoded (received). Usually, the mouse pointer indicates whether the data can be dropped. Note that you could use the dragMoveEvent() function instead of dragEnterEvent() if you don't want the whole widget to be able to receive data. See the Reference Documentation's "QWidget" section for information about how to use the dragMoveEvent() function.

- Finally, if the data can be decoded and is dropped, the dropEvent() function (lines 93 through 103) is called. This function includes the code that decodes the dragging object and inserts the result at the position it was dropped.

Note that Qt makes sure that the functions discussed in above list are called at the right time. This is nothing you need to worry about.

For more information about drag and drop, see the section titled "Drag and Drop" in the Qt Reference Documentation. For more information about mouse events, see the "QWidget" section of the Reference Documentation.

Summary

Both the Clipboard and the drag-and-drop feature have become standard on most GUI applications. Because they make many operations so much easier, you should consider both to be good features to have in an application. As a developer, you strive to create good applications that are as easy to use as possible, so the extra hours these features take to implement are in most cases (although not *all* cases) worth the effort.

The Clipboard feature is, by nature, very straightforward. Unless you want to create Clipboard functions for custom types of data, it doesn't take more than a few lines to implement.

On the other hand, drag and drop is by no means considered "straightforward." However, if you just make sure you have a good understanding of the mouse event functions, defined in QWidget (and therefore inherited by most other Qt classes), you will do fine. A great way of finding out when a functions actually is called is to use the qDebug() function (discussed in Hour 23, "Debugging Techniques"). By calling qDebug(), with a suitable string as an argument, in a function you're unsure about, the string will be outputted to stdout (or *standard output*—your monitor) when the function is called, and you can easily see exactly when this happens. You should also read the "Drag and Drop" section in the Reference Documentation; it includes some interesting information.

Q&A

Q Is there any way I can define my own key combinations for the Clipboard?

A Yes, the function QWidget::keyPressEvent() takes care of keypress events. There, you can define what happens when a certain key is pressed. See the Reference Documentation for more information.

Q Is there any way I can clear the Clipboard of data?

A Yes, just call the `QClipboard::clear()` function (`qApp->clipboard()->clear()`).

Q I feel a bit confused about the drag-and-drop feature. I just want to drag text from one text area in one Qt application to a text area in another application. Is there anything I need to do?

A No, there is absolutely nothing extra you need to do.

Workshop

You're encouraged to work through the following questions and exercises to help you retain what you've learned in this lesson. By working through these questions, you make sure you understand how to implement functions for program communication with Qt.

Quiz

1. What do you need to do to be able to copy and move text with the standard key combinations?

2. Is it possible to cut and paste images with the standard Qt Clipboard function?

3. Which class should you base your class on if you want to be able to use it with the Clipboard?

4. Is it possible to make only certain areas of a widget able to receive drag-and-drop objects?

5. Which function is called when you drop an object on an area that can receive the object?

6. Is it possible to make widgets that you can only drag objects from and not drop objects on as well as other widgets that you only can drop object on and not drag them from?

Exercises

1. Develop Listing 16.2 a little further so that it can send pixmaps in the other direction.

2. Implement a function in Listing 16.3 that doesn't start a dragging unless the object is moved more than three pixels (Hint: Use the `QMouseEvent::pos()` function).

3. Try to write a widget that can receive drag-and-drop objects, but only in one given area (for example, a square of 100×100 pixels in the widget's top-left corner).

PART IV

Qt Programming Techniques

Hour

Hour **17**

Writing KDE Applications: Lesson One

If you're a UNIX user (any clone or version), you've probably heard about the KDE desktop. This is a set of programs and libraries that gives UNIX users a more user-friendly desktop, quite similar the one provided in Microsoft Windows 98. KDE is a full-featured graphical working environment with all the components you'll ever need. Like Windows, KDE has its own file manager that also can be used as a Web browser. It includes text editors, graphics software, various network utilities (both for the Internet and your local network), games, and many other useful items. A special Office-like program suite is also under development.

As you probably know, KDE is built with Qt. However, the KDE has its own programming API, consisting of classes built on Qt classes. By using these

KDE classes, you follow the various KDE standards and make your applications fit in the KDE software family. To get a better view of what KDE actually is and what you can expect from the KDE standard, see Figure 17.1, which shows a basic KDE desktop.

FIGURE 17.1

A standard KDE desktop.

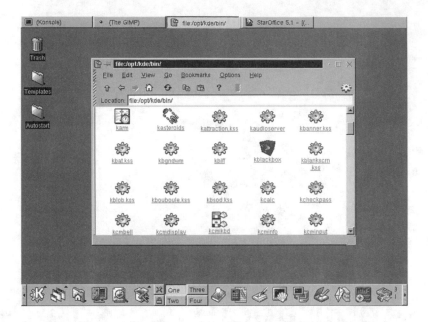

In Figure 17.1, you see the KDE panel at the bottom of the screen, from which you can start all the KDE programs and change which virtual desktop you want to work with. At the top of the screen is the taskbar, similar to the one in Windows 95 and 98. In the center of the screen, the KDE file manager is running.

This hour and the next one will give you a good introduction to KDE programming. These hours discuss the differences between *pure* Qt programming and KDE programming, and they provide a few simple KDE programming examples.

Learning the KDE Programming Basics

The first thing you need to do is to learn the very basics of KDE programming. In this section, you'll create a very simple KDE program. This section discusses the KDE classes you'll build this program on and compares the program to a regular Qt application.

In the screenshots shown in this hour and the next, the KDE Window Manager is used instead of the Motif Window Manager used in the other hours. You're advised to develop in a KDE environment to get access to all the features provided by the KDE library.

Installing KDE

Of course, the first thing you need to do before you can start developing KDE applications is to install KDE and its development libraries.

If you're using any of the larger Linux or UNIX distributions, KDE is most likely included on your distribution CD, and you can just install all KDE packages just like you install programs with your distribution. However, make sure you install the development libraries as well; these packages usually have the word devel in their filenames.

If KDE is not included in your Linux distribution or if you're using any other UNIX variant that doesn't ship with KDE, you can easily download the necessary files from www.kde.org, where you also find information on how to install (and compile, if necessary) the packages on your system.

Writing Your First KDE Program

You'll start by looking at a very simple KDE program that's similar to your first Qt program, discussed in Hour 1, "Introduction to Qt." Take a peek at Listing 17.1 and see whether you can find any differences.

LISTING 17.1 A Very Simple KDE Program

```
 1: #include <kapp.h>
 2: #include <ktmainwindow.h>
 3:
 4: int main( int argc, char **argv )
 5: {
 6:     KApplication a( argc, argv );
 7:
 8:     KTMainWindow *w = new KTMainWindow();
 9:     w->resize( 200, 100 );
10:     a.setMainWidget( w );
11:     w->show();
12:
13:     return a.exec();
14: }
```

As you see, this program looks a lot like a Qt program, although it has some important differences. To begin with, no Qt header files are included. This is simply because you won't use any Qt classes directly (KDE will take care of that). Instead, two KDE header files, kapp.h (line 1) and ktmainwindow.h (line 2), are included. kapp.h holds definitions for the KApplication class (a KApplication object is created on line 6), and ktmainwindow.h holds definitions for the KTMainWindow class (a KTMainWindow object is created on line 8).

The KApplication object has the same function in a KDE program as the QApplication object has in a pure Qt program. However, KApplication has some extra features that make your program follow the KDE standard. Initially, KApplication creates a KConfig object that's used to access KDE configuration entries. KApplication also provides various KDE resources, such as menu entries, accelerators, help invocation, and session management.

The KTMainWindow class creates a standard KDE main window. It provides toolbars and a status bar. KTMainWindow can also automatically set the icon, mini icon, and caption for your application (information that's received from QApplication).

Objects of these classes are then created in the main() function. As you can see, they're used just like the Qt classes. Now, you're ready to compile the program. How you do this depends how your system variables are set up. Here's a secure and reliable method:

```
$ g++ -I$KDEDIR/include -L$KDEDIR/lib -lqt -lkdecore -lkdeui 17lst01.cpp
       ➥    -o Listing-17.1
```

This makes sure your compiler looks in the right directories for the KDE header files and libraries. Note that you link with both the kdecore and kdeui library. You need to link with kdecore to get access to KApplication and with kdeui to get access to KTMainWindow. Figure 17.2 shows the program.

FIGURE 17.2
A very simple KDE program. It can't get more trivial than this.

As you can see, this is probably the easiest KDE program you can create. It has no buttons, no menus, and no status bar. Actually, it has no function at all.

Adding Buttons, Menus, Toolbars, and a Status Bar

As stated, KTMainWindow provides functions for adding buttons, menus, toolbars, and a status bar that follow the KDE standard. See Listing 17.2 for an example.

LISTING 17.2   A KDE Program with a Menu, a Toolbar, a Status Bar, and a Button

```
 1: #include <kapp.h>
 2: #include <ktmainwindow.h>
 3: #include <kkeydialog.h>
 4: #include <kstatusbar.h>
 5: #include <kmenubar.h>
 6: #include <qpopupmenu.h>
 7: #include <ktoolbar.h>
 8:
 9: class MyKDEProgram : public KTMainWindow
10: {
11: public:
12:     MyKDEProgram();
13: private:
14:     KKeyButton *exit;
15:     KStatusBar *sbar;
16:     KStatusBarLabel *slabel;
17:     KMenuBar *menu;
18:     QPopupMenu *file;
19:     QPopupMenu *help;
20:     KToolBar *tbar;
21: };
22:
23: MyKDEProgram::MyKDEProgram() : KTMainWindow()
24: {
25:     resize( 250, 150 );
26:
27:     //Create a keyboard-like button:
28:     exit = new KKeyButton( "exit", this );
29:     exit->setGeometry( 95, 70, 80, 40 );
30:     exit->setText( "Exit" );
31:
32:     //Create a status bar:
33:     sbar = new KStatusBar( this );
34:     //Add a label to the status bar:
35:     slabel = new KStatusBarLabel( "This is a status bar", 1, sbar );
36:     setStatusBar( sbar );
37:
38:     //Create the file-menu:
39:     file = new QPopupMenu();
40:     file->insertItem( "&Exit", kapp, SLOT( quit() ) );
41:     //Create the help-menu:
42:     help = kapp->getHelpMenu( TRUE, "Simple KDE Program" );
43:     //Create the menu bar and add the two menus to it:
44:     menu = new KMenuBar( this );
45:     menu->insertItem( "&File", file );
46:     menu->insertItem( "&Help", help );
```

continues

17

LISTING 17.2   continued

```
47:     //Set menu as the menubar of this KTMainWindow object:
48:     setMenu( menu );
49:
50:     //Create a toolbar:
51:     tbar = new KToolBar( this );
52:     //Insert three icons to the tool bar:
53:     tbar->insertButton( QPixmap( "fileopen.xpm" ), 0 );
54:     tbar->insertButton( QPixmap( "filesave.xpm" ), 1 );
55:     tbar->insertButton( QPixmap( "fileprint.xpm" ), 2 );
56:     //Set tbar as the status bar of this KTMainWindow object:
57:     addToolBar( tbar );
58:
59:     //Connect the KKeyButton to the quit() slot of kapp:
60:     connect( exit, SIGNAL( clicked() ), kapp, SLOT( quit() ) );
61: }
62:
63: int main( int argc, char **argv )
64: {
65:     KApplication a( argc, argv );
66:     MyKDEProgram w;
67:     a.setMainWidget( &w );
68:     w.show();
69:     return a.exec();
70: }
```

Again, the use of KDE classes is very similar to using Qt classes. The main difference is that the KDE classes follow the KDE standard, which is desirable. Here, you base your class on the KTMainWindow class (line 9), which is highly recommended for all your KDE projects.

In the class MyKDEPRogram, you create objects of a few common KDE classes. In the constructor (lines 23 through 61), you start by setting the size of the window (line 25). This is done just as with a Qt program—by using the resize() function. Then, the KKeyButton class is used to create a keyboard-like button (lines 28, 29, and 30). However, a QPushButton would have worked just fine here, but because this hour is about KDE, it will stick with KDE classes as much as possible. Note that you need to call the KKeyButton::setText() function to set the label of the button (line 30).

After that, an object of the KStatusBar class is created (line 33), which in turn creates a status bar at the bottom of the window. You also set a label for the status (line 35) bar and use the setStatusBar() function to tell KTMainWindow about the status bar (line 36). Note that this status bar shows the same text all the time. However, because a status bar's function is to inform the user about items the user is currently pointing to, this status bar implementation is not useful at all. You should implement code in some suitable mouse event function so that the text in the status bar changes depending on where the mouse is currently pointing.

The Qt class QPopupMenu is then used to create two menus: File and Help (lines 39, 40, and 42). The line that defines the Help menu is pretty interesting:

```
help = kapp->getHelpMenu( TRUE, "Simple KDE Program" );
```

This line lets the KApplication class take care of the menu definition. The TRUE argument indicates that you want to include an About QT item in the Help menu. The string that follows is the text that will be shown when the About <program name> menu item is selected. Although you could insert these menus in a QMenuBar object, a KMenuBar object is used instead (lines 44, 45, and 46) to make this program as KDE compatible as possible. Finally, a call to the KTMainWindow::setmenu() function is made (line 48) to tell KTMainWindow about the menu bar.

You use the KToolBar class to create a menu bar (line 51). The KMenuBar::insertItem() function is then used to insert three icons into the menu bar (lines 53, 54, and 55). Also, you tell KTMainWindow about the menu bar by calling the KTMainWindow::addToolBar() function (line 57).

The last task in the MyKDEProgram constructor is to connect the KKeyButton to the quit() slot of the KApplication object (line 60). Note that you use the kapp pointer to access the as-yet uncreated KApplication object. kapp works exactly like qApp.

Now, compile the program as described earlier. Figure 17.3 shows how your program should now look.

FIGURE 17.3

A fairly sophisticated KDE program that has a menu bar, a toolbar, a button, and a status bar, just like any other standard KDE program.

As you can see, the button looks a bit different, and both the menu bar and the toolbar have some textured areas along their left sides. These areas provide a pretty useful function. If you grab either one using your left mouse button, you can drag the bar to another position on the window or even drop it outside the window. See Figure 17.4 for an example.

17

FIGURE 17.4

*You can move the
menu bar and toolbar.
In this example, the
toolbar has been
moved to the bottom of
the window and the
menu bar is currently
outside the window.*

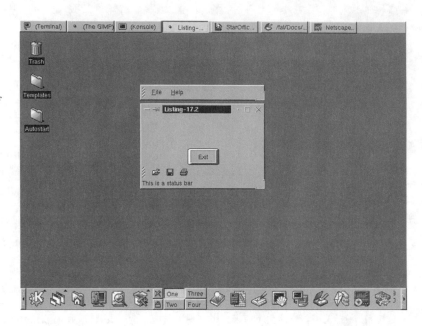

Now, take a look at the Help menu, which you let the KApplication::getHelpMenu()
create for you. This menu is shown in Figure 17.5.

FIGURE 17.5

The Help menu that
KApplication::
getHelpMenu()
created for you.

As you see, this menu holds three items: Contents, About Listing-17.2..., and About
KDE.... These three items were created by KApplication::getHelpMenu(). The first
item, Contents, opens the program documentation if documentation exists and is located
in the right place. If you click this item, program documentation is searched for in the
standard location for KDE program documentation. For this to work, you need to place
the documentation there. Click this item and see what happens. Figure 17.6 shows the
window that appears.

FIGURE 17.6

The information window that appears if you click the Contents item and no documentation can be found.

As you can tell from the window's text, the program tried to find the file `index.html` in the directory `/opt/kde/share/doc/HTML/default/Listing-17.2`. Why that directory, you might wonder? Here's why: In this case, KDE was installed under `/opt/kde` (`$KDEDIR` was set to `/opt/kde`) and the name of the program file was `Listing-17.2`. KDE program documentation is, by default, searched for in the `$KDEDIR/share/doc/HTML/default/<program name>` directory (and the filename `index.html`). If you install KDE under `/usr/local/kde` and your program file is named `kdeprogram`, the directory `/usr/local/kde/share/doc/HTML/default/kdeprogram` is searched for the `index.html` file instead.

17

> You can also set the program name by entering it as the third argument to the KApplication constructor. Therefore, if you want to call your application MyProgram, you would make the following call:
>
> KApplication a(argc, argv, "MyProgram");

If you click the second item, About Listing-17.2..., the window shown in Figure 17.7 appears.

FIGURE 17.7

The information window that appears when you click the About Listing-17.2... item.

The text shown in this window is the second argument you gave to the `KApplication::getHelpMenu()` function. This window is generally used to show some brief information about the program. It usually also includes the author's name and contact information.

The third item, About KDE..., is optional. However, because TRUE was passed as the first argument to KApplication::getHelpMenu(), it's included here. If you click this item, the KDE information window will appear (see Figure 17.8).

FIGURE 17.8

The standard KDE information window.

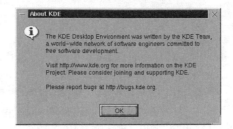

It's rare that programmers don't include the About KDE... option in their programs. It's considered a good thing to do, so you're encouraged to do so as well.

Taking Advantage of KDE's HTML Features

Given the Internet's growing popularity, it's only natural that the language used to create one of the Internet's most popular services, the World Wide Web, is also becoming more popular. These days, HTML isn't just used for creating Web sites; it's used for many other things as well, such as documentation (as in KDE's case).

KDE comes with a whole library, libkhtmlw, that's ready for you to use in your programs. libkhtmlw includes quite a few classes, but the only one you need to bother with is the KHTMLWidget class; the others are used internally by KDE. To show a Web page in your program, you need to create a KHTMLWidget object, start the HTML parsing, and fill the KHTMLWidget object with some HTML code. See Listing 17.3 for an example.

LISTING 17.3   A Simple HTML Viewer

```
 1: #include <kapp.h>
 2: #include <ktmainwindow.h>
 3: #include <html.h>
 4: #include <qstring.h>
 5:
 6: class MyKDEProgram : public KTMainWindow
 7: {
 8: public:
 9:     MyKDEProgram();
10: private:
11:     KHTMLWidget *mybrowser;
12: };
13:
```

```
14: MyKDEProgram::MyKDEProgram() : KTMainWindow()
15: {
16:     resize( 200, 200 );
17:
18:     QString htmlcode = "<html><head><title>My Web Browser</title></head>
19:                 <body bgcolor=\"#ffffff\"><center><h1>This is my
20:                 own WWW browser!</h1></body></html>";
21:
22:     mybrowser = new KHTMLWidget( this );
23:     mybrowser->resize( 200, 200 );
24:     mybrowser->begin();
25:     mybrowser->parse();
26:     mybrowser->write( htmlcode );
27:     mybrowser->end();
28: }
29:
30: int main( int argc, char **argv )
31: {
32:     KApplication a( argc, argv );
33:     MyKDEProgram w;
34:     a.setMainWidget( &w );
35:     w.show();
36:     return a.exec();
37: }
```

17

The concept is very simple. First, you create a KHTMLWidget object and set its size (lines 22 and 23). Then, the KHTMLWidget object is started by calling the KHTMLWidget::begin() function (line 24). If you want, you can enter a URL as an argument to this function, and that page will be shown. After this, the HTML parsing is started by calling the KHTMLWidget::parse() function (line 25). This is followed by a call to the KHTMLWidget::write() function (line 26). This function feeds the KHTMLWidget object with some HTML code (defined in the beginning of the MyKDEProgram constructor at lines 18, 19, and 20). Finally, you tell the KHTMLWidget object that you're finished inserting HTML code by calling KHTMLWidget::end() (line 27).

Exactly which linking parameters you need to add when compiling this program differs from one system to another. However, here is a quite safe one:

```
g++ -I$KDEDIR/include -L$KDEDIR/lib -lqt -lkdecore -lkdeui -lkhtmlw
-lkimgio -ljpeg -lpng -lgif -ltiff -ljscript 17lst01.cpp -o Listing-17.1
```

If you get errors about undefined symbols when compiling, try to find out which library these symbols are defined in and link with that library. The symbols' names usually refer to the library name. For example, if an undefined symbol's name includes the string Java or JS, you can assume it's a part of a Java library, maybe libjs or libjscript. On the other hand, if the linker says it can't find one of the libraries you want to link with, just remove that library from the list and try again.

A useful tool you should know about when searching for symbols is the nm program. It can list the symbols of a program or library. See man nm for details. Figure 17.9 shows what this program looks like.

Of course, KHTMLWidget also includes some interesting functions you should know about. These are described in Table 17.1.

TABLE 17.1   Useful KHTMLWidget Member Functions

Function	Description
KHTMLWidget::print()	Call this function to print out the HTML page.
KHTMLWidget::getSelectedText()	This function returns the text that the user has selected (as a reference to a QString object).
KHTMLWidget::isTextSelected()	Returns TRUE if any text is selected. Otherwise, FALSE is returned.
KHTMLWidget::getURL()	By passing a pointer to a QPoint object to this function, you can determine whether there's a URL on the spot that the QPoint object represents. If there is, it's returned as a char vector.
KHTMLWidget::docWidth()	Returns the width of the parsed HTML code in pixels.
KHTMLWidget::docHeight()	Returns the height of the parsed HTML code in pixels.
KHTMLWidget::getDocumentURL()	Returns a KURL object representing the URL of this HTML page.
KHTMLWidget::getSelectedFram()	Returns a pointer to a KHTMLView object describing the currently selected frame (if you're displaying a frame set, that is).
KHTMLWidget::isFrame()	Returns TRUE if the currently selected document is a frame. Returns FALSE if it's not.
KHTMLWidget::setDefaultFontBase()	With this function, you can set the default font base size. Just give it an integer argument between 2 and 5.

Function	Description
KHTMLWidget::setFixedFont()	This is used exactly as the preceding function, but it sets the fixed font instead of the default font.
KHTMLWidget::setDefaultFont()	Call this function if you want to change the default font. Enter the font you want to be used as a string argument.
KHTMLWidget::setDefaultBGColor()	With this function, you can set the default background color. Just give it a QColor object as an argument describing the color you want to use.
KHTMLWidget::setDefaultTextColors()	This takes two QColor objects as arguments. The first represents the default text color, and the second represents the default link color.

17

Actually, there are a lot more functions, but the ones listed here are the most popular. However, $KDEDIR/include/html.h (which will most likely be changed to khtml.h in KDE 2.0) includes information about all the functions. Even those you may find not so interesting!

KHTMLWidget is, in fact, a very powerful tool. By using it, you can easily implement functions in your programs for showing HTML pages that uses both CSS (cascading style sheets) and Java.

At the time of this writing, KDE 2.0 was not released yet. However, the KHTMLWidget class will be much improved in KDE 2.0, and if this is the KDE version you have, you'll find KHTMLWidget to be more like a full-featured Web browser than just a widget for showing HTML documents.

Summary

Now you've got a basic understanding of what the KDE project is and how to get started with KDE development. As you've noticed throughout this hour, working with KDE classes is pretty much the same as working with Qt classes. This might make you doubt whether it's really necessary to learn the KDE library as well. Of course, it's not necessary if you have no plans to make your applications KDE compatible, but it can be a good thing to do.

KDE makes it easier for newcomers to UNIX/Linux to learn how to use and take advantage of the system. If new users are presented with a GUI interface such as the one for KDE, the chances that they will adopt the system is much greater than if they were presented with the UNIX/Linux shell prompt. By making your applications follow the KDE standard, those already familiar with KDE will also feel familiar with your program, and they will have an easier time learning it. If your program is essential to many users, it could be included in the standard KDE distribution, and you'll therefore help to make KDE interesting to a wider range of people. Many would say that by contributing to the KDE project, you also contribute to the Linux/UNIX project(s), in general. Since you help making the KDE desktop environment better, you also make these platforms more interesting for wider range of people.

Keep in mind when you're developing under the KDE standard that you don't have to use KDE classes for everything (although that is possible). In most cases, it's enough if you use the KApplication and KTMainWindow classes. For everything else, the standard Qt classes will do just fine. However, this is totally up to you.

Q&A

Q My compiler can't find the KDE libraries or the header files, even though I follow the instructions exactly. What's wrong?

A To begin with, you need to make sure that KDE is installed. Then, you must make sure that the KDEDIR shell variable is set correctly. Check whether issuing the following command sets it:

```
$ echo $KDEDIR
```

If the output of this command is the directory where KDE is installed on your system, it's correct. For example, if KDE is installed under /opt/kde, KDEDIR should also be set to /opt/kde. If KDEDIR is not set, you can do so with the following command:

```
# export KDEDIR=/opt/kde
```

However, you'll probably want to add this to one of your startup files, such as /etc/profile.

Q When using the KHTMLWidget class, I can't get my HTML document to show up. What's wrong?

A Make sure you call the right functions at the right times. KHTMLWidget is quite sensitive about this.

Q When compiling a program that uses KHTMLWidget according to the instructions in this hour, my compiler says it can't find one of the image libraries (libgif, libpng, or libjpeg). Where can I find these libraries?

A These libraries and lots of other Linux software can be found at www.freshmeat.net. Also, ftp://sunsite.unc.edu is another good place to go.

Q When I call the `KHTMLWidget::print()` function, my printer prints, but it's unreadable junk. What's wrong?

A This problem is most likely not caused by your program. In most cases, this is caused by a bad printer driver or because you have no printer driver at all.

Workshop

You're encouraged to work through the following questions and exercises to help you retain what you've learned in this hour about the KDE programming essentials.

Quiz

1. What is KDE?
2. When writing a KDE program, which class should you use instead of `QApplication`?
3. What is `kapp`?
4. Which class should you use to create the main window in a KDE program?
5. What can you use the `KApplication::getHelpMenu()` for?
6. Is there a good way to show an HTML document in a KDE program?

Exercises

1. Write a program that creates a `KHTMLWidget` object and then shows the Qt Reference Documentation's main page in it.
2. Create program with a status bar and a toolbar. Create a few buttons on the toolbar. When the mouse pointer is over one of the toolbar buttons, the status bar should show some short information text about it (you'll need the KDE Library Reference for this).
3. Extend the program from the first exercise so that the user can select some text and then push a button to write the selected text to `stdout`.

17

HOUR 18

Writing KDE Applications: Lesson Two

This hour continues the discussion about developing GUI programs with the KDE library. It builds on your new knowledge of KDE development and provides a look at what the different KDE libraries have to offer.

In contrast to the Qt library, the KDE library is split up into a few separate libraries (which you learned in Hour 17, "Writing KDE Applications: Lesson One"). Each of these libraries holds one certain type of class, such as a class for working with files or a class for working with graphics. You've already learned about one of the libraries—libkhtmlw. In the last hour, you also looked at a couple classes from libkdecore and libkdeui, namely KApplication and KTMainWindow. However, both libkdecore and libkdeui have a lot more to offer, and this hour will cover a few more classes from these libraries (although not all the classes).

An invaluable resource when working with the KDE libraries is the KDE Library Reference, which can be found at `http://developer.kde.org`. The KDE Library Reference has the same importance to KDE developing as the Qt Reference Documentation has to Qt development.

Getting to Know KDE's Core Library

KDE's core library, `libkdecore`, contains the most basic KDE classes, such as `KApplication`. In this section, you'll look at some of the other classes. Keep in mind, though, that it's impossible to fully cover this library in this hour. You should view this and the other sections of this hour as introductions to the respective libraries. Also, remember that you need to tell your compiler to link with the library you're using classes from.

Creating Keyboard Shortcuts with the `KAccel` Class

The `KAccel` class can be used to easily define so-called *keyboard accelerators*. A keyboard accelerator is a function that lets the user access certain functions with his keyboard. Keyboard accelerators are usually accessed by holding down the Ctrl key and then press some other key. Listing 18.1 shows a simple example.

LISTING 18.1   Adding an Accelerator with `KAccel`

```
1: #include <kapp.h>
2: #include <ktmainwindow.h>
3: #include <kaccel.h>
4:
5: int main( int argc, char **argv )
6: {
7:         KApplication a( argc, argv );
8:         KTMainWindow w;
9:         w.resize( 100, 100 );
10:        a.setMainWidget( &w );
11:
12:        KAccel acc( &w );
13:        acc.insertItem( "Quit", "Quit", "CTRL+Q" );
14:        acc.connectItem( "Quit", &a, SLOT( quit() ) );
15:
16:        w.show();
17:        return a.exec();
18: }
```

The KAccel object, acc, is created on line 17. Then, the KAccel::insertItem() function is used to create a new accelerator item (line 13). The first two arguments ("Quit" and "Quit") to this function represent the local name of the action and the internal name of the action, respectively. The internal name can then be used to connect this accelerator to a slot. The last argument defines the key combination you want to use (Ctrl+Q, in this case). The KAccel::connectItem() function connects your newly created accelerator item to the slot KApplication::quit() on line 14.

Now, test this program. It doesn't do much; in fact, you'll see that the window is empty. However, if you hold down the Ctrl key and then press Q, the program will quit.

See the kaccel.h file, the ckey.h file, and/or the library reference for more information. Actually, KAccel include a few other features you might find useful. For example, the function for reading accelerator settings from file(s).

Managing Images with the KPixmap Class

This class is, of course, very similar to QPixmap. However, it adds two quite functional features to the standard QPixmap class: WebColor and LowColor. These two color modes are most useful on 256-color displays.

In WebColor mode, all images are always (yes, *always*) dithered to the Netscape palette. In other words, applications can share the Netscape palette, fewer colors will get allocated, and there will be more free color cells. WebColor is the default color mode for KPixmap.

In LowColor mode, images are checked against the KDE icon palette to see whether they match their color table. If they don't match, the image will be dithered to a minimal 3×3×3 color cube. By using the LowColor mode for background images, desktop icons, and so on, you make sure that the objects always visible on the desktop do not use more than 40 colors.

To load a KPixmap object with an image, you should use the KPixmap::load() function. However, see the kpixmap.h file or the library reference for more information.

Starting Subprocesses with the KProcess Class

KProcess is a class designed for starting a subprocess from within a KDE program. By using KProcess, you don't have to worry about the quite complex process system used on UNIX/Linux systems.

KProcess defines the << operator for inserting commands and arguments to these commands. To start the execution, the KProcess::start() function should be called, with

18

the appropriate arguments. For example, to execute the command ls -als /, you should implement the following code:

```
KProcess p;
p << "ls" << "-als" << "/";
p.start( KProcess::DontCare, KProcess::Stdout );
```

Here, you tell the KProcess object p to execute the command ls with the arguments -als and /. Then, the execution is started with the KProcess::start() function. This function takes zero to two arguments (both have default values).

The first argument is an enum value that represents what relation your program will have to this subprocess. In this case, it's defined as DontCare, which makes the program not care about when the subprocess is finished. The other choices are NotifyOnExit and Block. NotifyOnExit is the default. If this is used, the signal KProcess::processExited() will be emitted when the subprocess is finished. If you select Block, your program will get blocked until the subprocess is finished. In most cases, this is not what you want.

The second argument is also an enum value. This represents what kind of communication you want between your program and the subprocess. In this example, the choice is to only communicate with stdout of the subprocess. You have six choices here: NoCommunication, Stdin, Stdout, Stderr, AllOutput, and All. The default is NoCommunication.

If you've selected some kind of communication, you can get information from stdout and stderr by connecting to the signals KProcess::receivedStdout() and KProcess::receivedStderr(). You can also write data to the subprocess's stdin with KProcess::writeStdin(). See the library reference or the kprocess.h file for more information.

You should also take a look at the KShellProcess class, which is related to KProcess. KShellProcess is used to execute child processes through a UNIX/Linux shell.

Interacting with the Window Manager Through the KWM Class

The KWM class includes many functions for interacting with the Window Managers. Some handpicked KWM functions are presented in Table 18.1. Many of the functions work fine with window managers other than the K Window Manager (the Window Manager that is used by KDE), but it's recommended that you use the K Window Manager for best results. Many of these functions require you to define which window you want to work with; this is done by passing the Window object that represents the window you want to work with as argument to the function.

TABLE 18.1 Useful KWM Member Functions

Function	Description
KWM::setIcon()	Use this function to set the pixmap that you want to represent the window when it's minimized.
KWM::setDecoration()	With this function, you can set the decoration of a window. You have three choices: noDecoration makes the window totally undecorated, normalDecoration gives the window normal decoration, and tinyDecoration makes the window just a little frame.
KWM::currentDesktop()	This function returns the number of the current virtual desktop. This can be useful if you want your program to act differently depending on which desktop it is running.
KWM::switchToDesktop()	Here, you give the number of the virtual desktop you want to switch to as the argument to this function.
KWM::numberOfDesktops()	Returns the number of virtual desktops.
KWM::setNumberOfDesktops()	Sets the number of virtual desktops.
KWM::activeWindow()	This function returns the currently active window.
KWM::setWindowRegion()	This function takes two arguments: an integer representing which virtual desktop you're referring to and a QRect object representing the rectangle in which windows can appear. This can be useful if you have some static object on the screen that you want to be visible even if the other windows are maximized.
KWM::geometry()	Returns a QRect object representing the geometry of the window you gave as an argument.
KWM::geometryRestore()	This function restores a maximized window to its original size.
KWM::isActive()	Returns TRUE if the window you gave as an argument has focus.
KWM::moveToDesktop()	Moves a window to another virtual desktop.
KWM::setGeometry()	Sets a window's geometry with a QRect object.
KWM::setGeometryRestore()	Sets the original size for a window (with a QRect object).
KWM::move()	Moves a window to a certain position, defined by a QPoint object.
KWM::setMaximize()	Maximizes or sets a window's size to its original size. The function takes two arguments: a Window object and a bool value.
KWM::setIconify()	Takes the same arguments as the previous function. However, this function determines whether the window should be iconified.
KWM::close()	Used to close a window.

18

Everything you can do with the K Window Manager as a user you can also do through the KWM class as a programmer. Table 18.1 is a good place to start at when taking advantage of the KWM class. However, you also need to see documentation for the KWM class to investigate further the other powerful functions.

Getting to Know KDE's User Interface Library

KDE's user interface library, libkdeui, holds all the user interface classes, including classes for creating buttons and labels. You learned about the most used class from libkdeui, KTMainWindow, along with a few other classes in Hour 17. However, libkdeui has a lot more to offer. Actually, libkdeui includes so many classes that it would be impossible to describe them all in this section. Table 18.2 provides a listing of the more useful classes. It gives you a good idea of the classes available, and you can use the library reference to find out more information about them.

TABLE 18.2   Useful Classes in the KDE User Interface Library

Function	Description
KButtonBox	This is a button container class that can be used to place button horizontally or vertically.
KColorButton	This is a widget that can be used to let the user select a color.
KContainerLayout	This is a KDE class for laying out widgets.
KDatePicker	KDatePicker can be used to create a date-picker widget.
KEdit	KEdit is a great class that's based on QMultiLineEdit. It has predefined functions for opening and saving files, and a lot more. By using this class, you can write a full-feature text editor in no time!
KFontDialog	This is KDE's answer to QFontDialog.
KIconLoaderButton	This class creates a icon-loader button. Clicking the button will bring up the icon dialog (created by KIconLoaderDialog).
KLed	Creates a round light diode, which can actually be very useful. For example, if you want indicate that something is on or off in a program.
KListSpinBox	Lets the user cycle through a defined list of items.
KMsgBox	This is an enhanced QMessageBox. You can have up to four configurable buttons and internationalized button text.
KNoteBook	Provides a tabbed dialog with a lot of new features, compared to QTabDialog.
KNumericSpinBox	Lets the user cycle through a range of numeric values.
KPanner	A simple widget that lets the user control the size of two widgets.

Function	Description
KProgress	If you're striving to use KDE classes instead of Qt classes, use this class instead of QProgressBar and QProgressDialog.
KQuickHelpWindow	Use this class to create a window that shows some quick help text.
KQuickTip	Creates a KDE help system. At the time of this writing, this class was still under development.
KRadioGroup	A class for creating a group of radio buttons in a toolbar.
KSeparator	Used to create a horizontal line. You should use this class to make sure horizontal lines look exactly the same in all KDE programs.
KSlider	This class is almost exactly like QSlider. However, it's recommended that you use this class to make all the sliders in your KDE programs standard.
KStatusBar	Creates a status bar widget.
KTabBar	KTabBar is very similar to QTabBar. The only difference is that KTabBar provides scrolling buttons if the widgets don't fit in the tab bar.
KTabCtl	Very similar to QTabDialog. However, KTabCtl doesn't create a button and is therefore not limited to dialog boxes.
KTabListbox	Provides a multicolumn list box. The columns can be resized by the user.
KTreeList	Provides a widget that shows hierarchical data (directory trees, for example).
KWizard	This class can be used to create so-called *wizards*, similar to the installation wizards often used in Microsoft Windows or even configuration wizards, where the order in which the entries are filled is important.

As stated, libkdeui holds a lot more classes than those described in Table 18.2. See the KDE library reference for more information about libkdeui.

Using KDE's File Operation Library

KDE has its own file operation library, called libkfile. It includes all the necessary functions for working with files and directories. In this section, you'll look at the classes in libkfile and see how they can be used.

Selecting a Directory with the KDirDialog Class

The KDirDialog class is an enhanced version of QFileDialog. It provides a dialog that can be used to select a directory. Using KDirDialog is really simple. Listing 18.2 shows an example.

18

LISTING 18.2   Creating a Directory Dialog with `QDirDialog`

```
 1: #include <kapp.h>
 2: #include <ktmainwindow.h>
 3: #include <kfiledialog.h>
 4:
 5: int main( int argc, char **argv )
 6: {
 7:         KApplication a( argc, argv );
 8:         KTMainWindow w;
 9:         w.resize( 100, 100 );
10:         a.setMainWidget( &w );
11:
12:         QString dir = KDirDialog::getDirectory( "file:/" );
13:
14:         w.show();
15:         return a.exec();
16: }
```

This program calls the `KDirDialog::getDirectory()` (line 12) function, which makes the directory dialog appear onscreen so that the user can select a directory. When the user is finished and clicks the OK button, the directory name is stored in `dir` (also handled on line 12). On line 12, the `KDirDialog` object's starting point is also set, in this case, to `file:/`.

> KDE, like Windows 98, relies on URLs instead of directories. Therefore, the starting point of the KDirDialog object in Listing 18.2 is set to `file:/` instead of just `/`.

To compile the program, issue the following command:

```
# g++ -I$KDEDIR/include -L$KDEDIR/lib -lqt -lkdecore -lkdeui -lkfile -lkfm
   18lst02.cpp -o Listing-18.2
```

Note that you need to link with both `libkfile` and `libkfm`. Figure 18.1 shows this program.

Selecting a File with the `KFileDialog` Class

The `KFileDialog` class creates a dialog similar to the one shown in Figure 18.1. However, this one is used to select a file, not a directory. Look at the following line:

```
QString dir = KFileDialog::getOpenFileName( "file:/", "*" );
```

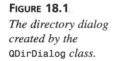

FIGURE 18.1

The directory dialog created by the `QDirDialog` *class.*

This will bring up the file dialog, let the user select a file, and then store the filename in `dir`. The two arguments given `KFileDialog::getOpenFileName()` represent where in the directory tree `KFileDialog` will start to look for a file and which filter you want to use. Here, the filter is set to * to make the file dialog show all files. If you just want to see files that end with `.txt`, you would change this to `*.txt`.

Getting File Information with the `KFileInfo` Class

`KFileInfo` can, like `QFileInfo`, be used to get various information about a file. Look at the following lines of code:

```
#include <qfilesimpleview.h>

KFileInfo file( "/vmlinuz" );
cout << "The file's size is: " << file.size() << endl;
cout << "The file belongs to the group " << file.group() << endl;
cout << "The file's owner is " << file.owner() << endl;
cout << "The access permissions for the file is " << file.access() << endl;
```

Implement these lines of code in a program, and you should get some output to `stdout`. Something like the following:

```
The file's size is: 444199
The file belongs to the group root
The file's owner is root
The access permissions for the file is -rw-r-r--
```

That was simple, wasn't it? The `KFileInfo` class can actually be easier to use than `QFileInfo` in many cases. See the library reference for `libkfile` to get more information about this class.

18

Previewing Files with the `KFilePreviewDialog` Class

File previewing is a great feature that lets the user see a small preview of a file before he opens it. KDE provides the `KFilePreviewDialog` class for this. As with all the other file dialogs, you can implement it with one single line of code:

```
QString file = KFilePreviewDialog::getOpenFileName();
```

This line will bring up the file preview dialog, as shown in Figure 18.2.

FIGURE **18.2**

The file preview dialog created by the `KFilePreviewDialog` *class. Currently, a text file is selected and being previewed on the dialog's right side.*

At the time of this writing, only text files and pixmaps could be previewed. However, if you want to preview a file in a format that's not supported, it's fully possible to implement support for that format yourself, although it can be quite a complex project.

As you can see, KDE offers a few dialogs that can be useful when you're working with files. However, for the actual file I/O operations, you must use the standard Qt classes.

Getting to Know the Remaining KDE Libraries

You've now seen `libkdecore`, `libkdeui`, `libkhtmlw`, and `libkfile`. However, there are few other small libraries you need to know.

To begin with, KDE also comes with a library called `libkimgio`. It's a library that holds KDE's various classes for image I/O. At the time of this writing, `libkimgio` doesn't include much that's useful. However, it is under development and will surely be more interesting in the future.

libkspell is another member of the KDE library family. At the time of this writing, the only class in libkspell was KSpell, a programming interface for the international spell-checker program ISpell.

The last library, libkab, holds functions for accessing the KDE address book.

 Note that these are the libraries in KDE 1.1.2. More libraries will be included in KDE 2.0.

Summary

As mentioned in Hour 17, you don't need to use KDE classes just because you're writing a KDE program. If you don't find any function in a KDE class that can make your program better, there's no reason to use it. Just use KDE classes when you feel they can make your program better, or if they follow a standard that's essential to a KDE program. By using KApplication and KTMainWindow and implementing the standard KDE Help menu, you have (in most people's opinion) the full right to call your program a KDE program.

However, as the KDE project develops and the KDE classes get better, you should take advantage of the great features that KDE classes provide. A good example of this is the KFilePreviewDialog class: By just changing one single line in your program, to make it use KFilePreviewDdialog instead of QFileDialog, you can make your program much easier to use.

Another point you should keep in mind is that KDE 2.0 is expected to be released in the spring of 2000. This is a major update, and it will include a lot of new features, for users as well as developers.

Q&A

Q I get error messages about unresolved symbols when I'm trying to compile a KDE program. What's wrong?

A You've forgot to link with a library that's needed by your program. Therefore, make sure this is correct. Also note that when you use the libkfile library, you also need to link with libkwm.

18

Q I have problems with the KWM class. Not all the functions seem to work. What can be wrong?

A You're probably using some Window Manager other than the K Window Manager. It's very possible that this Window Manager doesn't understand the instructions that the KWM class gives. You should use the K Window Manager instead.

Workshop

You're encouraged to work through the following questions and exercises to help you retain what you've learned in this hour. By working through these questions you can ensure that you understand what this hour has taught you about KDE programming.

Quiz

1. What can be found in the KDE core library?
2. Which class should you use if you want to start a subprocess in your program?
3. If your subprocess happens to be a shell command, which class should you use?
4. What advantages does KPixmap have over QPixmap?
5. Is it possible to minimize a window from within a KDE program?
6. What type of classes do you find in libkdeui?
7. When writing a KDE application, are you required to always build the user interface with the classes in libkdeui?
8. Should you use the classes in libkfile when you want to perform some file I/O operation?

Exercises

1. Write a KDE program that executes a subprocess by using the KProcess class and then inserts the output from this process into a KEdit object.
2. Use KFontDialog to let the user select a font. Then create a label that uses the selected font.
3. Create a KTabBar object. Insert some widgets that do not fit it. What happens?
4. Write a program that creates a few KFileInfo objects (all objects should refer to different files). Then create a function that sorts these files by size. Insert the filenames into a KEdit object, one file per line, with the largest files first. You might also want to show some extra information about the files, such as owners, groups, and so on.

HOUR 19

Learning to Use Qt's OpenGL Classes

OpenGL is a standard API for rendering 3D graphics. It's platform independent and is therefore used on many different systems. Both Windows NT and some commercial UNIX systems come with OpenGL libraries by default. However, on other systems, you need to install them by hand. Fortunately, there's a free OpenGL clone available, called MESA, for UNIX/Linux. This is the OpenGL implementation you'll work with in this hour. Although MESA usually doesn't include the latest features of OpenGL, it works well, and it's free! It's also possible to use some other implementation, such as SGI OpenGL.

Qt includes a few classes that make the integration of OpenGL functions in a Qt program easy. By doing this, you gain a lot because you can use Qt for creating the GUI for your OpenGL programs and don't need to reinvent buttons, menus, toolbars, and so on yourself.

In this hour, you'll learn what you need to do to get started with OpenGL programming with Qt. However, not all the OpenGL functions and terms are discussed here—that would be enough material for another book. For discussions about OpenGL and three-dimensional graphics, you should go to www.opengl.org, where you'll find lots of good documentation about OpenGL. You should at least have some basic OpenGL knowledge before studying this hour.

Preparing Your System for OpenGL Development

Before you can begin, you need to perform a few tasks. First, you need to download and install MESA (if you don't have any OpenGL implementation already). Then, you need to compile the OpenGL extension of Qt.

Getting and Installing MESA

You can always find the latest version of MESA at www.mesa3d.org. At the time of this writing, the latest version is 3.1. This may have changed recently, so be sure to get the latest version. It's between 1.5 and 2MB in size.

> It's possible that MESA comes with your UNIX/Linux distribution. If this is the case, you don't need to compile and install the source distribution; you can use the binary version that comes with the distribution instead.

When you've got the file on your hard drive, you need to untar the archive:

```
# tar xvfz MesaLib-3.1.tar.gz
```

This creates a directory called Mesa-3.1 on your hard drive. Change to this directory:

```
# cd Mesa-3.1
```

Then, start the configure utility that's provided:

```
# ./configure
```

The configure utility examines your system and makes sure MESA will be compiled to suit it. To start the compilation, run make:

```
# make
```

Now, the compilation starts, and you'll see a lot of cryptic output scrolling up your screen. This takes a while, especially if you're on a slow system, so be patient. When the compilation finishes, it's time to install the libraries:

```
# make install
```

This installs the MESA libraries in /usr/local/lib and the include files in /usr/local/include/GL.

> If you want to install MESA somewhere else, you can use the --prefix option with the configure utility. For example, if you want to install it under /usr/lib and /usr/include/GL instead, you would execute configure as follows:
>
> ```
> # ./configure --prefix=/usr
> ```

Now, the MESA libraries are installed and you're ready to compile the OpenGL extension of Qt.

Compiling Qt's OpenGL Extension

Qt's OpenGL extension is located in the directory $QTDIR/extensions/opengl/src. To compile and install it, run make in this directory:

```
# make
```

This will both compile and install the library in $QTDIR/lib. The library is of the static type, and its named libqgl.a. Now, you're all set.

19

Getting to Know Qt's OpenGL Classes

The OpenGL extension of Qt consists of three classes: QGLWidget, QGLContext, and QGLFormat. These three classes make it possible for you to use the Qt widgets for creating the user interface and at the same time use the OpenGL functions for creating the graphics. This section discusses these three classes to give you a good understanding of how and when to use them.

QGLWidget: The OpenGL Widget

The QGLWidget class is the most important part of Qt's OpenGL extension. In a subclass of QGLWidget, you can initialize and create OpenGL graphics. You should insert your OpenGL code into the three static functions QGLWidget::initializeGL(),

QGLWidget::paintGL(), and QGLWidget::resizeGL(). The following sections take a closer look at these functions.

Understanding the `initializeGL()` Function

In your implementation of the QGLWidget::initializeGL() function, you should put the code that initializes the OpenGL subsystem. This usually includes a few OpenGL function calls that set the color and the shape of your OpenGL graphic. Sometimes, this function can also include a call to some of the QGLWidget member functions. Here's an example:

```
void GLBox::initializeGL()
{
    qglClearColor( black );
    glShadeModel( GL_FLAT );
}
```

First, a call to Qt's function qglClearColor() is made (all functions starting with qgl are part of Qt's OpenGL implementation, not the actual OpenGL API). This function actually makes an appropriate call to the OpenGL function glClearColor(), which sets the clearing color (basically the background color). Although you could use glClearColor() here, the qglClearColor() function is easier to use because it can deal with QColor objects.

After this, the OpenGL function glShadeModel() is called. With this function, you can set the shading technique. In this example, make the shading technique "flat" to increase performance.

Note that you should put all OpenGL-specific initialization code in initializeGL() and not in the class constructor.

Understanding the `paintGL()` Function

QGLWidget::paintGL() is the most interesting function in your Qt-based OpenGL program. Here, you put the actual OpenGL drawing code. This function has the same purpose as the paintEvent() function, although paintGL() should use OpenGL instead of QPaint for drawing.

What you actually write in this function, of course, depends on what you want to draw. Because you should use OpenGL for drawing, you need be familiar with the OpenGL drawing function to create an implementation of paintGL(). This usually consists of a number of calls to various OpenGL drawing functions and a number of calls to the glEnd() function, to mark where certain drawing operations are finished.

You'll find a sample paintGL() function in Listing 19.1, later in this hour.

Understanding the `resizeGL()` Function

The `QGLWidget::resizeGL()` function is called each time the widget is resized. Its use is similar to the `QWidget::resizeEvent()` function, and you should use it to change size-specific parameters—for example, the size and position of your objects and the viewport size.

The `QGLWidget::resizeGL()` function is always called with two integers as arguments. The first argument represents the new width of the widget, and the second argument represents the new height of the widget.

`QGLContext`: Rendering OpenGL Graphics

As the Qt Reference Documentation states, "The `QGLContext` class encapsulates an OpenGL rendering context." So, what does this mean then? Well, an *OpenGL context* is basically an object that's used to output graphics to. This is usually a part of a window, but you can also set it to a pixmap or something similar.

The `QGLWidget` class automatically creates a rendering context for you (a `QGLContext` object), so if you don't need to change the context, you don't have to worry about it. However, suppose you want to output an OpenGL graphic to a pixmap. You could create a `QPixmap` object and then create a `QGLContext` object for it. Here's an example:

```
QPixmap pixmap;
QGLContext *pcx = new QGLContext( QGLFormat(), &pixmap );
```

As you can see, the `QGLContext` constructor takes two arguments. The first one is a `QGLFormat` object (see the next section for information about the `QGLFormat` class), and the second one is `QPaintDevice` object. Therefore, you can render an OpenGL graphic to any Qt class that inherits from `QPaintDevice`. Then, by changing the rendering context for your `QGLWidget` object and calling `QGLWidget::updateGL()`, the OpenGL graphic will be written to the pixmap. Here's an example:

```
MyQGLWidgetObject->setContext( pcx );
MyQGLWidgetObject->updateGL();
```

That's it! Note that you leave out two of the arguments to the `QGLWidget::setContext()` function because they have default values. See the Reference Documentation for more information about this function and its arguments.

`QGLFormat`: Setting a Context's Display Format

If you're not satisfied with the default settings of an OpenGL rendering context, you can use the `QGLFormat` class to set your own options. However, to take advantage of this class, you need to have a good understanding of OpenGL's more-advanced features, such

19

as alpha blending and stencil buffering. For changing the QGLFormat object for a QGLWidget object, you should use the QGLWidget::setFormat() function. You can also use the QGLFormat::format() function to retrieve the current QGLFormat object. Another way of setting a custom QGLFormat object for a context is to give it as the first argument to the QGLContext constructor.

After you've created a QGLFormat object, you can use the functions described in Table 19.1 to set the various options. All functions take a bool value as an argument.

TABLE 19.1 *QGLFormat* Member Functions

Function	Description
QGLFormat::setDoubleBuffer()	Give this function the argument TRUE to turn on double buffering. If you give it the argument FALSE, single buffering is used. *Double buffering* is a technique that makes the rendering to an off-screen buffer first; then, when the rendering is finished, the buffer is copied to the screen. This avoids flicker and help increases performance.
QGLFormat::setDepth()	Use this function to enable or disable the depth buffer. The depth buffer technique is also called *z-buffering*. This technique assigns pixels a z-value that represents the distance between the pixel and the viewer. The higher the z-value a pixel has, the closer it is to the viewer. The pixels with the highest z-values are drawn first.
QGLFormat::setRgba()	This function turns on RGBA color mode if it gets the argument TRUE, and it turns on color index mode if it gets the argument FALSE. *RGBA* is an extended version of RGB. It adds a fourth value to the color—the alpha quadruplet.
QGLFormat::setAlpha()	If this functions is called with the TRUE argument, it enables the alpha channel for the framebuffer. If this is enabled, the alpha quadruplet in RGBA specifies the transparency of a pixel.
QGLFormat::setAccum()	This function enables the accumulation buffer if you give it the argument TRUE. This feature is used to create blur effects and multiple exposures.
QGLFormat::setStencil()	This function turns on stencil buffering if the argument is TRUE. The stencil buffer can be used to mask away drawing from certain parts of the screen.
QGLFormat::setStereo()	By calling this function with the TRUE argument, you can turn on stereo buffering. The stereo buffer technique is used to provide extra color buffers to generate left-eye and right-eye images.

Function	Description
QGLFormat::setDirectRendering()	If you call this function with the argument TRUE, OpenGL will render directly from hardware to screen, bypassing the window system.
QGLFormat::setOverlay()	Use this function to enable the overlay plane. This will create an additional context in an overlay plane.

As you may have noticed, there are a lot of terms you need to know about when creating 3D graphics. However, all this is explained in the various OpenGL documents you can find at www.opengl.org.

Note that QGLFormat also comes with functions to retrieve all these options so that you can determine whether one options is currently enabled.

Writing, Compiling, and Running a Qt-Based OpenGL Program

In this section, you'll look at an example of how you can integrate Qt with OpenGL. The example creates a window with an OpenGL drawing area and three sliders, created with Qt's QSlider class. By using Qt's simple slot and signal function, you can make the OpenGL drawing change as the sliders are dragged.

You'll start by taking a look at the code. Although the code example is well commented, you'll need some basic understanding of OpenGL programming to follow it. After this, you'll learn how to compile and run the example, which libraries you need to link with, and so on.

Taking a Look at the Code

As stated, you won't be able to understand and follow this example without knowledge of OpenGL programming. Three-dimensional programming has a lot of special terms and complex techniques. Therefore, you should read one of the good tutorials on www.opengl.org, and you'll do just fine with this example.

Listing 19.1 is rather long, so you should split it up into separate files. At very least, you need to put the GLBox class declaration in a file of its own to be able to use the Meta Object Compiler (MOC) in it.

LISTING 19.1   An Example of How to Connect OpenGL and Qt

```
 1: /***** Start glbox.h *****/
 2: //Since the class includes custom
 3: //slots, remember to use MOC on it
 4: //and include the output in glbox.cpp
 5: #include <qgl.h>
 6:
 7: class GLBox : public QGLWidget
 8: {
 9: Q_OBJECT
10:
11: public:
12:         GLBox( QWidget* parent );
13:         ~GLBox();
14:
15: public slots:
16:         void setXRotation( int degrees );
17:         void setYRotation( int degrees );
18:         void setZRotation( int degrees );
19:
20: protected:
21:         void initializeGL();
22:         void paintGL();
23:         void resizeGL( int w, int h );
24:         virtual GLuint makeObject();
25:
26: private:
27:         GLuint object;
28:         GLfloat xRot, yRot, zRot, scale;
29: };
30: /***** End glbox.h *****/
31:
32: /**** Start glbox.cpp *****/
33: #include <qgl.h>
34: #include "glbox.moc"
35:
36: //In the constructor, we only set some values.
37: //We don't do any OpenGL function calls here:
38: GLBox::GLBox( QWidget *parent ) : QGLWidget( parent )
39: {
40:     //Set the default rotation:
41:     xRot = yRot = zRot = 0.0;
42:     //Set the default scale:
43:     scale = 1.25;
44:     //Set our OpenGL object to 0:
45:     object = 0;
46: }
47:
48: //Delete the display list:
49: GLBox::~GLBox()
```

```
50: {
51:     //The glDeleteLists() function is
52:     //used to delete the display list.
53:     //The second argument represent the
54:     //number of display lists to be deleted:
55:     glDeleteLists( object, 1 );
56: }
57:
58: //Paint the box using the OpenGL functions
59: //provided by MESA:
60: void GLBox::paintGL()
61: {
62:     //Clear the buffer and enable
63:     //color drawing:
64:     glClear( GL_COLOR_BUFFER_BIT );
65:
66:     //Replace the current matrix with
67:     //the identity matrix:
68:     glLoadIdentity();
69:
70:     //Translate the current matrix with
71:     //the following x, y, and z values:
72:     glTranslatef( 0.0, 0.0, -10.0 );
73:
74:     //Scale the current matrix with
75:     //the following x, y, and z values.
76:     //Use the predefined scale-value
77:     //for all axes (1.25):
78:     glScalef( scale, scale, scale );
79:
80:     //Rotate the matrix around its
81:     //x-axis by the angle xRot. The
82:     //value of xRot is changed as you
83:     //drag the top slider:
84:     glRotatef( xRot, 1.0, 0.0, 0.0 );
85:
86:     //Rotate the matrix around its
87:     //y-axis by the angle yRot. The
88:     //value of yRot is changed as you
89:     //drag the middle slider:
90:     glRotatef( yRot, 0.0, 1.0, 0.0 );
91:
92:     //Rotate the matrix around its
93:     //z-axis by the angle zRot. The
94:     //value of zRot is changed as you
95:     //drag the bottom slider:
96:     glRotatef( zRot, 0.0, 0.0, 1.0 );
97:
98:     //Executes a display list. This
99:     //function call will draw the new
```

19

continues

LISTING 19.1 continued

```
100:      //box to screen:
101:      glCallList( object );
102: }
103:
104: //Initialize the OpenGL sub-system:
105: void GLBox::initializeGL()
106: {
107:      //Use black as background color:
108:      qglClearColor( black );
109:
110:      //Generate an OpenGL display list.
111:      //A display list is a group of OpenGL
112:      //commands. On our case, these commands
113:      //are defined in the makeObject() function.
114:      //object is the integer name of the display list:
115:      object = makeObject();
116:
117:      //Set the shade model to flat.
118:      //This is usually done to increase
119:      //performance:
120:      glShadeModel( GL_FLAT );
121: }
122:
123: //This function will be called when the
124: //widget is resized. We access its new
125: //width and height through the variables
126: // w and h:
127: void GLBox::resizeGL( int w, int h )
128: {
129:      //Set the viewport. The first two
130:      //arguments (0, 0) represent the
131:      //lower left corner of the viewport.
132:      //The last two arguments represent
133:      //the width and height of the viewport.
134:      glViewport( 0, 0, (GLint)w, (GLint)h );
135:
136:      //This function sets the current matrix.
137:      //In this case, we set the current matrix
138:      //to the projection matrix.
139:      glMatrixMode( GL_PROJECTION );
140:
141:      //Replace the current matrix with the
142:      //identity matrix:
143:      glLoadIdentity();
144:
145:      //This function sets perspective of the matrix.
146:      //See the documentation found on www.opengl.org
```

```
147:        //for more information:
148:        glFrustum( -1.0, 1.0, -1.0, 1.0, 5.0, 15.0 );
149:
150:        //Set the current matrix to the modelview matrix:
151:        glMatrixMode( GL_MODELVIEW );
152: }
153:
154: //This function creates our OpenGL display list:
155: GLuint GLBox::makeObject()
156: {
157:        //Create a GLuint object that will represent
158:        //the display list:
159:        GLuint list;
160:
161:        //Create one empty display list and assign it
162:        //to list:
163:        list = glGenLists( 1 );
164:
165:        //This function starts the definition of the
166:        //new display list:
167:        glNewList( list, GL_COMPILE );
168:
169:        //Set the drawing color to white:
170:        qglColor( white );
171:
172:        //Set the width of the lines that
173:        //will be drawn:
174:        glLineWidth( 2.0 );
175:
176:        //Make the vertices we are about to
177:        //draw connected to each other:
178:        glBegin( GL_LINE_LOOP );
179:        //Draw three vertices. The three
180:        //arguments represent the x, y, and
181:        //z values of the vertices:
182:        glVertex3f(  1.0,  0.5, -0.4 );
183:        glVertex3f(  1.0, -0.5, -0.4 );
184:        glVertex3f( -1.0, -0.5, -0.4 );
185:        glVertex3f( -1.0,  0.5, -0.4 );
186:        //End the drawing:
187:        glEnd();
188:
189:        //Same as previous:
190:        glBegin( GL_LINE_LOOP );
191:        glVertex3f(  1.0,  0.5, 0.4 );
192:        glVertex3f(  1.0, -0.5, 0.4 );
193:        glVertex3f( -1.0, -0.5, 0.4 );
194:        glVertex3f( -1.0,  0.5, 0.4 );
195:        glEnd();
196:
```

19

continues

LISTING 19.1   continued

```
197:        //Now, treat each pair of vertices as
198:        //an independent line segment:
199:        glBegin( GL_LINES );
200:        //First pair:
201:        glVertex3f(  1.0,  0.5, -0.4 );
202:        glVertex3f(  1.0,  0.5, 0.4 );
203:        //Second pair:
204:        glVertex3f(  1.0, -0.5, -0.4 );
205:        glVertex3f(  1.0, -0.5, 0.4 );
206:        //Third pair:
207:        glVertex3f( -1.0, -0.5, -0.4 );
208:        glVertex3f( -1.0, -0.5, 0.4 );
209:        //Fourth pair:
210:        glVertex3f( -1.0,  0.5, -0.4 );
211:        glVertex3f( -1.0,  0.5, 0.4 );
212:        glEnd();
213:
214:        //End the display list definition:
215:        glEndList();
216:
217:        //Return the list so that we can
218:        //assign it to another GLuint object:
219:        return list;
220: }
221:
222: //The following three slots will be called when
223: //its corresponding slider is dragged:
224:
225: //Set the objects rotation angle around the X-axis:
226: void GLBox::setXRotation( int degrees )
227: {
228:        //Update xRot to the new value that
229:        //is set by the top slider:
230:        xRot = (GLfloat)(degrees % 360);
231:        //Update the drawing:
232:        updateGL();
233: }
234:
235: //Set the objects rotation angle around the Y-axis:
236: void GLBox::setYRotation( int degrees )
237: {
238:        //Update yRot to the new value that
239:        //is set by the middle slider:
240:        yRot = (GLfloat)(degrees % 360);
241:        //Update the drawing:
242:        updateGL();
243: }
244:
```

```
245: //Set the objects rotation angle around the Z-axis:
246: void GLBox::setZRotation( int degrees )
247: {
248:     //Update zRot to the new value that
249:     //is the by the bottom slider:
250:     zRot = (GLfloat)(degrees % 360);
251:     //Update the drawing:
252:     updateGL();
253: }
254: /***** End glbox.cpp *****/
255:
256: /***** Start glwindow.h *****/
257: class GLWindow : public QWidget
258: {
259: public:
260:         GLWindow( QWidget *parent = 0 );
261:
262: };
263: /***** End glwindow.h *****/
264:
265: /***** Start glwindow.cpp *****/
266: #include <qwidget.h>
267: #include <qpushbutton.h>
268: #include <qslider.h>
269: #include <qlayout.h>
270: #include <qapplication.h>
271: #include <qkeycode.h>
272:
273: #include "glbox.h"
274: #include "glwindow.h"
275:
276: GLWindow::GLWindow( QWidget *parent ) : QWidget( parent )
277: {
278:     resize( 400, 300 );
279:
280:     //Create our OpenGL widget:
281:     GLBox *glbox = new GLBox( this );
282:     glbox->setGeometry( 50, 10, 340, 280 );
283:
284:     //Create a slider for controlling the X-axis:
285:     QSlider *x = new QSlider ( 0, 360, 60, 0, QSlider::Vertical, this );
286:     x->setGeometry( 10, 30, 30, 75 );
287:     x->setTickmarks( QSlider::Left );
288:
289:     //Create a slider for controlling the Y-axis:
290:     QSlider *y = new QSlider ( 0, 360, 60, 0, QSlider::Vertical, this );
291:     y->setGeometry( 10, 115, 30, 75 );
292:     y->setTickmarks( QSlider::Left );
293:
```

19

continues

LISTING **19.1**   continued

```
294:      //Create a slider for controlling the Z-axis:
295:      QSlider *z = new QSlider ( 0, 360, 60, 0, QSlider::Vertical, this );
296:      z->setGeometry( 10, 200, 30, 75 );
297:      z->setTickmarks( QSlider::Left );
298:
299:      //Connect the slider to its appropriate slot on our GLBox object:
300:      connect( x, SIGNAL( valueChanged(int) ), glbox,
301:                    SLOT( setXRotation(int) ) );
302:      connect( y, SIGNAL( valueChanged(int) ), glbox,
303:                    SLOT( setYRotation(int) ) );
304:      connect( z, SIGNAL( valueChanged(int) ), glbox,
305:                    SLOT( setZRotation(int) ) );
306: }
307: /***** End glwindow.cpp *****/
308:
309: /***** Start main.cpp *****/
310: #include <qapplication.h>
311: #include <qgl.h>
312:
313: #include "glwindow.h"
314:
315: int main( int argc, char **argv )
316: {
317:          QApplication a(argc,argv);
318:          GLWindow w;
319:          a.setMainWidget( &w );
320:          w.show();
321:          return a.exec();
322: }
323: /***** End main.cpp *****/
```

Although each function is commented throughout this listing, it may be hard to get an overview of the entire program. It's a really simple concept though.

The GLBox class (declared in lines 7 through 29) is responsible for the actual OpenGL drawings. It defines the three static methods paintGL() (lines 60 through 102), initializeGL() (lines 105 through 121 and resizeGL() (lines 127 through 152). The use of these functions is the same as described earlier. GLBox also holds the function makeObject() (lines 155 through 220), which creates an OpenGL display list (starting at line 159) (a display list is a group of drawing operations) and then returns it (line 219). GLBox has three slots as well: setXRotation() (lines 226 through 233), setYRotation() (lines 236 through 243), and setZRotation() (lines 246 through 253). These functions are all connected to the valueChanged() signal of a QSlider object. However, that's done in the constructor of GLWindow (to be more precise, on lines 300 through 305).

The three slots set a new angle value for the x-, y-, or z-axes and then call updateGL() to draw the new picture (lines 232, 242, and 252).

Then you have the GLWindow class (defined in lines 257 through 262). This is just a regular Qt class, based on QWidget. In the GLWindow constructor (lines 276 through 306), an object of GLBox is created (line 281). The GLWindow constructor also creates three QSlider objects (lines 286 through 297) and connects their valueChanged() slots to one of the slots on the GLBox object (lines 300 through 305). This way, the new value of the slider will be passed on to the corresponding slot on GLBox, and that slot will make sure the view angle of the box changes equally.

An object of the GLWindow class is then created in main() (line 318) and set as the main widget (line 319). Despite that fact, GLWindow uses GLBox to create OpenGL graphics; it's implemented the same as any Qt widget.

Compiling and Running the Example

To compile the program in Listing 19.1, you need to split up the code into different .cpp and .h files (name the files as noted in the listing). Then, you should have five files to work with—glbox.cpp, glbox.h, glwindow.cpp, glwindow.h, and main.cpp.

Now, you should start by using the Meta Object Compiler on glbox.h. Because GLBox is the only class that includes custom slots, this is the only one you need to use MOC on, as follows:

```
# moc glbox.h -o glbox.moc
```

Note that if you choose to call the output anything other than glbox.moc, you need to change the following line in glbox.cpp:

```
#include "glbox.moc"
```

Therefore, it's best to name it glbox.moc. Then, you should create object files of each .cpp file:

```
# g++ -c glbox.cpp -o glbox.o
# g++ -c glwindow.cpp -o glwindow.o
# g++ -c main.cpp -o main.o
```

Actually, when creating object files, you don't have to tell g++ (or gcc) what you want to call the output. If you just enter the command

```
# g++ -c main.cpp
```

g++ will assume you want to call the object file main.o.

When the object files are ready, it's time to link them together into an executable program. This is done with the following command:

```
# g++ glbox.o glwindow.o main.o -o Listing-19.1 -lqt -lqgl -lGL
```

This command results in an executable file called Listing-19.1. Note that you link with the Qt standard library, Qt's OpenGL library, and the OpenGL library provided by MESA.

Now, start the program. If everything is correct, you should see the program shown in Figure 19.1.

FIGURE 19.1

The OpenGL program as it first appears onscreen. You can use the sliders to the left to change the view angle of the box.

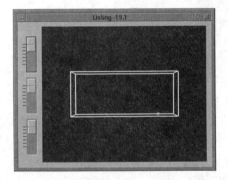

Now, try to drag the sliders so that the view angle changes. By doing that, you should accomplish something similar to what's shown in Figure 19.2.

FIGURE 19.2

An example of using the sliders to change the view angle.

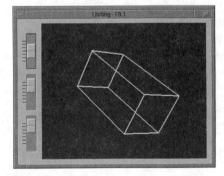

Although this program is not that useful, it certainly proves how easy it really is to connect the two libraries, Qt and OpenGL, together.

Summary

OpenGL's most obvious drawback is its lack of functions for user interaction (you should note, though, that OpenGL was never intended to be a GUI program). If you're a bit dramatic, you could say that Qt's most obvious drawback is its lack of high-performance drawing operations. However, by putting the Qt and OpenGL libraries together, you solve this problem completely. By using OpenGL for the graphic-intense operations and Qt for user interaction, the results are quite extraordinary.

However, although OpenGL is great for graphics, you should think twice before you use it. After all, OpenGL is a whole new library, and this of course means that all your users must have MESA (or some other OpenGL implementation) installed to be able to use your program. If they don't already have an OpenGL library, it's very possible that they won't install your software because of the extra effort they need to put in to get and install an OpenGL library. Therefore, for simple graphic functions, it's safest to stick with QPaint.

This problem, of course, only will occur if you're planning to distribute your software as source code. If you're planning to provide binaries only, it's simple to make a statically linked binary. This way, the users won't need to bother with getting and installing OpenGL libraries at all. Note that static libraries are not created by default when compiling MESA; you must add the `--enable-static` option to `configure` and then recompile to get static libraries.

Q&A

Q Actually, I don't understand much of this hour. Have I missed something?

A Yes and no. This hour assumes that you have at least a basic understanding of OpenGL programming. Without that, you'll find it very hard to follow the discussion. You can find good, free OpenGL documentation at `www.opengl.org`.

Q When compiling Listing 19.1, my compiler says it can't find any GL library. However, I am absolutely sure that I installed MESA correctly.

A MESA installs its libraries in `/usr/local/lib` by default. It's possible that your environment is not set to search for libraries in this directory. However, you can easily change this with the `-L` option. For example, `-L/usr/local/lib` will make sure that the compiler looks in `/usr/local/lib` for libraries.

19

Workshop

You're encouraged to work through the following questions and exercises to help you retain what you've learned in this hour about how to use OpenGL in a Qt program.

Quiz

1. What is OpenGL?

2. What is MESA?

3. What is `libqgl`?

4. When should you use OpenGL?

5. What is OpenGL's weakness?

6. What is the `QGLWidget` class used for?

Exercises

1. Find a good OpenGL tutorial at `www.opengl.org`. Then read and study it.

2. Build and test the examples found in the `$QTDIR/extensions/opengl/examples` directory. Also study the source code; it can give you some good ideas on how to use Qt in your OpenGL program (and vice versa).

3. Add a function to Listing 19.1 that makes it possible for the user to change the view distance. Add a bar that can control how far away the box appears to the user.

Hour **20**

Creating Netscape Plug-Ins

In this hour, you'll learn how to take advantage of Qt to easily write *browser plug-ins*, which are pieces of software (a shared object in UNIX; a DLL file in Windows) for many types of programs that easily extend the current features of these programs. An example of this is the popular Flash plug-in from Macromedia, which makes your Internet browser able to deal with Web sites that use Flash technology (for more information about this, see www.flash.com). If you have this plug-in installed, the browser will simply call the plug-in for help when it finds a file or a stream of data that the plug-in can handle. Keep in mind, though, that plug-ins for one program are not compatible with plug-ins for another program.

When creating plug-ins for Netscape Navigator, you'll generally use the Plugin SDK (Software Development Kit), which can be downloaded from Netscape's Web site, and write the plug-ins using the API (Application Programming Interface) provided by the Plugin SDK. However, the API provided by the Plugin SDK is considered pretty hard to use. That's where Qt comes in. Qt includes a few classes you can use to create Netscape plug-ins. By using these classes, you don't have to deal with the standard Plugin API; therefore, writing Netscape plug-ins becomes much easier.

This hour focuses on developing Netscape plug-ins by using Qt's plug-in classes. It does not cover how to use the Netscape Plugin SDK.

Preparing Your System for Plug-In Development

Before you can begin developing Netscape plug-ins with Qt, there are a few things you need to do first. The steps you'll need to take are covered in this section.

Getting the Netscape Plugin SDK

Although you won't directly use the Plugin SDK provided by Netscape, the plug-in extension in Qt uses parts of this SDK; therefore, you need to download it.

This can be done from Netscape's Web site (http://home.netscape.com/comprod/development_partners/plugin_api/). Make sure you get the right version for your system (Windows or UNIX). When the download is finished, you need to "untar" the archive and copy a few files to the $QTDIR/extensions/nsplugin/src directory. First, extract the archive:

```
# tar xvfz unix-sdk-3.0b5.tar.Z
```

This will untar the whole archive and place the files in a directory called PluginSDK30b5.

> As always, it's very possible that the version number has changed. At the time of this writing, the latest version was 3.0b5. If that has changed, it will affect both the name of the file and the name of the directory.

Now, you need to copy a few of these files to the $QTDIR/extensions/nsplugin/src directory. This can be done as follows:

```
# cd  PluginSDK30b5/common/
# cp npunix.cpp $QTDIR/extensions/nsplugin/src
```

```
# cp npwin.cpp $QTDIR/extensions/nsplugin/src
# cd ../include
# cp * $QTDIR/extensions/nsplugin/src
```

After this is done, you can delete the PluginSDK30b5 directory—you won't need it anymore.

Compiling the Qt Netscape Plug-In Extension

By default, the plug-in extension of Qt is not compiled—you need to do that manually. However, you can't compile it without the files you copied in the last section. This is not hard to do. Use cd to change the current directory to $QTDIR/extensions/nsplugin/src and run make from there, as follows:

```
# make
```

You'll see the following output:

```
g++ -c -I/usr/local/qt/include -I/usr/X11R6/include -pipe -O2 -fPIC
-o qnp.o qnp.cpp
/usr/local/qt/bin/moc ../../../include/qnp.h -o moc_qnp.cpp
g++ -c -I/usr/local/qt/include -I/usr/X11R6/include -pipe -O2 -fPIC
-o moc_qnp.o moc_qnp.cpp
rm -f ../../../lib/libqnp.a ; ar cqs ../../../lib/libqnp.a qnp.o moc_qnp.o
```

This will create a static library called libqnp.a. Copy this file to $QTDIR/lib so that you don't need to specify in which directory this library is located each time you compile your plug-in software.

Getting to Know Qt's Netscape Plug-In Classes

You first need to get an understanding of how the Qt plug-in classes work. This section goes through each of them, discussing how and when they are used. Note that only the most critical member functions of each class are covered. You should take a look in the Qt Reference Documentation for information about the functions not mentioned here.

20

QNPlugin: The Heart of the Plug-In

QNPlugin is the heart of the plug-in. There is never more than one object of this plug-in. For each of your plug-ins created with Qt, you need to create a subclass of QNPlugin and reimplement a few functions that the browser calls to get various information about the particular plug-in.

Understanding the `getMIMEDescription()` Function

`QNPlugin::getMIMEDescription()` is called by the browser when it needs to know what MIME type and which filename extensions the plug-in can handle.

MIME types are used by Internet browsers to determine what kind of data they're dealing with. It's up to the Web server to tell the browser what MIME type a file or stream of data belongs to. The browser then checks its configuration to see whether there's a *handler* (either a program or a plug-in) defined for this MIME type. If a handler exists, the browser uses it to work with the data.

A MIME type consists of a major and a minor type, separated by a slash (/). For example, the MIME type `text/plain` represents text of the type plain, and the MIME type `image/gif` represents an image of the type GIF.

However, to define a new MIME type, you need to have access to the Web server's configuration file, and that's not something you usually have. Fortunately, file types can also be determined by looking at the filename extension. For example, text files usually end with `.txt`, and GIF images with `.gif`.

Here's a sample implementation of `QNPlugin::getMIMEDescription()`:

```
const char *getMIMEDescription()
{
    return "image/gif:gif:GIF Image";
}
```

As you can see, this string is divided into three parts, separated by colons (`:`). The first part represents the MIME type, the second part represents the filename extension, and the last part represents a description of the type. Note that the filename extension can include more than one extension. If you want to register more than one filename extension for a type, you should separate each instance with a comma (`,`).

Understanding the `getPluginNameString()` Function

`QNPlugin::getPluginNameString()` returns the name of the plug-in as a string. This string appears in the Description column on the About Plug-Ins page in Netscape Navigator. The About Plug-Ins page can be accessed from the Help menu (located on the right side of the browser window). You can also access it by typing **about:plugins** in the URL field. A sample implementation of `QNPlugin::getPluginNameString()` follows:

```
const char *getPluginNameString() const
{
    return "This is the full name of my plugin";
}
```

Understanding the `getPluginDescriptionString()` Function

`QNPlugin::getPluginDescriptionString()` also returns a string that's shown on the About Plug-Ins page. However, this function returns a short description of the plug-in instead of the name of the plug-in. A sample implementation of `QNPlugin::getPluginDescriptionString()` follows:

```
const char *getPluginDescriptionString() const
{
    return "Here is a short description of my plugin";
}
```

Understanding the `newInstance()` Function

`QNPlugin::newInstance()` is used by the browser to get a new object of the `QNPInstance` class (that is, a subclass of the `QNPInstance` class that you have created). For example, if your subclass of `QNPInstance` is called `MyPluginInstance`, `QNPlugin::newInstance()` would look like this:

```
QNPInstance *newInstance()
{
    return new MyPluginInstance;
}
```

`QNPInstance`: The Link Between the Browser and the Plug-In

As stated previously, there's never more than one `QNPlugin` object. Instead, `QNPInstance` objects are created by calling the `QNPlugin::newInstance()` function. After a `QNPlugin` object is created and `QNPlugin::newInstance()` is called, `QNPInstance` takes care of the communication between the plug-in and the browser. This is done through a few static functions, which you will go through now.

Understanding the `newWindow()` Function

`QNPInstance::newWindow()` returns a pointer to an object of a subclass of the `QNPWidget` class. This function is called once by the browser when the plug-in should be shown onscreen. A sample implementation of this function follows:

```
QNPWidget *newWindow()
{
    return new MyPluginWidget;
}
```

In this case, the subclass of `QNPWidget` is called `MyPluginWidget`.

20

Understanding the `newStreamCreated()` Function

`QNPInstance::newStreamCreated()` is used by the browser to tell the plug-in that data is available for it. With this function, you can also tell the browser whether you want the data as a file or a stream. `QNPInstance::newStreamCreated()` returns TRUE if the data is accepted. Here's a sample implementation:

```
bool newStreamCreated( QNPStream*, StreamMode &smode )
{
    smode = AsFileOnly;
    return TRUE;
}
```

In this example, the plug-in accepts the data and tells the browser that it wants the data in a file. In this case, because the browser is told to provide the data as a file, the `QNPInstance::streamAsFile()` function will be called later. This function includes the code that will process the data in the file.

If you set smod to any of the other three values you can choose from (Normal, Seek, or AsFile), it's possible that the data will be received as a stream instead. Then, the browser would have to call `QNPInstance::writeReady()`, to inquire about the minimum amount of data the instance is willing to receive from the given stream, and `QNPInstance::write()`, which should take care of the actual processing (or call the appropriate function or functions that will take care of the processing) instead.

The code in `QNPInstance::streamAsFile()`, `QNPInstance::writeReady()`, and `QNPInstance::write()` varies a lot depending on what type of data you're processing. Therefore, this section won't cover any sample implementations of these functions. However, the Qt Reference Documentation includes some interesting information about them.

`QNPWidget`: Creating the Visual Part of the Plug-In

Your subclass of `QNPWidget` should include the event and drawing code for the plug-in. `QNPWidget` is a subclass of `QWidget` and should be considered equal to any other Qt widget. Actually, the code in this class is often just regular Qt programming code (and you don't need an example of that, do you?).

`QNPStream`: Receiving Data Streams from the Browser

A subclass of `QNPStream` should only be implemented if you're using streams instead of files to receive data. `QNPStream` is an abstraction of a data stream and is used by the `QNPInstance::writeReady()` and `QNPInstance::write()` functions to stream data. However, the implementation of this class also varies a lot depending on the kind of data you're working with. The Reference Documentation includes useful information about this class and its members.

Creating Your First Netscape Plug-In

This section provides a very simple Qt-based plug-in example. You'll learn how to compile this example, how to make Netscape aware of it, and, finally, how to test it.

Investigating the Code

You should now be ready to write a simple plug-in. Listing 20.1 shows a very basic example.

LISTING 20.1   A Very Simple Qt-Based Netscape Plug-In

```
 1: //We need to include qnp.h to get the
 2: //plugin definitions:
 3: #include <qnp.h>
 4: #include <qpainter.h>
 5:
 6: //This is our QNPWidget sub-class. It will
 7: //create the actual plugin widget:
 8: class MyPluginWidget : public QNPWidget
 9: {
10: public:
11:
12: //We reimplement the paintEvent() function
13: //to take care of the painting:
14: void paintEvent(QPaintEvent* event)
15: {
16:     QPainter p( this );
17:     p.setClipRect( event->rect() );
18:     int w = width();
19:     p.drawRect( rect() );
20:     p.drawText( w/8, 0, w-w/4, height(), AlignCenter,
➡ "Your first Qt-based plugin!" );
21: }
22:
23: };
24:
25: //This is our QNPInstance sub-class. This simple
26: //version only includes the newWindow() function,
27: //which returns an object of the MyPluginWidget
28: //class:
29: class MyPluginInstance : public QNPInstance
30: {
```

20

continues

LISTING 20.1 continued

```
31: public:
32:
33: QNPWidget *newWindow()
34: {
35:     return new MyPluginWidget;
36: }
37:
38: };
39:
40: //MyPlugin is the heart of our plugin.
41: //Its members are called by the browser
42: //to get various information about the plugin
43: //and to get an object of the MyPluginInstance
44: //class:
45: class MyPlugin : public QNPlugin
46: {
47: public:
48:
49: QNPInstance *newInstance()
50: {
51:     return new MyPluginInstance;
52: }
53:
54: const char *getMIMEDescription() const
55: {
56:     return "basic/very:bas:A very basic plugin";
57: }
58:
59: const char *getPluginNameString() const
60: {
61:     return "A very basic Qt-based Plugin";
62: }
63:
64: const char *getPluginDescriptionString() const
65: {
66:     return "A very simple Qt-based plugin that can't do anything useful";
67: }
68:
69: };
70:
71: //The extern function that will feed the
72: //browser with an object of the MyPlugin
73: //class:
74: QNPlugin* QNPlugin::create()
75: {
76:     return new MyPlugin;
77: }
```

As you can see, this is a very simple example. Because the functions are so short, the function definitions are placed inside the class definitions (lines 8 through 23 and lines 29 through 69; this is known as *inline programming*). This makes the code easier to follow. Most of the parts of this program were discussed in the section "Getting to Know Qt's Netscape Plug-In Classes." Also, the paintEvent() function (lines 14 through 21) doesn't present anything new, so there's not much to say about it. However, note that the MIME type basic/very and the filename extension .bas (for basic) are used (line 56).

Actually, the fact that you don't need any further explanation of Listing 20.1 is the big reason why you should use Qt to develop Netscape plug-ins. If, on the other hand, you choose to use the standard API provided by the Netscape Plugin SDK instead, you have to learn and understand all the functions in that API. Now, the only thing you actually need to learn is how the communication between your plug-in and the browser works. For the actual plug-in implementation, you can use the usual Qt classes, which you should already be familiar with at this point.

Compiling and Installing the Plug-In

As stated earlier, a plug-in is a shared object (UNIX) or a DLL file (Windows). To make it a shared object, you need to compile it in a way compared that's different from how you've compiled your other Qt programs.

First, you need to make an object file out of the source code:

```
# g++ -c 20lst01.cpp -o 20lst01.o
```

This creates an object file named 20lst01.o. Then, you need to link this object file with some other libraries and make a shared object out of it. To do this, issue the following command:

```
# g++ -L/usr/local/qt/lib -L/usr/X11R6/lib 20lst01.o -lqt -lXext -lX11
 -lm -L/usr/local/qt/lib -lqnp -lXt -lm -shared -o 20lst01.so
```

Note the -lqnp options, which tell your linker (probably ld) to link with the libqnp library created earlier in the "Preparing Your System for Plug-in Development" section. Also, note the -shared option. This option makes the output of the command a shared object.

However, this will result in a file called 20lst01.so. You should copy this file to the plugins directory of your Netscape installation, which is probably something like /usr/lib/netscape/plugins, /usr/local/netscape/plugin, /usr/netscape/plugin, or /opt/netscape/plugins. To copy the file, issue the following command:

```
# cp 20lst01.so /usr/lib/netscape/plugins
```

20

If you want more information about linking and compiling, you are encouraged to pick up another book in this series, *Sams Teach Yourself Linux Programming in 24 Hours*, by Warren W. Gay (ISBN 0-672-31582-3). It includes an extensive discussion about compiling and linking with g++ (gcc) and ld.

If Netscape is already running, you need to restart it. Then, select the About Plug-Ins item from the Help menu in the browser window. Now, if everything is alright, you should see information about your basic plug-in at the top of the page. This is shown in Figure 20.1.

FIGURE 20.1

The About Plug-Ins page of Netscape Navigator, showing the sample plug-in.

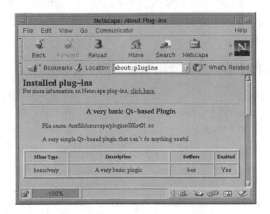

The heading "A very basic Qt-based Plugin" is taken from the `QNPlugin::getPluginNameString()` function. The description under the filename comes from the `QNPlugin::getPluginDescriptionString()` function, and the three fields in the table are defined in the `QNPlugin::getMIMEDescription()` function.

Testing the Plug-In

Because this simple plug-in doesn't deal with any data at all, you won't use a file with the correct filename extension (`.bas`) to test the plug-in. Instead, you'll use the HTML tag `<EMBED>` to call the plug-in. Because this is not an HTML book, this section only discusses the `<EMBED>` tag just enough to teach you how to use it to show the plug-in.

To test your plug-in, you first need to create a HTML document. Here's an example:

```
<HTML>
<HEAD>
<TITLE>A Very Basic Qt-Based Plugin Called With the EMBED Tag</TITLE>
</HEAD>
<BODY BGCOLOR="#ffffff">
<CENTER>
<EMBED TYPE=basic/very WIDTH=300 HEIGHT=100>
</CENTER>
</BODY>
</HTML>
```

Now, if you open this document in Netscape, your plug-in will paint a rectangle that's 300 by 100 pixels (defined by the `<EMBED>` tag) with the text "Your first Qt-based plugin!" in it. This is shown in Figure 20.2.

FIGURE 20.2

Your plug-in embedded in an HTML document using the `<EMBED>` *tag.*

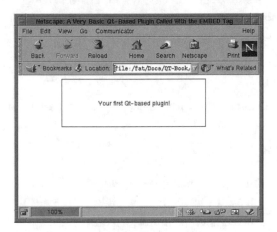

This example is not that useful; it just draws a rectangle that contains some text. However, suppose you've created a plug-in for showing AVI movies. You could easily embed an AVI movie in a HTML document, like this:

```
<EMBED SRC="movie.avi" WIDTH=320 HEIGHT=200 AUTOSTART=true LOOP=true>
```

For more detailed information about the `<EMBED>` tag, you might want to look into one of the many free HTML courses on the Internet.

20

Summary

Developing Netscape plug-ins with Qt can make many aspects of plug-in programming easier. By choosing Qt over the standard API provided by the Netscape Plugin SDK, you also save yourself a lot of time. The API provided by the Netscape Plugin SDK is quite complicated and difficult to use. By now, it should be clear to you that this is *not* the case with Qt.

You'll find three interesting examples of plug-ins in the `extensions/nsplugin/ examples` directory of your Qt installation. Perhaps the most useful of the three is the `qtimage` plug-in. It extends Netscape's capabilities to show any of the image formats supported by Qt! You're encouraged to take a look at the source code for this plug-in. It shows how easily you can create a useful plug-in with Qt.

When you create a Netscape plug-in, you'll find it hard to debug through Netscape. Therefore, you should make a regular Qt program of the plug-in first; then, when it's tested and ready to use, you can convert it into a plug-in very easily.

Q&A

Q When I'm trying to link with `libqnp`, my compiler says it can't find any library with that name. What's wrong?

A You probably forgot to copy the library from `$QTDIR/extensions/nsplugin/src` to `$QTDIR/lib`. The library will not be found if you don't do that.

Q When executing the command that makes the shared object, my compiler says it can't find one of the libraries it was told to link with. What's wrong?

A It's possible that you have the library in a directory that's not searched by the compiler. Try to find the library manually (with `find` or `locate`). If you find it, tell the compiler to search in that directory by using the `-L` option. If you can't find the library, try removing it from the linking list and see whether the plug-in works anyway. If that doesn't work, try to install the library from your distribution or search for it on `www.freshmeat.net`.

Q When compiling the `qtimage` plug-in, the compiler says it can't find the `qimgio` library. Where do I find that library?

A This library can be found in the `extensions` directory of your Qt installation. It's not compiled and installed by default—you have to do that manually.

Workshop

You're encouraged to work through the following questions and exercises to help you retain what you've learned about how the Qt plug-in classes work and how to take advantage of them.

Quiz

1. Why should you use Qt to develop Netscape plug-ins?

2. What does the QNPlugin::getMIMEDescription() function do?

3. What is a MIME type?

4. Suppose you've created a plug-in for showing BMP images. You open a document with many BMP images in it. How many QNPlugin objects are created?

5. In the scenario from question 3, how many QNPInstance objects are created?

6. What is the QNPInstance::newWindow() function used for?

7. When does the browser call the QNPInstance::newStreamCreated() function?

8. What kind of code should you find in a subclass of QNPWidget?

9. When do you need to create a subclass of QNPStream?

10. What is the <EMBED> HTML tag used for?

Exercises

1. Compile, install, and test the qtimage plug-in.

2. Write a plug-in that reads some text from a file (with a special filename extension) and then shows (draws) the text in the browser window. An idea would also be to present the text in such way that is beyond usual HTML, so that your plug-in can be of any use. (Note that you'll need to study the Reference Documentation for this.) For example, you could make a plug-in that case draw circles of text, or something like that.

20

PART V
Learning to Improve Your Programs

Hour

HOUR 21

Internationalizing Your Qt Programs

One of the things you can do to make your Qt programs easier to use for a wider range of people is to make them available in other languages. Although many people speak English as a second language, they'll usually find it is easier to fully understand your programs in their native languages. If English isn't your native language, you know how frustrating it can be to find one or two words in a program that you do not understand.

Fortunately, Qt comes with an extensive collection of tools and functions for making the internationalization of your programs easier. This not only includes language translation but also character encoding, input techniques, and presentation conventions.

In this lesson, you'll take a look at the functions and utilities that can help you create international Qt applications.

Understanding the Importance of `QString`

To begin with, you're encouraged to use the `QString` class for any user-visible text (that is, text that in any way will be visible to the user).

`QString` uses, in contrast to `char`, Unicode encoding internally. This makes `QString` able to process any of the world's languages without problems. If you use `char` instead, it's very possible that some systems won't be able to present the text in the way it was intended. By using `QString` for text that's visible for the user, you make sure this problem won't occur.

Another good reason to use `QString` is speed. All Qt functions that present some kind of text to the user take a `QString` as an argument. Although it's possible to use `char` with these functions as well, do so will force a `char-to-QString` conversion, and this conversion takes a certain amount of CPU time. By using `QString` instead of `char`, you avoid this conversion. However, you won't recognize any change in speed by just changing a few `char` instances to `QString`. The speed change will only be obvious if your program is forced to do a large amount of `char-to-QString` conversions.

For strings that the user never sees (also known as *programmer space text*), it's safe to use `char`.

Creating Translation Files

When creating translation files in Qt, you need to perform a number of tasks. These include changes to the source code as well as using Qt's utilities to create the special translation files for you, which are used to find a translation for specific words or terms. In this section, you'll learn everything you need to know to create your own translation files.

Using the `tr()` Function

The `QObject::tr()` function must be used everywhere in your program where you want to have a string translated. It's a simple function to use; you just pass the string you want to translate as an argument. Because it's a subclass of `QObject`, it's included in all classes that inherit from `QObject`.

For example, if you want to translate the label `Password:` in a password login widget, you would use something like this:

```
QLabel *label = new QLabel( tr("Password:"), this );
```

What happens here is that the `tr()` function searches for a translation of the string `Password:`. If a translation is found, that string is used. If no translation is found, `Password:` is used. However, you'll of course need translation files to make this work (see the following sections). Without a translation file, the call to the `tr()` function will always return `Password:`.

If the text you want to translate is not in a subclass of `QObject` (for example, it's in a global function), you can use the `tr()` function of some other appropriate class. Here's an example:

```
void MyGlobalFunction()
{
    QLabel *label = new QLabel( MyQObjectSubClass::tr("Text to be translated:")
                              , parent );
}
```

This has the same function as the previous example, although the function is not a member of a `QObject` subclass. Note that the function name and class name are fictive.

Therefore, by using the `tr()` function on all text that will be presented to the user in your program, you make sure that translation will be preformed if it's available. However, as mentioned earlier, you need to create translation files that hold the translations to make the `tr()` function useful.

Extracting Text for Translation with the `findtr` Utility

To make use of the calls to the `tr()` function, you need to create translation files. These files work as databases for your program's translations—one file for each language. The steps you need to take in this process are all covered in this section.

 You're not required to use the filename conventions used in this section. However, it's recommended that you do so to follow the Qt translation file standard. This makes it easier for others to understand how your program is organized.

21

To begin with, you need to find all `tr()` function calls in your program and extract a PO file (a file with a `.po` extension) out of them. This is done using the `findtr` utility, located in the $QTDIR/bin directory. This program searches one or more files for tr() function calls and makes an entry for each call in a PO file.

It's then up to you to edit this file so that each entry in it has a valid translation. Consider the example of a password widget, as shown in Listing 21.1.

LISTING 21.1 A Typical Password Widget

```
 1: #include <qapplication.h>
 2: #include <qwidget.h>
 3: #include <qlabel.h>
 4: #include <qlineedit.h>
 5:
 6: class MyWidget : public QWidget
 7: {
 8: public:
 9:         MyWidget();
10: private:
11:         QLabel *label;
12:         QLineEdit *edit;
13: };
14:
15: MyWidget::MyWidget()
16: {
17:     resize( 200, 50 );
18:
19:     label = new QLabel( "Password:", this );
20:     label->setGeometry( 10, 10, 60, 30 );
21:
22:     edit = new QLineEdit( this );
23:     edit->setGeometry( 70, 10, 120, 30 );
24:     edit->setEchoMode( QLineEdit::Password );
25: }
26:
27: main( int argc, char **argv )
28: {
29:     QApplication a( argc, argv );
30:     MyWidget w;
31:     a.setMainWidget( &w );
32:     w.show();
33:     return a.exec();
34: }
```

This program creates a small window with a label to the left (lines 19 and 20) and a QLineEdit object to the right (lines 22, 23, and 24)—a typical widget for retrieving a password (see Figure 21.1).

FIGURE 21.1

A typical widget for retrieving a password.

Wouldn't it be a nice gesture to all your users who don't know English very well to change the Password: label to whatever language the user is running? Fortunately, this is easy.

To begin with, you need to implement the tr() function discussed earlier. Just change the line

```
label = new QLabel( "Password:", this );
```

so that it looks like this:

```
label = new QLabel( tr("Password:"), this );
```

Now, you need to create a PO file to hold a translation for the Password: label. Execute the following command:

```
# findtr 21lst01.cpp > 21lst01.po
```

This command will search through the file 21lst01.cpp for tr() function calls and output one entry for each call to the file 21lst01.po. If you followed the instructions on how the implement the tr() function in Listing 21.1, your output from findtr will look like this:

```
# This is a Qt message file in .po format.  Each msgid starts with
# a scope.  This scope should *NOT* be translated - eg. "Foo::Bar"
# would be translated to "Pub", not "Foo::Pub".
msgid ""
msgstr ""
"Project-Id-Version: example-Qt-message-extraction\n"
"POT-Creation-Date: 1999-02-23 15:38+0200\n"
"PO-Revision-Date: 1999-02-23 15:38+0200\n"
"Last-Translator: \n"
"Content-Type: text/plain; charset=iso-8859-1\n"

#: 21lst01.cpp:19
msgid "MyWidget::Password:"
msgstr ""
```

The first 10 lines contain standard data that's outputted by findtr in all cases. However, what comes after this depends on the files you have findtr investigate. In this case, it's the last three lines that are important. Take a look at the following line:

```
#: 21lst01.cpp:19
```

21

This lines tells you that a tr() function call was found in the file 21lst01.cpp at line 17. Then, you see this line:

```
msgid "MyWidget::Password:"
```

This is the ID of the translation entry. MyWidget is the scope of the entry (that is, the name of the class in which the tr() function call was made). Password is the key of the translation entry (that is, the text that should be translated). Then there's the translation string line:

```
msgstr ""
```

On this line, you should insert the string that you want to replace the key with (Password:, in this case). However, you usually don't edit the original PO file. A common way of doing this is to make copies of the original PO file, one copy for each language, and then edit the copies instead. For example, if you wanted to make a Swedish translation for this widget, you would copy the original PO file to another suitable filename, such as 21lst01_se.po, and then make any needed changes to that file. In this case, the last three lines of 21lst01_se.po would be this:

```
#: 21lst01.cpp:19
msgid "MyWidget::Password:"
msgstr "Lösenord:"
```

Now, if you used this translation in your program, every call to tr("Password:") would return the string Lösenord:.

It's easy to make findtr search for tr() function calls in multiple files without needing to issue one command for each of them. For instance, the following example would search all files that end with .cpp or .h and output the results in a file called MyClass.po:

```
# findtr *.cpp *.h > MyClass.po
```

Creating Binary Translation Files with the msg2qm Utility

Now that you've created a valid PO file (21lst01_se.po), you need to create a binary database file out of it. This is done via the Qt utility msg2qm. By using binary databases instead of regular text files, the translation will occur much faster. What's more, you must do this to make the translation work anyway.

Like `findtr`, the `msg2qm` utility can be found in the `$QTDIR/bin` directory. It takes two command-line arguments: the PO file you want to work with, and the name of the file you want to store the output in (that is, the binary database file). So, to create a binary database file of the `21lst01_se.po` file you created in the previous section, you would issue the following command:

```
# msg2qm 21lst01_se.po 21lst01_se.qm
```

This creates the file `21lst01_se.qm`, which you can then use in your program to retrieve translations from.

Merging Changes with the `mergetr` Utility

As you develop a program, it's very possible that its text will change. It's easy to update the original PO file with `findtr`. However, you also need to edit the changed entries in all your other language-specific PO files. If you've made translations for a lot of languages, this can be a time-consuming task to do by hand.

Fortunately, the `mergetr` utility is a great help for this problem. It simply searches the original (and updated) PO file for changes and then edits the other PO file accordingly. For example, it's very possible that the line numbers change as your program gets larger. Because of this, the line numbers in the PO files won't be correct anymore. However, `mergtr` fixes this for you.

To use `mergetr` for updating your PO files, you first need to update the original PO file, like this:

```
# findtr *.cpp *.h > MyClass.po
```

`MyClass.po` will now contain the updated information. Then, you can use `mergtr` to update all your language-specific PO files as well. Here's an example:

```
# mergetr MyClass.po MyClass_fr.po
```

This updates the `MyClass_fr.po` file. If any line numbers were changed, they would be updated. If any translations were deleted, they would be commented out (using # signs) in `MyClass_se.po`. Also, if any entries were added, they would be added to `MyClass_se.po` as well.

Keep in mind, though, that if you change a translation (for example, you decide to remove the colon in `Password:`), `findtr` will interpret this as a new entry; it can't see that it's an old, changed entry. This also applies to `mergetr`: If it finds an entry in the original PO file that doesn't exactly match one of the old entries, it will interpret this as a new entry (and new entries always have empty translation strings, so you need to insert them again). Because `mergetr` won't find an exact match for the old entry, it will be commented out (in the language-specific PO file).

21

So, `mergtr` updates the line numbers automatically, it deletes (or comments out) any entries that are not used anymore, and if there are any new entries in the original PO file, they will be automatically added to the language-specific PO file as well. However, it interprets changed translation entries as new entries.

Implementing a Translation Function in Your Program

After the binary translation files are created and ready to use, it's time to tell your program to use them; this is not done automatically. However, the `QTranslator` class makes this process really simple. Here are the steps you need to take:

1. Create a `QTranslator` object.

2. Tell the `QTranslator` object which binary translation file to use (which you've created with the `msg2qm` utility).

3. Tell the `QApplication` object about your new translator.

4. Implement a call to the `Q_OBJECT` macro in the class declaration and use `moc` on the header file.

Start by creating a `QTranslator` object. Then tell it which binary translation file to use and tell the `QApplication` object that a translator is available. You also need to include the file `qtranslator.h` to get access to the `QTranslator` class declaration, as follows:

```
#include <qtranslator.h>

QTranslator translator( this );
translator.load( "21lst01_se.qm", "." );
qApp->installTranslator( &translator );
```

The first line creates a `QTranslator` object (`translator`) and sets its parent to the `this` pointer (a pointer to an uncreated object of the currently defined class). On the second line, the `QTranslator::load()` function is called to tell the `QTranslator` object which binary translation file to use. The first argument given to this function is the name of the binary translation file, and the second argument defines in which directory the program should search for this file. In this case, the current directory (`.`) will be searched. On the third line, the `QApplication::installTranslator()` function is called to tell the `QApplication` object about this translator. The memory address to `translator` is passed as an argument.

Because the translation function, `tr()`, is implemented by `moc`, you also need to make a call to the `Q_OBJECT` macro and create a MOC file of the class declaration (and, as always, include the MOC file in the CPP file).

After these changes are made, the class declaration and definition in Listing 21.1 should look as shown in Listing 21.2.

LISTING 21.2 An International Password Widget

```
 1: class MyWidget : public QWidget
 2: {
 3:         Q_OBJECT
 4: public:
 5:         MyWidget();
 6: private:
 7:         QLabel *label;
 8:         QLineEdit *edit;
 9: };
10:
11: #include "21lst01.moc"
12:
13: MyWidget::MyWidget()
14: {
15:         resize( 200, 50 );
16:
17:         QTranslator translator( this );
18:         translator.load( "21lst01_se.qm", "." );
19:         qApp->installTranslator( &translator );
20:
21:         label = new QLabel( tr("Password:"), this );
22:         label->setGeometry( 10, 10, 60, 30 );
23:
24:         edit = new QLineEdit( this );
25:         edit->setGeometry( 70, 10, 120, 30 );
26:         edit->setEchoMode( QLineEdit::Password );
27: }
```

However, in reality, you should make two files out of this. Now, it's time to test the translation. First, use moc on the class declaration:

```
# moc 21lst01.h -o 21lst01.moc
```

Make sure you've included the MOC file in the CPP file and then recompile the edited version of Listing 21.1:

```
# g++ -lqt 21lst01.cpp -o Listing-21.1
```

If you already created the QM file (out of the PO file) with the msg2qm utility, you could test the program now. However, because you have added a few lines to the source code, the line numbers in the PO file doesn't match any longer. The translation will work anyway, and in this case, where you just have one translation, it really doesn't matter.

21

However, in a large PO file with many translations, it's more convenient to have matching line numbers, and it's a lot easier to find a specific entry. So, whether you use the old QM file, based on an old version of the 21lst01_se.po file, or re-create it from an updated version of 21lst01_se.po, running the program in Listing 21.1 presents you with what's shown in Figure 21.2.

FIGURE 21.2

The Swedish version of the password widget. The translation is taken from the binary translation file 21lst01_se.qm.

You've just completed your first international Qt program! Although this example is a very simple one, the techniques used here are the same no matter how many tr() function calls you make.

Working with Date and Time Values

Date and time values don't exactly constitute an internationalization matter. However, they do differ depending on where on the planet you live; therefore, they're considered an international matter in this book.

Qt's support for date and time values consists of three classes: QDate, QTime, and QDateTime. All three are defined in the qdatetime.h file.

Using the QDate Class for Date Values

By far the most popular function in the QDate class is QDate::currentDate(), which returns the current date. After the current date is returned by the currentDate() function, you'll usually use the QDate::toString() function to convert the date to a QString. Listing 21.3 provides an example of this.

LISTING 21.3   A Widget Showing the Current Date

```
1: #include <qapplication.h>
2: #include <qwidget.h>
3: #include <qdatetime.h>
4: #include <qlabel.h>
5:
6: class MyWidget : public QWidget
7: {
```

```
 8: public:
 9:         MyWidget();
10: private:
11:     QLabel *label;
12: };
13:
14: MyWidget::MyWidget()
15: {
16:     resize( 150, 50 );
17:
18:     //Get the current date and store it
19:     //in date:
20:     QDate date = QDate::currentDate();
21:
22:     //Use the QDate::toString() function to make
23:     //a string out of the date and show it in a
24:     //QLabel:
25:     label = new QLabel( date.toString(), this );
26:     label->setGeometry( 0, 0, 150, 50 );
27:     label->setAlignment( AlignCenter );
28: }
29:
30: main( int argc, char **argv )
31: {
32:     QApplication a( argc, argv );
33:     MyWidget w;
34:     a.setMainWidget( &w );
35:     w.show();
36:     return a.exec();
37: }
```

This example creates a QDate object and uses the QDate::currentDate() function to define the new object (QDate::currentDate() actually returns a QDate object representing the current date). Then, the QDate::toString() function is used to make a string of the date and insert it into a QLabel object. Figure 21.3 shows this example.

FIGURE 21.3

A small widget showing the current date.

Some other QDate member functions you might find useful are presented in Table 21.1.

21

TABLE 21.1   Useful `QDate` Member Functions

Function	Description
`QDate::year()`	Returns an integer representing the current year.
`QDate::month()`	Returns an integer representing the current month (1 for January; 12 for December).
`QDate::day()`	Returns an integer representing the day of the month (1 through 31).
`QDate::dayOfYear()`	Returns an integer representing the day of the year (1 through 365).
`QDate::daysOfMonth()`	Returns an integer representing the number of days in the month (28, 29, 30, or 31).
`QDate::daysInYear()`	Returns an integer representing the number of days in the year (365 or 366).
`QDate::monthName()`	This function takes an integer (1–12) as an argument and returns the name of the month in a `QString`.
`QDate::dayName()`	This function takes an integer (1–7) as an argument and returns the name of the day as a string.
`QDate::daysTo()`	This function takes a `QDate` object as an argument and returns an integer representing the number of days between this date and the date that was passed as an argument.

The `QDate::currentDate()` function uses the day/month/year standard. However, it's easy to accomplish your desired standard by using the functions described in Table 21.1.

Another great feature of `QDate` is that you can use the ==, !=, <, >, <=, and >= operators with it. This makes it very simple to compare multiple `QDate` objects.

Using the `QTime` Class for Time Values

`QTime` is built very similarly to `QDate`. However, it's intended for time values, not date values. You can use the `QTime::currentTime()` function to retrieve the current time, and you can use the `QTime::toString()` function to make a string of the time. Listing 21.4 shows a simple example of this.

LISTING 21.4   A Widget Showing the Current Time

```
1: #include <qapplication.h>
2: #include <qwidget.h>
3: #include <qdatetime.h>
4: #include <qlabel.h>
5:
6: class MyWidget : public QWidget
7: {
```

```
 8: public:
 9:         MyWidget();
10: private:
11:     QLabel *label;
12: };
13:
14: MyWidget::MyWidget()
15: {
16:     resize( 150, 50 );
17:
18:     //Get the current date and store it
19:     //in time:
20:     QTime time = QTime::currentTime();
21:
22:     //Use the QTime::toString() function to make
23:     //a string out of the time and show it in a
24:     //QLabel:
25:     label = new QLabel( time.toString(), this );
26:     label->setGeometry( 0, 0, 150, 50 );
27:     label->setAlignment( AlignCenter );
28: }
29:
30: main( int argc, char **argv )
31: {
32:     QApplication a( argc, argv );
33:     MyWidget w;
34:     a.setMainWidget( &w );
35:     w.show();
36:     return a.exec();
37: }
```

Here, a QTime object is created and set to the current time by using the QTime::currentTime() function (line 20). Then, it's shown in a QLabel object by using the QTime::toString() (line 25) function (see Figure 21.4).

FIGURE 21.4

A small widget showing the current time.

As is the case with QDate, you can use the various comparison operators to compare different QTime objects. QTime also has a few member functions you can use to perform various operations with your QTime object. Table 21.2 describes those functions.

21

TABLE 21.2   Useful `QTime` Member Functions

Function	Description
`QTime::hour()`	Returns in integer representing the current hour (1–23).
`QTime::minute()`	Returns an integer representing the current minute (0–59).
`QTime::second()`	Returns an integer representing the current second (0–59).
`QTime::msec()`	Returns an integer representing milliseconds (0–999). This is not very useful when you just want to display the current time. A possible use would be if you need to measure an amount of time very precisely.
`QTime::addSecs()`	Takes an integer as an argument and adds this number of seconds to the time. The new time is then returned.
`QTime::secsTo()`	Takes a `QTime` object as an argument and returns another `QTime` object representing the time between the argument's time and the time of this object.
`QTime::addMSecs()`	Takes an integer as an argument that represents the number of milliseconds you want to add to the time. The new time is returned as a `QTime` object.
`QTime::msecsTo()`	Takes a `QTime` object as an argument and returns another `QTime` object representing the time between the argument's time and the time of this object.
`QTime::start()`	If you want to use a `QTime` object as a timer, you start the timer by calling this function. You can then check how much time has elapsed with the `QTime::elapsed()` function and then restart the timer with the `QTime::restart()` function.

`QTime` is a very useful class. Actually, it's used a lot in non-Qt programs because of its simplicity. It's recommended that you use it, whether you want to show the current time or measure how long a certain task takes.

Using the `QDateTime` Class for Combining Date and Time Values

Qt's `QDateTime` class combines `QTime` and `QDate` into one single class. This class is usually used to show the current date and time. It's built pretty much like `QDate` and `QTime`. However, it can't get the current date and time by itself; you need to use `QDate` and `QTime` for that. See Listing 21.5 for an example.

LISTING 21.5   A Widget Showing the Current Date and Time

```
1: #include <qapplication.h>
2: #include <qwidget.h>
3: #include <qdatetime.h>
4: #include <qlabel.h>
```

```
 5:
 6: class MyWidget : public QWidget
 7: {
 8: public:
 9:          MyWidget();
10: private:
11:     QLabel *label;
12: };
13:
14: MyWidget::MyWidget()
15: {
16:     resize( 150, 50 );
17:
18:     //Create a QDateTime object:
19:     QDateTime datetime;
20:
21:     //Set the date the current date:
22:     datetime.setDate( QDate::currentDate() );
23:
24:     //Set the time to the current time:
25:     datetime.setTime( QTime::currentTime() );
26:
27:     //Use the QDateTime::toString() function to make
28:     //a string out of the date and time and show it
29:     //in a QLabel object:
30:     label = new QLabel( datetime.toString(), this );
31:     label->setGeometry( 0, 0, 150, 50 );
32:     label->setAlignment( AlignCenter );
33: }
34:
35: main( int argc, char **argv )
36: {
37:     QApplication a( argc, argv );
38:     MyWidget w;
39:     a.setMainWidget( &w );
40:     w.show();
41:     return a.exec();
42: }
```

Here, the QDateTime::setDate() (line 22) and QDateTime::setTime() (line 25) functions are used to set the date and time. These functions take a QDate and a QTime object
as arguments. In this case, the QDate::currentDate() (line 22) and
QTime::currentTime() (line 25) functions are used to get objects for the current date
and time. Then, the QDateTime::toString() function (line 30) is used to insert the current date and time into the QLabel object.

QDateTime also has a few useful member functions; these are presented in Table 21.3.

21

TABLE 21.3   Useful `QDateTime` Member Functions

Function	Description
`QDateTime::date()`	Returns a `QDate` object representing the date part of the `QDateTime` object.
`QDateTime::time()`	Returns a `QTime` object representing the time part of the `QDateTime` object.
`QDateTime::setTime_t()`	Takes an `uint` argument representing the number of seconds that have passed since 00:00:00 January 1, 1970. This can be useful if you want to use `QDateTime` with the standard C/C++ time and date functions (declared in `time.h`) that uses this method.
`QDateTime::addDays()`	Takes an integer argument representing the number of days you want to add to the `QDateTime` object. The new `QDateTime` object is returned.
`QDateTime::addSecs()`	Takes an integer argument representing the number of seconds you want to add to the `QDateTime` object. The new `QDateTime` object is returned.
`QDateTime::daysTo()`	Takes a `QDateTime` object as an argument and returns an integer representing the number of days between the argument and the `QDateTime` object.
`QDateTime::secsTo()`	Same as the previous function, but this one works with seconds instead of days.

You should now have enough information to cover all your needs regarding date and time values. However, you should note that all three classes covered in this section have constructors that can be used to set the date and/or time of the objects in addition to the member functions. `QTime`'s constructor can take two to four integer arguments, representing the hour, minute, second, and millisecond. However, the last two arguments have default values, so they can be skipped. `QDate`'s constructor takes three integer arguments, representing the year, the month, and the day. `QDateTime` has two overloaded constructors. One of them takes a `QDate` object as an argument and the other one takes a `QDate` and a `QTime` object as arguments. Which you choose depends on whether you want to set just the date or both the date and the time.

Summary

Qt's functions for making programs in multiple languages can certainly improve the usefulness of your applications—especially if you create Qt programs in a language other than English.

Of course, most people don't have the knowledge to translate their programs into more than two, maybe three, languages. However, by using English as the default language in your program and creating a translation file out of the source code, you can send this file to someone who knows the language you want to translate your program into and have him or her fill in the blanks in the translation file and send it back to you. Also, many of the standard terms used in a program can most likely be found in some other program translated into your desired language.

You should also consider which languages you're actually going to translate your program into. Start with the most widespread languages, such as English, German, French, Spanish, Portuguese, Chinese, and Japanese. Of course, you should also consider what people would appreciate the translation the most.

There's not much to say about the date and time values except that Qt's date and time classes are exceptionally well made and easy to use. They save you a lot of work compared to the standard date and time functions defined in time.h.

Q&A

Q My program refuses to use the translation file I just created. What can be wrong?

A Many things. However, the most likely problem is that you've forgotten to run the Q_OBJECT macro and to use moc in the class declaration. Some other things that could be wrong include forgetting to create a binary translation file with the msg2qm utility and making changes to the program and then forgetting to update the translation file(s).

Q Is there any way I can search the translation file for a particular entry?

A Yes, this is very easy to do with the QTranslator::find() function. It takes two strings as arguments. The first represent the scope (usually the name of the class in which this translation should be made) and the second represents the key (the string that should be translated).

Q When working with the current time, will the time automatically change to the local time of the area where the program is started?

A Yes, this depends on the computer system's clock. Therefore, if it's set to your local time, QTime will get the local time when QTime::getCurrent() is called. This means that if your system's clock is set wrong, QTime::getCurrent() will also return the wrong time.

21

Workshop

You're encouraged to work through the following questions and exercises to help you retain what you've learned in this lesson about how to internationalize your Qt programs and how to use Qt classes for date and time values.

Quiz

1. What is user-space text?

2. Why should you use QString for all user-space text?

3. When do you need to use the `tr()` function?

4. What is the `findtr` utility used for?

5. When do you need to use the `msg2qm` utility?

6. When can the `mergetr` utility be useful?

7. Which class takes care of the actual translation inside your program?

8. What does the `QApplication::installTranslator()` function do?

9. Why is it required that you call the `Q_OBJECT` macro and use the Meta Object Compiler on a class that uses translations?

10. What can the `QDate` class be used for?

11. What can the `QTime` class be used for?

12. When should you consider using the `QDateTime` class?

Exercises

1. Write a standard program based on `QMainWindow`. Add the standard menu (File, Edit, and Help) to it. Also add a toolbar with a few buttons and a status bar that shows the description of a button if the user points at it with the mouse. Then, translate the entire program to another language. An interesting function of program would be a dialog that lets the user select a language when the program is started. Remember to follow all the necessary steps described in the sections "Creating Translation Files" and "Implementing a Translation Function in Your Program."

2. As stated, the `QDate` function uses the day/month/year system to show dates. However, many people use the month/day/year system. Therefore, use `QDate`'s member functions to show a date as month/day/year.

Hour **22**

Portability

If a program or library, created on one platform, can easily be converted to another platform, it's considered *portable*. Just as you reach out to a wider range of people by translating your program into multiple languages, you also reach out to more people by making your program available on multiple platforms. Therefore, portability should, after functionality, be a top priority in the development of your applications.

One of Qt's biggest strengths is its portability. At the time of this writing, Qt could easily be compiled on 16 different UNIX versions and clones with various compilers. Of course, with the commercial version of Qt, your program can also be compiled on Microsoft Windows as well—and that's not bad at all! In fact, this means you can make your programs available for a great majority of all computers on this planet.

However, a few precautions need to be taken to make your Qt programs portable. This is the topic of this hour. It will help you write good, portable applications that you can make widely available. If you're working on a commercial project, this hour might even help you earn more money.

Although portability is desirable in most cases, in some situations there's no need to strive for portability. For example, if you're creating a GUI configuration tool for compiling the Linux kernel, portability is not important at all, because the program will most likely never be used on platforms other than Linux. If you're developing a GUI installation tool for your new device driver on Windows NT, portability will never be something you need to think of. However, portability is very important in most cases and therefore you'll most likely find this hour very interesting.

Writing Portable Qt Applications

As stated earlier, Qt's portability is excellent, but keeping a Qt program portable takes a little effort from you, as the programmer, as well. In this section, you'll get some general information on what you should to do keep your Qt programs portable.

Using Qt's Classes

Using Qt classes and functions when writing a Qt application might sound pretty obvious to you. However, in cases where GUI-specific functions aren't needed, you might have to use some other library to get a fully functional program. By implementing another library into your program, you also make it much harder (although not impossible) to achieve portability. The worst-case scenario would be that this other library exists only on your development platform, thus making your program impossible to use on platforms other than your primary one. You should always keep in mind that Qt not only consists of GUI widgets but that it also functions for many other programming tasks, such as accessing the file system.

Using Qt's Streaming Functions

As you learned in Hour 12, "Working with Files and Directories," Qt provides extensive support for text streaming. These streaming functions, in most cases, are more than enough to fulfill your needs. Qt's streaming functions are actually important to use if you want to keep your program portable.

Although C++'s standard classes for streaming, defined in iostream.h, exist in all C++ implementations and therefore should be okay to use and still remain portable, there are always a few small differences that make the various implementations more or less incompatible with each other. These small differences are actually differences in size between the implementations of the built-in types, such as int, long, and double. For example, int can be two bytes on one system and four bytes on another. Because these types are used by the standard streaming classes, the small differences can actually cause big problems in a program that uses standard streaming, and they can make a program that's valid on one platform invalid on another. Therefore, it's highly recommended that you stick with Qt's streaming classes; they can help you avoid lots of problems.

If you want to create a special file type for your program, the QDataStream class is the perfect class to use. Although you could use C++'s standard classes for this as well, QDataStream stays exactly the same on all platforms that are supported by Qt, thus keeping your program portable. For example, if you're writing a word-processing program, you could easily create a special file format for storing documents with the QDataStream class. Then, if you save a document on one platform, the same file could be opened with no problems on any of the other supported platforms (maybe even all platforms supported by Qt).

Using Qt's Classes for Dealing with Files and Directories

The classes QFile and QDir are Qt's classes for dealing with files and directories. These are discussed in Hour 12. If you've worked with the standard C or C++ library, you're well aware that structures for this already exist. However, these structures have the same problem as the standard streaming classes, so you're encouraged to use QFile and QDir to keep your programs portable. The fact that QFile and QDir are much easier to use than C and C++'s standard structures is probably reason enough to use them anyway.

Using QPainter for Painting

Hour 19, "Learning to Use Qt's OpenGL Classes," contains a short discussion about thinking twice before implementing OpenGL functions in your Qt programs. This is a reminder of that discussion. Using QPainter instead of a whole new painting library makes things easier for your users and makes sure the painting functions in your programs will work on all platforms supported by Qt.

Using QPrinter for Printing

Using Qt's QPrinter class is by far the easiest way of implementing a printing function in a program. If you, against all odds, happen to be thinking of implementing a printing function without using this class, you should get rid if that thought as quickly as you can! QPrinter is not just easy to use, it also makes sure your programs' printing functions work on all platforms (if a printer is installed and set up correctly, that is).

Using Qt for Working with Sockets

Qt's socket classes can be used to deal with various input sources, such as network connections. Qt's socket support consists of three classes: QSocket, QSocketAddress, and QSocketNotifier. By using these three classes, you can create a platform-independent communication system using sockets. At the time of this writing, Qt's socket support wasn't fully implemented yet. However, it's expected to be in the near future. Imagine your own platform-independent Internet browser!

Also at the time of this writing, Qt's socket library was not a part of the standard Qt library. If this will still be the case when you read this book is hard to say. However, it will be quite obvious when you try to compile a program that uses one of Qt's socket classes. If your compiler whines about undefined symbols regarding one of the three socket classes, the library is not part of the standard Qt library. However, it's very simple to fix this. Here's how:

```
# cd $QTDIR/extensions/network/src
# make
```

By running make, you install and compile the library in $QTDIR/lib as libnetwork.a (a static library). You then need to link against this library when you want to use one of the socket classes.

Following the POSIX Standard

POSIX, an acronym for *IEEE Portable Operating System Interface for Computing*, is a operating system standard. POSIX.1, one specific part of the POSIX standard, defines the functions that should be available for accessing system-specific features. If you use functions that follow this standard, you can use non-Qt classes and functions and still keep your programs quite portable.

All well-known UNIX systems, as well as Windows NT, follow the POSIX standard. If you need a function that Qt can't offer, you're forced to use an outside function or class. However, if your non-Qt functions or classes follow the POSIX standard, you can still be sure that your program will be portable.

If you want to learn more about POSIX, as well as which functions are a part of the POSIX standard, call IEEE at 732-981-1393 and order the POSIX standards and drafts (inside the U.S, you can also call toll-free at 1-800-678-IEEE).

Isolating Platform-Specific Calls

Sometimes, the only solution to a problem is to use platform-specific functions that don't even follow the POSIX standard. In these cases, you're forced to write two or more versions of certain parts of your program to make it available on multiple platforms.

It's important that you don't spread the platform-specific code all over your source code. This will make the porting process much harder and time consuming. If you do spread it all over your source code, you'll have to search it all through it to find platform-specific calls and make small changes here and there. On the other hand, if you isolate the part of your source code that has to be platform specific into one or more classes or files, the porting will be much easier because you then know exactly which part of the code needs to be changed.

For example, you could isolate all the platform-specific code into the class PlatformSpecificClass and just make one version of this class for each platform you want to support. You could then have one global header file, PlatformSpecificClass.h, that would hold the class declaration for PlatformSpecificClass, and one CPP file for each platform that holds the platform-specific class definitions. If your program supports Linux and Windows NT, you could simply make two CPP files— PlatformSpecificClass-Linux.cpp and PlatformSpecificClass-NT.cpp—and copy one of them to PlatformSpecificClass.cpp, depending on whether you're compiling on Linux or Windows NT.

By following these simple isolation rules, porting a program that uses platform-specific code can still be quite easy (although never as easy as if only Qt classes were used).

Another way of doing this is to make two classes with the same name, place the class declaration for them in separate files and then let the preprocessor decide which header file to include. Consider the following example:

```
#ifdef LINUX
#include "platform-linux.h"
#else
#include "platform-nt.h"
#endif
```

By making sure that LINUX is defined only if the program is compiled on Linux, and then add this code to the beginning of the cpp file, you'll make sure that the correct header file will be included.

Nonportable Qt Functions

Although the Qt developers strive to keep Qt as platform independent as possible, it is, in some cases, impossible to fully do so. Therefore, the functionality of a few Qt methods differs between UNIX and Windows. These differences are not big, but they can still cause problems in some cases. However, if you're aware of these differences, you can easily work around them. Table 22.1 presents the methods that behave differently on UNIX and Windows in Qt 2.0.2. Note that these functions are listed in alphabetic order.

TABLE 22.1   Nonportable Qt Functions

Function	Explanation
debug()	The debug() function is used to output debugging information to the programmer. However, its functionality differs a bit between UNIX and Windows. In UNIX, the arguments given to debug() are outputted to stderr (usually the screen); on Windows, they're sent to the debugger. However, you'll probably want to remove the calls to debug() in the final version of your program, so this will rarely be a problem.
QApplication::flushX()	On X11 systems (UNIX), a call to this function will flush the X event queue. However, it does nothing on Windows.
QApplication::setColorSpec()	The functionality of this function differs depending on whether it's called on UNIX or Windows. This is described in the "Working with Colors" section of Hour 9, "Creating Simple Graphics."
QApplication::setDoubleClickInterval()	With this function, you can set the maximum amount of time in milliseconds that can elapse between two mouse clicks and still interpret this action as a double click. In Windows, this functions sets the double click value for all windows, but on UNIX, it sets the double click value only for your Qt application.
QApplication::setMainWidget()	On UNIX systems, calling this function will also set the position and size of the window according to the -geometry command-line option. This is not the case in Windows.
QApplication::syncX()	On UNIX systems, this function processes all outstanding events and flushes all queues. However, there's no need to do this on Windows, so this function does nothing on that platform.

Function	Explanation
QDir::convertSeparators()	In Windows, this functions is used to convert the slashes (/) in a path to backslashes (\). For example, QDir::convertSeparator("c:/windows/system") would return c:\windows\system. On UNIX, this function does nothing. However, QDir::convertSeparators() should be considered an advantage rather than a problem.
QDir::setFilter()	This function can be used to set a file filter. This means you can determine what types of files should be returned by QDir::entryList() and QDir::entryInfoList(). You do this by passing one or more values to the function. However, two of these values—Modified (list modified files) and System (list system files)—have no effect on UNIX. Also, on UNIX, the value Hidden results in listing files that start with a dot (.).
QFile::open()	The value IO_Translate, which you can pass on to this function, enables carriage return and linefeed translation. This is not necessary on UNIX, so the IO_Translate value has no effect.
QWidget::setSizeIncrement()	The two integer arguments you pass to this function define the least number of horizontal and vertical pixels the window can be resized to. In other words, you can define how large you want the resizing steps to be. This has no effect on Windows. Some Window Managers on X11 also ignore it.
QWidget::winId()	This function returns the window ID (of the type Wid) of this widget. Although it's fully possible to use this function on both UNIX and Windows, the returned value differs and is therefore not portable.

22

These functions are the ones you should avoid if you want to keep your programs portable. If you're forced to use one of them—for example, QApplication::setMainWidget() is hard to avoid—you should be aware that the Windows and UNIX implementations are not fully compatible, so you might want to take some further precautions to solve your problem. Fortunately, none of the functions in Table 22.1 will cause any devastating problems. What's more, if a problem should occur, these functions are usually very simple to get rid of.

Building a Portable Project with the `tmake` Utility

You've probably noticed that there's almost always one or more files called `Makefile` in a source distribution of a program. These files hold information about how the program should be compiled. This includes information about what compiler to use, which libraries to link with, in which order the source files should be compiled, and so on. Then, when you run the `make` utility in the directory containing the makefile, `make` reads the makefile and ensures that the program is compiled as defined in the makefile. This way, anyone who wants to compile the source just has to enter `make` and then press Enter.

Makefiles can be generated in many different ways. However, although you can certainly write all makefiles manually, it's more convenient to have some kind of tool that does this for you. If you've ever compiled an application on UNIX, you're probably familiar with the configure script, which is often used to get various types of information about the system and then create one or more makefiles based on this information.

However, this only applies on UNIX platforms. When working with a cross-platform library such as Qt, you need some tool that can be used on both UNIX and Windows and can also generate makefiles for both platforms. Fortunately, this tool has already been created by Troll Tech; it's called `tmake`. This tool creates makefiles for either UNIX or Windows, depending on which platform it's currently running on. In fact, this is an extraordinary tool that can save you hours of boring work (such as writing makefiles for multiple platforms manually). Here's how Troll Tech describes it:

> `tmake` automates and streamlines the process of managing makefiles and lets you spend your valuable time on writing code, not makefiles.

Getting and Installing `tmake`

`tmake` is free software and can be downloaded from Troll Tech's FTP archive (`ftp://ftp.troll.no/freebies/tmake/`). Here, you'll find two versions of the tool—one for Windows and one for UNIX. The Windows version ends with `.zip` (it's a zipped archive), and the UNIX version ends with `.tar.gz` (it's a tarred and gzipped archive). At the time of this writing, the latest version of `tmake` is 1.3.

When you've downloaded one of the `tmake` distributions, you need to unzip or untar the file. On Windows, this can easily be done with WinZip (`www.winzip.com`) or pkzip (`www.pkware.com`). If you're on UNIX, issue the following command in the directory containing the file you just downloaded:

```
# tar xvfz tmake-1.3.tar.gz
```

This will create a subdirectory called `tmake`, with the whole `tmake` distribution in it. You'll probably want to move this directory to `/usr/local/qt` or somewhere that suits you better. To execute `tmake` easily, you should make a symbolic link to `/usr/local/qt/tmake/bin/tmake` in a directory that's included in your PATH variable, such as `/usr/bin`. Here's an example:

```
# ln -s /usr/local/qt/tmake/bin/tmake /usr/bin/tmake
```

On Windows, you'll probably want to add the `c:\tmake\bin` directory to your path so you don't have to enter the full path every time you want to use `tmake`.

On both UNIX and Windows, you also have to set the TMAKEPATH variable, which should point to the directory where `tmake`'s template files for your system are located. The template files are a set of files that holds various information about your system. `tmake` uses this information to generate a makefile. Therefore, if you're on UNIX, using the Bourne shell, and your compiler is g++, add the following lines to one of your startup files:

```
TMAKEPATH=/usr/local/qt/tmake/lib/linux-g++
export TMAKEPATH
```

If you're using C shell, here's what you should use:

```
setenv TMAKEPATH /usr/local/qt/tmake/lib/linux-g++
```

If you're using Windows and the Visual C++ compiler, you should preferably set your TMAKEPATH and PATH variables in `autoexec.bat`:

```
set TMAKEPATH=c:\tmake\lib\win32-msvc
set PATH=%PATH%;c:\tmake\bin
```

For a complete list of platforms and compilers that have predefined template files, just run `dir` in the `/lib` directory of your `tmake` installation.

When you've followed one of these steps to set the TMAKEPATH variable and installed the `tmake` distribution correctly, you're all set.

Note that when you add something to your startup files, such as `/etc/profile`, you always need to log out and then log in again to activate your changes. If you don't want to log out and log back in, you can use the `source` command on the file in question. Here's an example:

```
source /etc/profile
```

This will read the file `/etc/profile` and execute all the commands in it, including the line that sets the TMAKEPATH variable.

tmake is a script written in Perl. Therefore, if you're using UNIX, you need to have the Perl interpreter, perl, installed to be able to use tmake. Fortunately, perl is often installed by default in modern UNIX systems. If it's not, it's most likely included in your Linux/UNIX distribution.

Using tmake for Creating Makefiles

When tmake is correctly set up on your system, you're ready to start using it. In this section, the most common uses of tmake are covered. For a complete description, see the HTML documents tmake.html (user's guide) and tmake-ref.html (reference documentation). Both are located in the doc subdirectory of the tmake distribution.

When tmake creates a makefile for you, it does so based on the template files it finds in the directory entered in the TMAKEPATH variable and from a project file (which ends with .pro) that you need to create. Creating a project file is really simple, and it usually doesn't take long. Here's an example:

```
CONFIG   = qt release
HEADERS  = MyWidget.h
SOURCES  = MyWidget.cpp main.cpp
TARGET   = MyWidget
```

In the first line, the CONFIG variable is set. This variable can have a few predefined values that determine what kind of project this is. In this case, the options qt and release are set. This tells tmake that this project is a Qt project and that it should be considered a release version and not a debug version. However, both these options are set by default (if no CONFIG variable is set). They are just included here as an example. For a complete list of options you can enter in the CONFIG variable, see Table 22.2.

TABLE 22.2 Qt Functions That Aren't Portable

Option	Explanation
qt	This options tells tmake that the project is a Qt project. When this is set, any needed MOC files will be generated and included. This is the default.
release	This options tells tmake that the project should be considered a release version. This means that no debugging symbols will be included and that the binary will be compiled for full optimization. This is also the default.
debug	This options tells tmake that the project should be considered a debugging version and therefore include debugging symbols. This should only be set if you want to compile a binary used for debugging.

Option	Explanation
warn_on	If this options is set, tmake will show as many warnings as possible during the compilation. However, this is the default if no CONFIG variable is set.
warn_off	This options tells tmake that as few warnings as possible should be shown during the compilation. However, this is not recommended because it can hide some serious problems from you.
opengl	Set this options if your project is using the OpenGL extension of Qt.

Next, the HEADERS variable is set to MyWidget.h. Here, you should list all the headers in your program. In this example, though, there is only one. The SOURCES variable should include all source files (CPP files). In this example, there are two source files—one containing a Qt class definition and one containing the main() function. The last variable, TARGET, defines what you want to call the executable output (the actual program). Here, TARGET is set to MyWidget.

Now you have the TMAKEPATH variable set to the corresponding directory for your system and you have a simple (but useful) project file. You're now ready to let tmake generate a makefile for you. For this, issue the following command:

```
tmake MyWidget.pro -o Makefile
```

If everything is set up correctly, tmake will now generate a fully usable makefile (called Makefile) for you.

Note that if you want to execute make without any arguments, you have to name the makefile Makefile.

If TMAKEPATH is set to use the Linux/g++ template files on your system, the makefile you'll generate will look like the one shown in Listing 22.1.

LISTING 22.1 A Makefile Generated by tmake

```
#############################################################################
# Makefile for building MyWidget
# Generated by tmake at 09:02, 2000/01/29
#     Project: MyWidget
```

continues

LISTING 22.1 continued

```
#     Template: app
#############################################################################

####### Compiler, tools and options

CC     =    gcc
CXX    =    g++
CFLAGS =      -pipe -O2 -DNO_DEBUG
CXXFLAGS=     -pipe -O2 -DNO_DEBUG
INCPATH   =     -I$(QTDIR)/include
LINK   =    g++
LFLAGS    =
LIBS   =      -L$(QTDIR)/lib -lqt -L/usr/X11R6/lib -lXext -lX11 -lm
MOC    =    moc

TAR    =    tar -cf
GZIP   =    gzip -9f

####### Files

HEADERS =    MyWidget.h
SOURCES =    MyWidget.cpp \
        main.cpp
OBJECTS =    MyWidget.o \
        main.o
SRCMOC   =    moc_MyWidget.cpp
OBJMOC   =    moc_MyWidget.o
DIST    =
TARGET  =    MyWidget

####### Implicit rules

.SUFFIXES: .cpp .cxx .cc .C .c

.cpp.o:
    $(CXX) -c $(CXXFLAGS) $(INCPATH) -o $@ $<

.cxx.o:
    $(CXX) -c $(CXXFLAGS) $(INCPATH) -o $@ $<

.cc.o:
    $(CXX) -c $(CXXFLAGS) $(INCPATH) -o $@ $<

.C.o:
    $(CXX) -c $(CXXFLAGS) $(INCPATH) -o $@ $<

.c.o:
    $(CC) -c $(CFLAGS) $(INCPATH) -o $@ $<
```

```
####### Build rules

all: $(TARGET)

$(TARGET): $(OBJECTS) $(OBJMOC)
    $(LINK) $(LFLAGS) -o $(TARGET) $(OBJECTS) $(OBJMOC) $(LIBS)

moc: $(SRCMOC)

tmake: Makefile

Makefile: MyWidget.pro
    tmake MyWidget.pro -o Makefile

dist:
    $(TAR) MyWidget.tar MyWidget.pro $(SOURCES) $(HEADERS) $(DIST)
    $(GZIP) MyWidget.tar

clean:
    -rm -f $(OBJECTS) $(OBJMOC) $(SRCMOC) $(TARGET)
    -rm -f *~ core

####### Compile

MyWidget.o: MyWidget.cpp \
        MyWidget.h

main.o: main.cpp \
        MyWidget.h

moc_MyWidget.o: moc_MyWidget.cpp \
        MyWidget.h

moc_MyWidget.cpp: MyWidget.h
    $(MOC) MyWidget.h -o moc_MyWidget.cpp
```

This is not a make how-to, so you won't find a complete explanation of this listing here. However, makefiles use a very simple syntax, so you should be able to understand the listing without any explanation. The most interesting part is the last few lines; they make sure a MOC file is generated and included correctly.

Note that if you use tmake, you don't have to include or generate MOC files manually; instead, tmake will take care of this. In this case, you would just need to include the MyWidget.h file in MyWidget.cpp and main.cpp and make sure a call to Q_OBJECT is included in MyWidget.h.

When the makefile is generated, start the compilation:

```
# make
```

Then, you'll see the following output:

```
g++ -c -pipe -O2 -DNO_DEBUG -I/usr/local/qt/include -o MyWidget.o MyWidget.cpp
g++ -c -pipe -O2 -DNO_DEBUG -I/usr/local/qt/include -o main.o main.cpp
moc MyWidget.h -o moc_MyWidget.cpp
g++ -c -pipe -O2 -DNO_DEBUG -I/usr/local/qt/include
-o moc_MyWidget.o moc_MyWidget.cpp
g++  -o MyWidget MyWidget.o main.o moc_MyWidget.o -L/usr/local/qt/lib -lqt
-L/usr/X11R6/lib -lXext -lX11 -lm
```

Note that a MOC file is generated on the third line and compiled on the fourth. On the fifth and sixth lines, the three object files (including the object file that was generated from the MOC file) are linked together to the executable binary called `MyWidget`.

> To compile this project, you'll need to have the files `MyWidget.cpp`, `MyWidget.h`, and `main.cpp` in your current directory, with some real C++ code in them. However, you can use one of the earlier examples for this.

You've just completed your first `tmake`-generated makefile. As stated in the beginning of this section, the two HTML documents `tmake.html` and `tmake-ref.htm` in the `doc` sub-directory of your `tmake` installation hold a complete user's guide and some reference documentation, respectively. You should check them out for further information about `tmake`.

Using progen for Generating Project Files

If you're on a large Qt project with many files, it can be quite cumbersome to list all the files manually in a project file. Fortunately, Troll Tech has developed a tool that solves this; it's called `progen` (for Project Generator). `progen`, like `tmake`, is a Perl script, and it's included in the `tmake` distribution. If you're on UNIX and didn't add the `/usr/local/qt/tmake/bin` directory to your `PATH` variable, you'll probably want to make a symbolic link to `progen` in `/usr/bin`, just as you did with `tmake`. Here's how:

```
# ln -s /usr/local/qt/tmake/bin/progen /usr/bin/progen
```

This way, you can execute `progen` from anywhere on your file system without entering the full path to it.

What progen does is to search through a given set of source files and then generate a project file based on the information it finds in these files. However, it's impossible for progen to know exactly what options you want to use (like what libraries you want to link with), so that you need to edit by hand.

Here's an example using the files from the previous section (MyWidget.cpp, MyWidget.h, and main.cpp). Place these files in a directory of their own (without subdirectories) and issue the following command:

```
# progen -n MyWidget -o MyWidget.pro
```

Now, progen will search the current directory and all subdirectories for files that end with .cpp or .h. A project files are then created (what's included in the project file depends on which files progen finds). The -n option is used to define the name of this project (that is, what value the TARGET variable will have on the project file). With the -o option, you define the name of the project file. In this case, progen will create the following project file:

```
TEMPLATE        = app
CONFIG          = qt warn_on release
HEADERS         = MyWidget.h
SOURCES         = MyWidget.cpp \
                  main.cpp
TARGET          = MyWidget
```

As you can see, progen found all three files and placed them correctly in the HEADERS and SOURCES variables. However, in this example, progen wasn't of much help because the project only consists of three files. However, image how useful this tool is when your projects include few hundred files!

> On the first line of the progen-generated project file, there's a new variable you haven't seen before, called TEMPLATE. This variable defines the name of the template file to use. In this case, the /usr/local/qt/tmake/lib/ linux-g++/app.t template file will be used. This is the default, though, so you don't need to define the TEMPLATE variable if you're developing an application. However, there are a few other files (other than app.t) in each subdirectory of /usr/local/qt/tmake/lib that should be used if your project is not an application. For example, the lib.t file should be used if your project is a library.

The progen utility is covered in the tmake user's guide, so you're encouraged to take a look there for complete coverage of this tool.

Summary

Regardless of whether you're developing Qt programs professionally or just for fun, you'll probably want as many people as possible to use and take advantage of your software. If you're selling your programs for money, the reason to strive for portability is quite obvious (more users means more money). Also, as a free-software programmer, it feels good to know that many people can use the software you've worked so long and hard to create.

Qt is, by nature, very portable, so you don't need to do anything special to keep it that way. However, you should be aware of those special cases in which there are small differences between the Windows and UNIX implementations. Many of these differences you'll most likely never experience. However, if a problem does occur, it's good to understand the problem so that you can easily write a workaround. This rarely takes more than one or two lines of code.

Many Qt programmers claim that they can't live without tmake, and chances are that once you get to know it, you'll feel the same way. To fully understand the greatness of tmake, you need to start a large project that consists of at least 200 source and header files. Then, you need to make the software available on at least five different UNIX platforms as well as for Microsoft Windows. Also, during the development you should write all your makefiles by hand, one for each subdirectory of your source tree and one version for each platform. Well, you get the picture—creating all the makefiles would take almost as long as writing the code! On the other hand, you could start using tmake and progen right away.

Q&A

Q **When trying to execute tmake or progen, I get a message stating that perl can't be found. What's wrong?**

A You probably don't have perl installed. Install it from your distribution or download it from www.perl.com.

Q **The tmake utility just don't work for me. It just says that it can't find a file called tmake.conf!**

A This happens if the TMAKEPATH variable is not set correctly. Make sure you've added it to one of your startup files and then log out and log in again. Alternatively, you can use the source utility. If you're using bash, remember that you have to export the variable with the export keyword. If you're using any of the C shells, remember to use the setenv keyword.

Q I'm developing a GUI installation program for my new Linux device driver. Is portability really important for me?

A No, obviously it's not. Device drivers are always platform specific, and the chance that anyone would ever want to install your device driver on any other platform is very small. However, if you ever want to write a similar program for Windows, it may be a good idea to make this installation GUI portable anyway, so it can be easily adopted to Windows. This way, you can save yourself some work.

Q Is it possible to create makefiles for platforms other than my own with `tmake`?

A Of course it is. Just change the TMAKEPATH variable. For example, to create a makefile for Borland C++ on Windows, set TMAKEPATH as follows:

```
# export TMAKEPATH=/usr/local/qt/tmake/lib/win32-borland
```

Then, to create the makefile, just use `tmake` as usual:

```
tmake MyWidget.pro -o Makefile
```

It's as simple as that!

Workshop

You're encouraged to work through the following questions and exercises to help you retain what you've learned in this hour.

Quiz

1. Is it possible to write network applications with Qt?
2. What is POSIX?
3. What is POSIX.1?
4. Are there any functions in Qt that are not fully compatible between UNIX and Windows?
5. What is `tmake`?
6. What is a project file?
7. What is `progen`?

Exercises

1. Try setting the TMAKEPATH variable to a few different subdirectories of `/usr/local/qt/tmake/lib`. Create a makefile for each time you change TMAKEPATH and then investigate the makefiles to see the differences that exist.

2. Go to the `src` directory of your Qt installation (for example, `/usr/local/qt/src`). Execute the command `progen -o MyProject.pro` there. When `progen` is finished, take a look in the resulting `MyProject.pro` file. How would it be to write this by hand?

3. You could also use the project file created in the previous exercise to let `tmake` generate a makefile. When `tmake` is done, take a look at the makefile. Think about writing that by hand! With some minor changes to this makefile, you could actually use it to compile the entire Qt library.

Hour **23**

Debugging Techniques

When developing computer software, you must always consider that there will be more or less serious errors (knows as *bugs* among programmers) in your software. These bugs can present themselves in many different ways. If you're using Linux, you've most likely experienced a program exiting with a *segmentation fault*, which is usually caused by bad memory management. However, the definition of a bug extends beyond just memory problems. Actually, anything unwanted in a program can be called a bug. A bug in a computer program has the same meaning that *corrosion* has in chemistry; you can use these terms whenever something unwanted happens (an unwanted program function or an unwanted chemical reaction).

One thing that often causes bugs is a lack of understanding of a library or function that the programmer is trying to use. For example, you most likely had many more problems getting your Qt programs to work correctly in the beginning of your learning curve than you have now, at the end of it. Now that you have a broader understanding of how the Qt library works, you find it much easier to avoid problems because they appear obvious to you. Therefore, the best way to avoid bugs is to be sure of what you're doing.

However, no matter how experienced you are, there are always bugs that can't be fixed, or even found, right away. Fortunately, Qt offers a few functions and macros that can be of help in this situation. They won't fix the actual bug, but they will help you find it. After all, the biggest problem with bugs is simply finding them!

In this hour, you'll learn how to use Qt's facilities for finding bugs. You'll also learn how to use a debugger to go through a Qt program, step by step. In the last section of this hour, you'll find a discussion about the command-line options that can be useful when running a Qt program through a debugger.

Using Qt's Debugging Functions

Qt comes with a few functions that can be used to make a program easier to debug. By making a call to one of these functions in a particular part of your program, you can easily determine when this part is executed. You could, for example, use one of these functions to determine at which point an `if` statement is true or how many times the code inside a `while` loop is executed. By doing this, you get a better overview of your program and can more easily avoid bugs.

This section discusses three Qt functions: `qDebug()`, `qWarning()`, and `qFatal()`. They're all global, so there's no need to include any extra header file to use them.

All three debugging functions are limited to 512 bytes of output, including the zero byte (the byte that marks the string as finished).

Using the `qDebug()` Function

The first and probably most used of the three functions is `qDebug()`. It prints out a debugging message to `stdout` (the screen), which you can use to get information about what the program is doing.

On Windows, `qDebug()` prints the message to the debugger, not to `stdout`.

qDebug() takes one or more arguments; the first is always a format string, and the rest are arguments that should be inserted in the format string. If you've worked with the printf() function from the standard C library, you know how this works. Consider the following example:

```
qDebug( "This is the widget's ID = %x", myWidget->id() );
```

This would replace %x in the first argument with the second argument, myWidget->id(). For example, if the widget myWidget has the ID 3, the output of this line would be as follows:

```
This is the widget's ID = 3
```

However, for you to make any use of the qDebug() function, any calls to it need to be placed in the right parts of your program; implementing a call to qDebug() globally in your program is normally not of any use. Instead, you should use it to check if and when a certain part of the program is executed. You could, for example, use it to check when the body of a while statement is executed, as follows:

```
while( YourVariable != Something )
{
    qDebug( "Now the body is executed,
        so the developer must be warned!" );
}
```

Here, the text Now the body is executed, so the developer must be warned! is printed to stdout (the debugger on Windows) every time the while statement is true. Now, you can see exactly when this part of the program is executed. If the body is executed at a point where it shouldn't be executed, this will be very easy for you to see. On the other hand, if it isn't executed at a point where it should be executed, this will be easy for you to see as well. Both scenarios help a lot in your search for bugs!

Using the qWarning() Function

The qWarning() function works exactly like qDebug(). However, from a programming perspective, there's an important distinction between the two. By using the qDebug() function to inform yourself about certain events and the qWarning() function to inform yourself about program faults, you create an obvious distinction between event information and fault information in your program.

If qDebug() were used for both tasks, it would be harder for you to determine whether a call to qDebug() is to inform you about a program fault or a program event. Therefore, use qWarning() to inform yourself when a fault occurs in your program. Here's an example:

```
QPushButton b1( "Hello!", this );
if( !QPushButton )
{
    qWarning( "The QPushButton object b1 was
            not created correctly!" );
}
```

Here, a QPushButton object, b1, is created in the first line. However, if some problem occurs, the if statement will be true and the qWarning() function call will be made. This way, you will be informed when there's a problem with the creation of b1. This is a typical example of when the qWarning() function should be used.

> Another thing you should consider doing when working with qDebug() and qWarning() is to mark the output so that you can easily see, when running the program, which of these functions is executed. Here's an example:
>
> ```
> qWarning( "WARNING: The QPushButton object
>     b1 was not created correctly!" );
> ```
>
> By inserting the word WARNING at the beginning of the output, you can easily see that this is a call to qWarning(). In the same style, you should insert the word DEBUG or something similar as the first word in the output from the qDebug() function.

Using the `qFatal()` Function

The last of Qt's debugging functions is qFatal(). You use it just like qDebug() and qWarning(). However, qFatal() also exits the program; therefore, it should be used only when some serious problem has occurred.

For example, suppose you're program is about to divide one integer (x) by another integer (y), and both are controlled by the program. Now, if y is 0, the division can't be made, and you can assume that some serious problems with the program will occur. In this case, you should use the qFatal() function, as follows:

```
if( y == 0 )
{
qFatal( "FATAL: Can't divide x by 0!" );
}
```

Here, if y is 0, the call to qFatal() will be made and the program will exit after the information FATAL: Can't divide x by 0! has been printed to stdout (the debugger

on Windows). As you see, the word FATAL is used to mark that this is a call to qFatal().
However, because the program will exit, this will be quite obvious anyway.

Understanding Qt's Debugging Macros

Although qglobal.h includes definitions for many debugging macros, only the two most
important ones, ASSERT() and CHECK_PTR(), are covered in this section. These two
macros (as well as all the others in qglobal.h) use the qDebug(), qWarning(), and
qFatal() functions to create debugging information for certain events. By using these
macros instead of the debugging functions directly, you can save yourself some work.

23

Using the ASSERT() Macro

The ASSERT() macro takes a Boolean value as an argument. If the value is FALSE, it
prints out a line with debugging information that follows a certain standard. Here's an
example:

```
ASSERT( x != 0 ); //This is line 48
```

Here, if x is 0 (remember, ASSERT() outputs information about the statement if FALSE),
the following will be printed if the program file is test.cpp and the line number is 48:

```
ASSERT: "x == 0" in test.cpp (48)
```

Using the CHECK_PTR() Macro

The CHECK_PTR() macro can be used to check whether a program has run out of memory.
It takes a pointer as an argument, and if this pointer is NULL, CHECK_PTR() calls the
qFatal() function to inform you that the program has run out of memory and then exits
the program. Consider the following example:

```
char *string = new char[100];
CHECK_PTR( string );
```

Here, CHECK_PTR() will call qFatal() if the string variable is not created correctly.

Never create an object inside the CHECK_PTR() macro, as follows:

```
CHECK_PTR( char *ch = new char[10] );
```

The problem is quite tricky to understand. However, if you feel you need to
know why this doesn't work, see the Qt Reference Documentation. Just be
sure not to do this in your programs.

Using the gdb Debugger for Debugging Qt Programs

A *debugger* is a piece of software that can be used to step through a program and discover any possible bugs. gdb, the GNU debugger, comes with most free UNIX systems, including Linux. gdb is a classic among the GNU programs. It doesn't provide any GUI interface, but it is, however, an invaluable tool when debugging a program.

When you're using gdb on a program, it's important that the program is compiled with debugging symbols turned on. With gcc, you do this with the -g option.

Getting and Installing gdb

gdb most likely comes with your UNIX/Linux distribution, and you can easily install it with the standard package utilities on your system (for example, the rpm utility on Red Hat Linux).

However, if gdb is not included in your distribution, you need to download it from ftp://ftp.gnu.org/pub/gnu/gdb/. The installation procedure is the same as for most GNU software: Run ./configure, run make, and then run make install.

> At the time of this writing, the latest gdb source distribution (4.18) is over 11MB in size. Therefore, if you're on a slow dial-up connection, the download time can be an hour or more.

Whether you install a binary version of gdb from your distribution or compile the source yourself, you must make sure the gdb is correctly installed to be able to follow the example in this section.

Getting Started with gdb

When you want to use gdb to step through a program, you must first tell gdb what file should be executed. The easiest way of doing this is to enter the filename as the first command-line argument to gdb, as follows:

```
# gdb <filename>
```

So, if you want to use gdb with your Qt program MyQtProgram, the command would be this:

```
# gdb MyQtProgram
```

Now, when you press Enter, gdb will start and provide the following output:

```
GNU gdb 4.18
Copyright 1998 Free Software Foundation, Inc.
GDB is free software, covered by the GNU General Public License, and you are
welcome to change it and/or distribute copies of it under certain conditions.
Type "show copying" to see the conditions.
There is absolutely no warranty for GDB.  Type "show warranty" for details.
This GDB was configured as "i686-pc-linux-gnu"...
(gdb)
```

23

The first seven lines show some information about gdb. The last line, (gdb), indicates that gdb is started and is ready to receive commands from you. Note that MyQtProgram is not started yet.

Now, you'll usually want to set a breakpoint. This means that you instruct gdb to stop the program at a specific point (at a point where you know a problem will occur). For this, you need to know the internal name of the function. The internal name differs a bit from the name you use in the source file, but with the nm utility, this name is easy to find. Therefore, start a new xterm or switch to another virtual console and use cd to go to the directory containing the MyQtProgram file. To list all functions in the MyQtProgram program, issue the following command:

```
# nm MyQtProgram
```

A lot of entries will now scroll up your screen (the bigger the program is, the more entries included in it). It's quite impossible to find one single entry in this large list. However, with the grep command, you can easily find what you're looking for. Suppose you want to know the internal name of the function MyProblematicFunction(). You would then enter this:

```
# nm MyQtProgram | grep MyProblematicFunction
```

The grep command will now make sure that only lines that contain the string MyProblematicFunction will be listed. If more than one line is listed, choose the one that has a T beside the memory address (the memory address is the eight-digit long hexadecimal number at the left side of the listing).

Then, switch back to the xterm or virtual console that's running gdb and set the breakpoint, as follows:

```
(gdb) break <name you found with nm>
```

Here, <name you found with nm>, of course, is the internal name that you located with the nm utility. If the name is correct, gdb will answer with something like this:

```
Breakpoint 1, 0x804f29c in MyQtProgram::MyProblematicFunction ()
```

Now when a breakpoint is set, you're ready to start the program. To do this, enter the command run:

```
(gdb) run
Starting program: /fat/docs/qt-book/Ch23/MyQtProgram
Qt: gdb: -nograb added to command-line options.
        Use the -dograb option to enforce grabbing.
```

Now, gdb will start the program and give you detailed information about what's happening. On the second line, gdb says that it is about to start the program. On the following two lines, Qt gives the message that the -nograb command-line argument is added (this is because you're running the program through gdb; see the next section for details).

When the program is started, you should make the program call the breakpoint function (MyProblematicFunction() in this case). When it does, the program will stop, and the (gdb) prompt will come up again. Now, you can use the various gdb commands for investigating the state of the program. Unfortunately, the topic of gdb commands is far too big a subject to be covered in this section. However, gdb includes a help function you can use to get short information about all the commands. First, type **help** at the (gdb) prompt; you'll get the following output:

```
(gdb) help
List of classes of commands:

aliases -- Aliases of other commands
breakpoints -- Making program stop at certain points
data -- Examining data
files -- Specifying and examining files
internals -- Maintenance commands
obscure -- Obscure features
running -- Running the program
stack -- Examining the stack
status -- Status inquiries
support -- Support facilities
tracepoints -- Tracing of program execution without stopping the program
user-defined -- User-defined commands

Type "help" followed by a class name for a list of commands in that class.
Type "help" followed by command name for full documentation.
Command name abbreviations are allowed if unambiguous.
```

Now, select one of the listed topics and enter **help** followed by that topic. For example, if you want to know more about how to examine data, enter the following command:

```
(gdb) help data
Examining data.

List of commands:

call -- Call a function in the program
```

```
delete display -- Cancel some expressions to be displayed when program stops
disable display -- Disable some expressions to be displayed when program stops
disassemble -- Disassemble a specified section of memory
display -- Print value of expression EXP each time the program stops
enable display -- Enable some expressions to be displayed when program stops
inspect -- Same as "print" command
output -- Like "print" but don't put in value history and don't print newline
print -- Print value of expression EXP
printf -- Printf "printf format string"
ptype -- Print definition of type TYPE
set -- Evaluate expression EXP and assign result to variable VAR
set variable -- Evaluate expression EXP and assign result to variable VAR
undisplay -- Cancel some expressions to be displayed when program stops
whatis -- Print data type of expression EXP
x -- Examine memory: x/FMT ADDRESS

Type "help" followed by command name for full documentation.
Command name abbreviations are allowed if unambiguous.
```

These gdb commands can be used to examine your program's data. For example, you can use the call command to execute one specific function of your program. With these commands, as well as the ones covered in the other gdb help sections, you get full control over your program.

For more information about the GNU debugger, see the gdb man page (man gdb).

Useful Command-Line Options

When debugging a Qt program, you can use a few command-line arguments to make the debugging easier.

First, the -nograb argument tells the program to never grab the mouse or the keyboard (it will always allow other programs to use the mouse and the keyboard simultaneously). If the mouse or keyboard is grabbed during a run, it will be impossible to enter commands or click on other programs (such as a debugger). Fortunately, this argument is set automatically when a Qt program is run through the gdb debugger.

The -dograb argument makes a program ignore the -dograb argument, in case you want the program to grab the mouse and the keyboard even when it's run through gdb (however, this is very rare).

The -sync command-line argument tells the X11 server (it only works with X11) to run in synchronous mode. This means that the X server will not use any buffer optimization but rather perform each client request immediately. This often makes the program run much slower and therefore easier to debug.

23

Summary

Using Qt's debugging functions and macros gives you, the developer, a better understanding of how a program works without using a debugger. By reading the information these functions and macros output to stdout (X) or the debugger (Windows), you increase your chances of finding the bug. When you run a program that gives no output at all, it's much harder to get an overview of what's actually happening, such as how and when the functions are called.

Of course, the information given by the debugging functions and macros is not limited to function calls; you can give yourself much more detailed information. Because the debugging functions use the same outstanding argument lists as the printf() function, it's easy to embed various program variables in the output string as well.

In this hour, you learned the basics about the gdb debugger. This program is great when you feel the debugging functions and macros are not enough for you, such as when you need more inside information. By mastering gdb, you get full control over your program and can defeat any possible bugs, no matter how complex they are.

Finally, remember to always remove all calls to debugging functions and macros in the final version of your program.

Q&A

Q Where can I find information about all those other debugging macros not mentioned in this hour?

A Unfortunately, there isn't any detailed information about these macros at the time of this writing. However, they are briefly described in the "Debugging Techniques" section of the Qt Reference Documentation.

Q I don't get it. Why should I use the debugging macros instead of the debugging functions?

A The debugging macros do much of the work for you. By using them, you don't have to create the output string yourself—it's handled by the macro. The only thing you need to do is feed the macro with a pointer or a Boolean value so it can determine whether a debugging string should be outputted.

Q I don't like text-based programs. Is there a GUI interface for the gdb debugger?

A Actually, there is. It's written in Tcl/Tk and can be found at http://sourceware.cygnus.com/insight/.

Workshop

You're encouraged to work through the following questions and exercises to help you retain what you've learned in this hour about what Qt has to offer when it comes to debugging. By answering these questions, you also make sure you understand the basics of the gdb debugger.

Quiz

23

1. When should the qDebug() function be used?
2. When should the qWarning() function be used?
3. When should you use the qFatal() function?
4. What does the ASSERT() macro do?
5. What does the CHECK_PTR() macro do?
6. What is a debugger?
7. How do you tell gdb which file you want to work with?
8. With what gdb command do you set a breakpoint?
9. What does the command run do in gdb?
10. If you were to guess, which command do you think quits the gdb debugger?

Exercises

1. Start the gdb debugger with one of your Qt programs as an argument. Set a breakpoint for the program, start the program, and make sure it reaches that breakpoint. When the program has stopped, try some of the gdb commands that you get descriptions of by entering **help data**. For example, use the call command to execute one particular function in your program.

HOUR 24

Use the Qt Builders

As Qt has become more and more popular, the need for some kind of GUI builder has become more obvious. A *GUI builder* is a program that graphically enables you to create a GUI interface, often without writing one single line of code! However, these programs are limited to just creating GUI interfaces; they can't create the actual program functions for you.

In this hour, you'll get a good introduction to three of these builders: QtEz, QtArchitect, and Ebuilder. These three programs can all be used to build Qt GUI interfaces easily. Which one you choose is often just a matter of taste.

Note that only the Qt-specific GUI builders are covered in this hour. A few are available for KDE building as well, but those are not covered here (after all, this is a Qt book).

Getting Started with QtEz

QtEz is considered by many to be the best Qt GUI builder. In this section, you'll learn how to get, compile, and install QtEz as well as how to create a simple GUI with it. You'll be amazed how simple it can be to create a professional Qt project!

Getting and Installing QtEz

The first thing you need to do is to get the latest QtEz distribution, which can easily be downloaded from the QtEz Web site (`http://www.ibl.sk/qtez/`). At the time of this writing, the latest version of QtEz is 0.85.2. You'll find both binary and source distributions of QtEz.

If a binary distribution is available for your system, you should choose that one. However, if that's not the case, you need to download the `.tar.gz` source distribution.

If you've downloaded the source distribution, the first thing you need to do is to uncompress the archive, as follows:

```
# tar xvfz qtez-0.85-2.tar.gz
```

This will create a directory called `qtez-0.85-2`, where the whole source distribution will reside. Then, you need to prepare the source to be compiled on your system. For this, there are a few things you need to do. First, run the `autogen.sh` script included in the base directory of the QtEz distribution:

```
# ./autogen.sh
```

You'll now see the following output slowly scrolling up your screen:

```
Creating Makefile.in in all subdirectories...
Creating modifications for MOC files...
Creating script ./configure
Creating include links...
complete, please run ./configure or ./configure --help for help
```

As the last line instructs, you should now run the `configure` script:

```
# ./configure
```

The `configure` script will examine your system and create makefiles according to the information it finds. This can take a while. However, when it's finished, you need to run a Perl script called `automoc`, which also resides in the top-level directory of the QtEz distribution, as follows:

```
# perl automoc
```

This will make sure that the MOC files are handled correctly. Finally, you're ready to start the compilation. As usual, you do this by simply running make:

```
# make
```

Now, the compilation will start. This might take some time, depending of the speed and load of your system. After the compilation finishes, you're ready to install the binaries into your system. This is done with the following command:

```
# make install
```

All necessary files will now be copied to their correct places on your file system. After this is finished, you need to set the QTEZ environment variable. This should be set to the directory holding the QtEz template files. These are not installed automatically, so you need to do that by hand:

```
# cd qtez-0.85.2/templates
# mkdir /usr/local/share/qtez
# cp -r * /usr/local/share/qtez
```

Then, set QTEZ to the directory you just created. If you're using bash, use this command:

```
# export QTEZ=/usr/local/share/qtez
```

If you're using C shell, here's the correct command:

```
# setenv QTEZ=/usr/local/share/qtez
```

If you're planning to use QtEz more than once, you'll probably want to add a line to one of your startup files that sets the QTEZ variable.

Creating a Simple GUI with QtEz

In this section, you'll learn the QtEz basics. You'll find step-by-step instructions on how to created a simple GUI. This information is intended to get you started with QtEz.

First, you need to start QtEz:

```
# qtez
```

QtEz should now start, and two quite large windows will appear on your screen. These windows are shown in Figure 24.1.

The top window is the main QtEz window, from which you control the entire program. The bottom window is for setting environment options. As you can see in the main QtEz window (the one at the top), this is a large program with many options and features. However, despite all these features, QtEz is very straightforward and easy to use.

FIGURE **24.1**

The two standard QtEz windows.

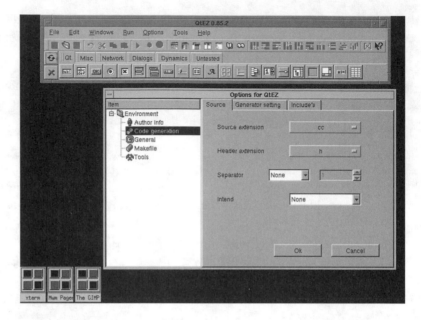

Creating a New Project

To create a new project, click the File menu on the main QtEz window; then select New, Project. Now, another window will show up. This window is shown is Figure 24.2.

FIGURE **24.2**

The Project Settings window of QtEz. In this window you set the general information about your new project.

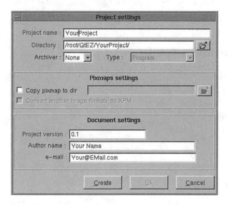

This is the Project Settings window. Here's where you set the general information about your project, such as the project's name, where to store the project, and the creator's name and email. Enter this information and then click the Create button.

Now, two new windows pop up, as shown in Figure 24.3.

Figure 24.3

The window representing your empty project (the one at the top), and the window that shows all the compiling output for your project.

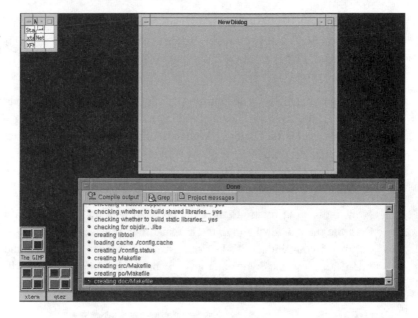

24

When these two windows appear, QtEz will immediately start to investigate your system and create makefiles and other standard files and directories. The output of this work is shown in one of the new windows. The other window represents (or actually is) your project. As you can see, this is still empty.

To get a view of what QtEz does when you choose to create a new project, take a look in the directory that you choose for your project in the Project Settings window. Running `ls` there will give you the following output:

```
# ls
total 790
    1 AUTHORS           1 README           3 config.cache       6 install-sh*
   19 COPYING           1 YourProject.lsm  30 config.guess*    114 libtool*
    1 ChangeLog         1 YourProject.qtz   5 config.log        90 ltconfig*
    8 INSTALL          93 acinclude.m4      7 config.status*   106 ltmain.sh
   14 Makefile         95 aclocal.m4       21 config.sub*        7 missing*
    1 Makefile.am      38 am_edit*         96 configure*         1 mkinstalldirs*
   14 Makefile.in       1 autogen.sh*       1 configure.in       1 po/
    1 NEWS             11 automoc*          1 doc/               1 src/
```

Actually, this is a complete Qt project with makefiles, a `configure` script, and also directories where the source, documentation, and translation files will be placed. However, the project still doesn't have any actual function. That is still up to you!

Adding Widgets to the Project

Once a new project is created, you can start adding widgets to it. This involves two steps: choosing a widget from the QtEz main window and then drawing it on your empty window (the project).

Start by choosing a Qt widget from the QtEz main window. The widgets are shown at the bottom of the window, separated into a few categories on a tab bar. The tabs are labeled Qt, Misc, Network, Dialogs, Dynamics, and Untested. For now, stick with the widgets in the tab labeled Qt. From the set of widgets included in the Qt tab, click the icon representing a pushbutton (if you're unsure which one it is, hold the mouse pointer over one of the icons, and a description text will soon appear).

Now, move your mouse to the empty project window, hold the left mouse button down, drag the mouse down and to the left, and then release it. Now you've created a pushbutton on your widget; it's as simple as that! You can now resize the button by dragging one if its corner, and you can move the button by dragging somewhere in the middle of it. An example of what this button will look like is shown is Figure 24.4.

FIGURE 24.4

A project window with a simple pushbutton in it.

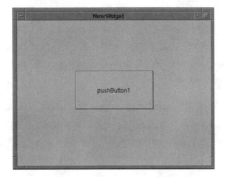

To change the settings for the button, such as the text label, click with your left mouse button on the button, and choose Attributes from the menu that appears. Now, the Attributes window for the button will appear (all widgets have an Attributes window from which you easily can change their attributes). This window is shown in Figure 24.5.

In this window, scroll down to the row labeled Text and click on the right cell of this row. This cell will become editable, and you can enter your own label for the button here. When you've entered a new label, press Enter to activate the change and then close the Attributes window. Now, the label of your pushbutton is changed.

The concept used here to add and customize a pushbutton is the same for all widgets. Therefore, if you've followed and understood everything in this section, you'll have no problem adding other widgets as well.

FIGURE 24.5

*The Attributes window
for a pushbutton.*

Connecting Signals and Slots

With the Signal/Slot editor that comes with QtEz, connecting signals to slots has never been easier. The Signal/Slot editor is started from the main QtEz window; just click the fourteenth item from the left on the toolbar (the toolbar is the bar located right beneath the menu bar). Now, the Signal/Slot Editor window will appear, as shown in Figure 24.6.

FIGURE 24.6

*The Signal/Slot Editor
window.*

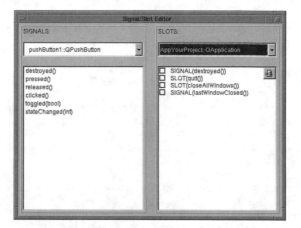

At the top of this window, you see two drop-down menus. With these, you can choose which widget you want to work with. Click the left drop-down menu and choose the pushbutton (probably named pushButton1). The signals for the pushbutton will now appear in the list box. In this list box, choose the clicked() signal. Now, choose the QApplication object (named AppYourProject, if your project name is YourProject) and then double-click the quit() slot (so that a green cross appears in the box at the left side of the slot name).

The clicked() signal should now be selected on the left side and the quit() slot on the right side. When this is done, close the Signal/Slot editor. You've just connected the clicked() signal on the pushbutton to the quit() signal on the QApplication object. Although you've done this many times before, this is the first time you've done it graphically.

Creating the Source Files of a QtEz Project

To compile your new QtEz project, you first need to create source files out of it. This is done via the Run, Create, Source Files menu item. By selecting this item, QtEz will create valid source files of the project and place them in the src subdirectory of the project's base directory (the directory you chose on the Projects Settings window). So, if your project's base directory is /home/user/QtEz/YourProject, the source files will be created in /home/user/QtEz/YourProject/src. If you've followed the instructions for creating a simple QtEz project with one single pushbutton, the contents of the directory should look like this:

```
# ls
total 34
   14 Makefile        14 Makefile.in     1 main.h        1 widget1.h
    1 Makefile.am      1 main.cc         1 widget1.cc    1 widget1_data.cc
```

Just to see that there's actually Qt code inside these files, take a look in the main.cc file. This file holds the main() function, as shown in Listing 24.1.

LISTING 24.1   A main() Function Generated by QtEz

```
 1: /*************************************************
 2: ** Source Dump From QtEZ http://www.ibl.sk/qtez **
 3: **-------------------------------------------**
 4: **   Dumped: Wed Feb 13 14:18:20 2000
 5: **       To: main.cc
 6: ** Project: YourProject
 7: ** Version: 0.1
 8: **   Author: Your Name
 9: **   e-mail: Your@Name.com
10: *************************************************/
11:
12: /*** Main Include ****/
13: #include "main.h"
14:
15: /*** Top Level Widget Includes ***/
16: #include "widget1.h"
17:
18: int
19: main(int argc,char **argv)
20: {
```

```
21:   QApplication AppYourProject(argc,argv);
22:   AppYourProject.setStyle(new QWindowsStyle);
23:   Cwidget1 widget1(0, "widget1");
24:
25:   QObject::connect(widget1.pushButton1,SIGNAL(clicked()),
26:        &AppYourProject,SLOT(quit()));
27:   AppYourProject.setMainWidget(&widget1);
28:   widget1.show();
29:   int retCode = AppYourProject.exec();
30:   return(retCode);
31: }
```

The first few lines of all QtEz-generated source files hold some information about the file (lines 2 through 9), such as when it was created (line 4), which project it belongs to (line 6), who the author is (line 8), and so on. As you can see, this also applies to this sample file. The lines are just common C++/Qt code, and although they don't follow the same style you're used to in this book, they are fully valid.

If you want to, investigate the other source files as well to see how QtEz has built the project. Although you don't need to have the same control over the source code when you're using a GUI builder, it's always good to get an overview of the files so that you can more easily fix possible problems that QtEz can't fix automatically.

Compiling and Running a QtEz Project

You can compile and run a QtEz program in one of two ways: directly from QtEz or manually from the command prompt.

To compile and run a QtEz project from the command prompt, you just follow the standard used by most UNIX/Linux source distribution—that is, run configure, run make, and then run make install. Of course, you should do this in the base directory of your project. However, note that performing a make install is probably not what you want to do in this test project; instead, you probably just want to run it directly from the src directory. Therefore, to compile and run the project manually, use cd to go to the project's base directory and issue the following command:

```
# ./configure
# make
# cd src
# ./YourProject
```

Of course, you need to change YourProject to the real name of your project.

Compiling and running the project from within QtEz is even easier: It's just a matter of clicking a button. So, locate the green item on the toolbar (the eighth from the left) and click it. You'll probably want to have the Compile window visible now so that you can see what's happening. If it's not already visible, click the Compile Window item from the Windows menu. The Compile window should now appear, showing the compiling information that's outputted by your compiler as the compilation moves on. When the compilation is finished, the program will be automatically executed and shown onscreen (see Figure 24.7).

FIGURE 24.7
A simple Qt program created with QtEz. Clicking the button will exit the program.

This is your first Qt program created with QtEz! It consists of a QWidget object, a QPushButton object, and, of course, a QApplication object. The clicked() signal of the QPushButton object is connected to the quit() slot of the QApplication object. Not a new concept for you, but this time it's created with QtEz.

Getting Started with QtArchitect

Another popular Qt GUI-building tool is QtArchitect. It's a well-developed piece of software, although not quite as big as QtEz (yet). However, you might like the interface better than the one used in QtEz, and QtArchitect sure will do the job for you. It should be noted, though, that QtArchitect is not a complete Qt project builder; it's just used to build dialogs. Therefore, you still need to do some of the coding yourself (such as writing the main() function).

Getting and Installing QtArchitect

QtArchitect is available both in a binary and a source distribution at http://www.qtarch.intranova.net/. As always, choose the binary version if one is available for your system. However, if this is not the case, compiling the source will be no problem for you; just follow the instruction throughout this section.

First, download the latest source distribution, which is 2.0-1 at the time of this writing. The file is just around 700KB, so the download won't take more than a few minutes even if you're on a slow connection.

When the download is complete, uncompress the archive:

```
# tar xvfz qtarch-2.0-1.tar.gz
```

This will create a directory called `qtarch-2.0`, where all sources will be placed. Use `cd` to go to this directory. Now, if your `QTDIR` variable is set correctly and you don't have any uncommon settings for your system, QtArchitect will be ready to compile. However, it's best to check the file `Makefile` to see whether anything needs to be changed. Then, start the compilation:

```
# make
```

The compilation will take a while. When it finishes, you have a binary in the `qtarch-2.0` directory called `qtarch`; this is the actual program. If you want to, you can also install the binary (in `/usr/local/bin`) and a few other files (in `/usr/local/lib/qtarch`) by running `make install`. However, it's fully possible to run the binary directly as well.

Creating a Simple GUI with QtArchitect

Now you're ready to start using QtArchitect. If you chose to install it in `/usr/local/bin`, you can start it from anywhere on your file system. If you didn't install it, you must explicitly tell your shell where the binary is located. So, use `cd` to change to the `qtarch-2.0` directory and issue the following command:

```
# ./qtarch
```

The main QtArchitect window will now appear on your screen. This window is shown in Figure 24.8.

FIGURE 24.8

The main QtArchitect window.

Now, the first thing you need to do is to create a new project. This is easily done by choosing the New Project... item from the File menu. A little icon will now appear in the white area of the window. This icon represents your new project.

Then, you need to add a dialog to the project. To do this, select the New Dialog... item on the File menu. When you do, the dialog creation window will appear, as shown in Figure 24.9.

24

FIGURE **24.9**

*The dialog creation
window of QtArchitect.*

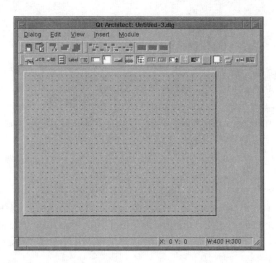

As you can see, this dialog is still empty. However, it's very easy to add widgets to it. To
add a pushbutton, select the Insert menu and then choose Buttons, Push Buttons. A new
button will appear in the upper-left corner. Drag the button to the middle of the widget
and then drag one of its corners so that it's a size you're satisfied with. Next, right-click
the button and choose Properties. The Properties window for the button will now appear
(see Figure 24.10).

FIGURE **24.10**

*The Properties win-
dow for your newly
created pushbutton.*

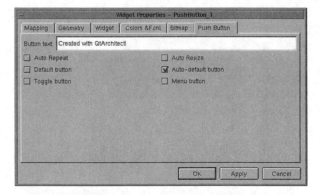

Now select the tab labeled Push Button in the properties window, as shown in Figure
24.10. Add a text label for your button in the text edit line at the top of the window; then
click OK. You'll now go back to the dialog creation window, but this time with a label
added to the button (see Figure 24.11).

FIGURE 24.11

The dialog creation window showing a dialog with a labeled pushbutton on it.

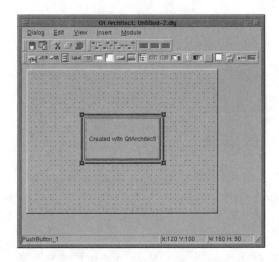

Right-click the button and choose Properties again. This time, choose the tab labeled Mapping. From here, you can connect the pushbutton's signals to slots. Click the Add button to make the Signal/Slot Connection window appear. Here, click the pushbutton's signal clicked() at the left side of the window and then enter the name of the slot you want to connect it to in the text edit box at the bottom of the window. Figure 24.12 shows how the Signal/Slot Connection window now should look.

FIGURE 24.12

The Signal/Slot Connection window. The clicked() signal of the push button is currently connected to the quit() slot of the QApplication object.

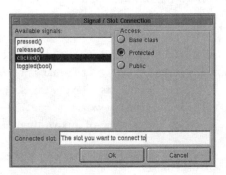

Next, click OK in the Signal/Slot Connection window and then click OK in the Properties window. You should now be back at the dialog creation window. Here, select the Generate Files option from the Dialog menu. The Generate Source window will now appear. From this window you can tell QtArchitect what you want to call the source files. See Figure 24.13 for an example.

FIGURE 24.13

*The Generate Source
window. You should
enter appropriate file-
names as shown here.*

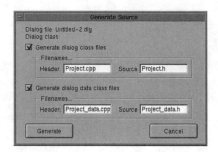

When you're finished, click the OK button. QtArchitect will generate the source files in the directory where you executed qtarch. So, you should now have your newly created widget divided into four files, ready to use. However, to compile and use this widget, you need to write a main() function manually.

As stated, QtArchitect hasn't come as far as QtEz in its development. It is, however, a very good application, and it gets better and better all the time.

Getting Started with Ebuilder

The last builder you'll learn to use in this hour is called Ebuilder. Although the source distribution is still quite small (the archive is around 100KB), it's both useful and user friendly. In this section, you'll learn how to install and use this neat little program.

Getting and Installing Ebuilder

As always, you need the one of the Ebuilder distributions. If a binary distribution is available for your system, that's preferred. However, if that's not the case, you need to compile the source yourself, which is what's described in this section. Both source and binary distributions of Ebuilder can be found at www.fys.ruu.nl/~meer/Ebuilder/. Just make sure you get the latest version! At the time of this writing, the latest version is 0.56c.

When the file is downloaded, uncompress as usual:

```
# tar xvfz evuilder-0.56c.tar.gz
```

This will create a directory called ebuilder-0.56c, where the whole distribution will reside. Use cd to go to this directory and edit the file config.mk in your favorite editor (vi, for example):

```
# vi config.mk
```

If your QTDIR variable is already set, the only thing you may need to do is to change the name of your compiler and the path to the flex utility. The compiler is set to CC by default. However, you'll probably need to change this to gcc, g++, or something similar. The path to the flex utility is set to /usr/local/bin/flex by default. However, you'll probably need to change this to /usr/bin/flex. If you're unsure about the name of your compiler and the path to flex, search your system for gcc and flex with the find utility (see man find for more information).

When config.mk is edited and ready, you can start the compilation by running make:

```
# make
```

The compilation will now start and, hopefully, not end until everything is finished. This will take a while.

When the compilation is finished, two binaries are created in the bin directory of the ebuilder-0.56c directory: ebuilder and convert. The only one you need to worry about is ebuilder; this is the actual program (convert is a utility for converting old Ebuilder projects to the new format). To install Ebuilder, simply copy the ebuilder binary to a suitable directory (for example, /usr/local/bin).

Creating a Simple GUI with Ebuilder

Once Ebuilder is correctly installed on your system, it's time to start it. If you copied the ebuilder binary to a directory that's included in your PATH variable, you only need to enter ebuilder at the prompt and press Enter:

```
# ebuilder
```

Now, the main Ebuilder window, shown in Figure 24.14, will appear on your screen.

FIGURE 24.14

The main Ebuilder window, as it first appears onscreen.

24

To create a new widget, click the File menu and choose New…. Then, the class creation window will appear. Here, you need to tell Ebuilder what you want to call your new class and which class it should be based on. Optionally, you can also enter some documentation for the class here as well (see Figure 24.15).

FIGURE 24.15

The class creation window of Ebuilder.

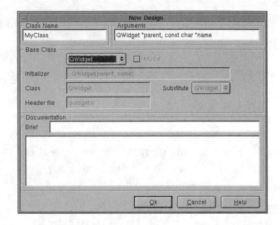

When you've chosen a name and base class for your new class, click the OK button. Now, an empty window will appear. This is your new window that you can add widgets to. Adding widgets in Ebuilder is done by clicking the Edit menu in the main window and then choosing Add. Once you do this, a list of widgets appears. From this list, select PushButton. Now, Ebuilder asks what you want to call the new button. This is shown in Figure 24.16.

FIGURE 24.16

The window in which you enter the name of your new pushbutton. Here, the name MyButton *is entered.*

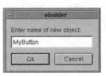

When you've entered a name for the button, click the OK button. Now, the Properties window for the new button will appear. This window is divided into a few tabs. Click the tab labeled Button and enter a label for the button in the text edit box that appears at the top of the window (see Figure 24.17).

When you've entered a label for the button, click the OK button. Now, the buttons will appear in the top-left corner of the project window. Click the button to give it focus and then drag it to the position you want it. You can also resize it by dragging one of its corners. When this is done, your window should look something like the one shown in Figure 24.18.

FIGURE 24.17

The Properties window for the push-button. The Button tab is currently selected, and a label has been entered.

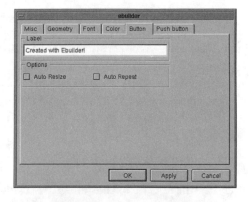

FIGURE 24.18

Your newly created window with a labeled pushbutton on it.

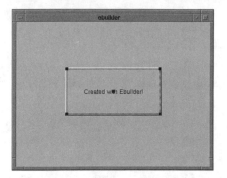

Now, to export this widget to a source file, click the File menu and choose Export. Ebuilder will now ask for the base filename of the source and header files. This could, for example, be MyClass. When you've entered a base filename, click the OK button. One source and one header file will now be created in the directory where you executed ebuilder. You should take a look at these two files to see how Ebuilder has arranged the project. This widget is now ready for you to use in your projects.

Summary

The GUI builders covered in this hour can (and will) be a great help to you when creating GUI interfaces. Although you still have to write the code that will give your program actual functions (a GUI builder can't write the HTML parser in a WWW browser), the GUI builders take care of the GUI interface. This includes tasks such as placing out and setting the size of widgets and creating dialogs. If your program uses a complicated layout and many dialogs, this can be quite time consuming to do by hand. Therefore, GUI builders can save you lots of work.

However, although GUI builders are a great help, you still can't create Qt programs without actually knowing how the library works. There's a chance that a GUI builder has bugs that will make it output bad code in certain situations. Therefore, it's important that you know and understand the library so that you can fix any problems. Because of this, the GUI builders were not even mentioned prior to this hour. However, if you've followed the first 23 hours successfully, you've certainly earned the right to use GUI builder by now.

Q&A

Q If I understood it right, I need `perl` to compile QtEz. I don't have `perl`. Where can I get it?

A A `perl` distribution is probably included in your UNIX/Linux distribution. If that's not the case, you can download it from www.perl.com.

Q When I'm trying to run QtEz, it says that the `QTEZ` environment variable is not set, but I'm absolutely sure that I did set it. What's wrong?

A If you set the `QTEZ` environment variable in one xterm or virtual console and then try to start QtEz in another console, QtEz won't find the variable. To be sure that this variable is set in all xterms and virtual consoles, you need to set it in one of your startup scripts (for example, `/etc/profile`).

Q I'm compiling QtEz (or QtArchitect), and it's taken a few hours now. Something must be wrong!

A No, if the computer is still compiling, nothing is wrong. It's just that both QtEz and QtArchitect are quite large applications and therefore take quite some time to compile. If your computer is a few years old, it's quite possible that this process will take a few hours.

Q I don't know which GUI builder to choose. What do you think?

A If you don't have anything against the QtEz interface, it's currently the best choice. It has the most features and takes care of much of the work in actually building the GUI. However, it's possible that this will change in the future as the other GUI builders develop.

Workshop

You're encouraged to work through the following questions and exercises to help you retain what you've learned in this hour about GUI builders.

Quiz

1. What is a GUI builder?

2. Is there more than one Qt GUI builder available?

3. What can't a GUI builder help you with?

4. Why do you still have to know how Qt works even though you're using a GUI builder?

Exercises

1. Start your favorite GUI builder. Create a new project and a new widget (which are the same thing in some GUI builders). Create a GUI for a simple text editor, complete with a menu bar (with File, Edit, and Help menus), a status bar, and a toolbar. In the middle, there should be one big `QMultiLineEdit` object. Export this project to source files and then compile and run it.

24

PART VI
Appendix

Appendix

A   Quiz Answers

APPENDIX A

Quiz Answers

Quiz Answers for Hour 1

1. What is Qt?

   Qt is a C++ class library for creating GUI programs.

2. What advantages does Qt have over other similar products?

   Qt is fast, portable, and easy to use.

3. What is a `QPushButton` class?

   `QPushButton` is a class that provides you with a clickable button. It can be labeled with text or a pixmap.

4. How is the `QWidget` class used?

   `QWidget` is used as the workspace in a Qt application. `QWidget` is the underlying window on which you can add other objects, such as buttons.

5. What does `a.setMainWidget( &mainwindow );` mean?

This piece of code tells Qt that the `mainwindow` object is the program's main widget. When the main widget is closed, the entire program is finished.

6. Where do you find the Qt Reference Documentation?

The Qt Reference Documentation is included in the Qt distribution in the subdirectory `doc`.

Quiz Answers for Hour 2

1. What does OOP stand for?

OOP stands for *object-oriented programming*.

2. What is a class?

A *class* is a description of a special type of data. You can describe what data and what functions the class will consist of.

3. What is an object?

If you write a class describing a car, an object of that class is one particular car. You create one object for every single car. However, this could be a house, a dog, or a graphical button in a GUI program as well.

4. What is a method?

A method is the same as a member function, a function that belongs to a class.

5. What is class inheritance?

Class inheritance is a way of building new classes based on existing ones. You can use old tested code and just add the features you need at the time. By using class inheritance, you don't need to reinvent code over and over again.

6. Why do you need OOP knowledge to use Qt?

Qt is a C++ class library. It is an OOP library, which uses the OOP features included in the C++ library. Therefore you need OOP knowledge to use Qt successfully.

Quiz Answers for Hour 3

1. What does the `setMaximumSize()` function do?

The `setMaximumSize()` function sets the maximum size of the widget in question.

2. What does the `setMinimumSize()` function do?

The `setMinimumSize()` function sets the minimum size the widget can have.

3. What is the `setGeometry()` function used for?

The `setGeometry()` function is used to set the size and position of the widget. If the widget is a window, it can be moved and resized later.

4. What can you do if you include the `qfont.h` header file in your source file?

You can use the `QFont` class to format text.

5. What does the line `MyMainWindow w;` do?

It creates a `MyMainWindow` object and executes the class's constructor.

6. Why don't you need to call the `show()` function for each object?

When you call `show()` for a parent widget, its child widgets are automatically shown.

7. What do you do when you enter the `this` pointer as a parent widget?

The `this` pointer represents the uncreated object of the current class. Therefore, if you're setting the `this` pointer as the parent widget, the parent will be the object you then create in the `main()` function.

8. What is qApp?

qApp was created in the same spirit as the `this` pointer. It's a pointer to the uncreated `QApplication` object (which is created in `main()`).

9. Why do you need to make a call to `a.exec()` in `main()`?

On this line, the program control is passed onto the Qt library. From here, Qt takes care of user interaction as well as other operations that make the program work.

Quiz Answers for Hour 4

1. What is a slot?

A slot is a special type of member function that can be connected to a signal. When the signal is emitted, the slot (function) will be executed.

2. What is a signal?

A signal is a special type of function that can be connected with a slot. The signal notifies the slot when a certain event occurs, and the slot is then executed.

3. How do you connect a signal to a slot?

By using the `QObject::connect()` function.

4. Can you connect multiple slots to one signal?

Yes, this is possible. Just make a call to the `connect()` function for each connection.

5. When can you call the connect() function without specifying in which class it's defined?

When you make the call from a member function of a class derived from QObject or one of its subclasses.

6. Is it possible to disconnect a connected slot from a signal?

Yes, this is possible. Just use the QObject::disconnect() function.

7. What does it mean to leave out the name of the object holding the slot in a call to the connect() function?

That means that the slot is defined in the current class (that is, the class that's currently defined). Therefore, this kind of call can only be made from within a member function of the class holding the slot.

8. Is it possible to connect a signal to another signal? If so, how?

Yes, this is possible. You just use the connect() function as usual, as shown in the following:

```
connect( button, SIGNAL( clicked() ), this, SIGNAL( anothersignal() ) );
```

Quiz Answers for Hour 5

1. What can the QScrollView class be used for?

The QScrollView class can be used to create a window with scrollbars.

2. Which member function is used to add objects to the QScrollView class?

The QScrollView::addChild() function is used to add objects to the QScrollView class.

3. What does *scroll-on-demand* mean?

Scroll-on-demand means that the scrollbars are shown only when they're needed (that is, they're not shown when all the widgets are fully visible).

4. What are QMenuBar and QPopupMenu?

QMenuBar and QPopupMenu are the Qt classes that should be used to create pull-down menus. The QMenuBar object represents the entire menu bar, and QPopupMenu represents a single menu.

5. When do you need to call the QMenuBar::insertItem() function?

You need to call the QMenuBar::insertItem() function when you want to add a menu to the menu bar.

6. What are `QToolBar` and `QToolButton`?

   `QToolBar` and `QToolButton` are the Qt classes you should use to create toolbars. `QToolBar` represents the actual toolbar, and `QToolButton` represents a button on the toolbar.

7. What is the `QMainWindow` class good for?

   The `QMainWindow` class is of great help when you want to create an application with a standard look and feel.

8. What is the central widget in a `QMainWindow` object?

   The central widget is the widget that `QMainWindow` will add a menu bar, toolbars, and a status bar around. For example, in a text editor, the central widget is the white area you add text to.

9. Do you need to call any special functions to add a toolbar to a `QMainWindow`-based class?

   No, the `QMainWindow` class will take care of this as you create the toolbar.

10. What is `QPixmap`?

    `QPixmap` is a class for managing pixmap files. See Listing 5.5 for details on how this works.

Quiz Answers for Hour 6

1. What are the different types of buttons used for?

   Pushbuttons are often used to explicitly make something happen in your programs. Radio buttons are used for making one selection out of multiple choices, and check buttons are used to make one or more selections out of multiple choices.

2. What signal should be used to check whether a `QPushButton` object is clicked?

   The `clicked()` signal.

3. Which class should be used for arranging buttons?

   The `QButtonGroup` class.

4. Which function sets the alignment of the text in a `QLabel` object?

   The `setAlignment()` function. This function is used to set the alignment of many other Qt widgets as well.

5. How do you change the size, font, and style of the text in a `QLabel` object?

   By calling the `QPushButton::setFont()` function. This function takes a `QFont` object as an argument. Here's an example:

   ```
   b1->setFont( QFont( "Times", 16, QFont::Bold ) );
   ```

A

6. When creating a subclass based on `QTableView`, which function do you need to implement other than the constructor?

The `paintCell()` function.

7. Why do you need to implement this function?

If you don't implement this function in a valid way, `QTableView` will not know how to paint its cells.

8. Which class should be used to create a table header?

The `QHeader` class.

Quiz Answers for Hour 7

1. What is a selection widget?

A *selection widget* is, as its name implies, a widget that lets the user select text, a pixmap, or a numerical value.

2. What two types of text-selection widgets does Qt provide?

List boxes (`QListBox`) and combo boxes (`QComboBox`). They're very similar to each other, but a combo box takes up less space.

3. What is the `QSplitter` class used for?

The `QSplitter` class is used when you want the user of your program to be able to control the size of two or more widgets.

4. What can you use the `QWidgetStack` class for?

You can add widgets to a `QWidgetStack` object and then control which of these widgets is currently shown.

5. When would it be useful to use an integer ID instead of a widget pointer when working with a widget stack?

This feature can be useful at compile time when you're not absolutely sure which widget you want to work with. Perhaps events in the program will decide which widgets will be inserted in the widget stack. If so, the integer ID feature is required!

6. Although they're not explicitly referred to as *selection widgets* in this hour, you learned about two selection widgets for numerical values. Can you name them?

The slider widget (`QSlider`) and the spin box widget (`QSpinBox`).

7. What advantage does a slider have over a spin box?

It's easier to convey to the user the possible values when you use a slider instead of a spin box. On the other hand, a spin box takes up less space.

Quiz Answers for Hour 8

1. What's the difference between QLineEdit and QMultiLineEdit?

   QLineEdit is for retrieving short text strings, such as a password, from the user. QMultiLineEdit is for showing large amounts of text to the user or for letting the user type in large amounts of text.

2. Which class should you use to show a text file to the user?

   Most likely the QMultiLineEdit class.

3. If you look only at member functions, what is the most essential difference between QLineEdit and QMultiLineEdit?

   QMultiLineEdit includes functions for programmatically inserting text at exact positions.

4. If you don't use the insertItem() function to insert items to a list view, which method is used?

   The parent-child method.

5. Which signal is emitted when you double-click an item in the list view?

   The doubleClicked() signal.

6. Which signal is emitted when you press Return or Enter in a list view?

   The returnPressed() signal.

7. What is a progress bar?

   A progress bar is a smart widget that gives the user a view of how much time is left before one or more tasks are finished.

8. When should you implement a progress bar in your application?

   When your application is about to perform a time-consuming task.

Quiz Answers for Hour 9

1. What class is used for creating graphics?

   The QPainter class is used for creating graphics.

2. What does the setPen() function do?

   With the setPen() function, you can change the type of pen you're working with.

A

3. What is the brush used for?

The brush is used for filling the inside of figures.

4. Is there more than one fill style to select from?

Yes, there is. A description of all the fill styles can be found in Table 9.1.

5. Why should you use `QPainter` to show text?

Yes, why should you? If your goal is just to show text, it's better to use `QLabel`.

6. What is RGB?

RGB stand for Red/Green/Blue. It is a method for defining colors.

7. What is a palette?

A palette contains three color groups and makes a complete set of colors for your application—one for each state (active application, disabled application, and normal application).

8. What would you do to print a circle on a piece of paper?

Just draw the circle, as usual, to a `QPrinter` object.

Quiz Answers for Hour 10

1. What is a dialog?

A *dialog* is a widget that interacts with the user in some way (for example, asking the user whether he or she wants to proceed).

2. Does Qt provide any dialog for choosing a file?

Yes, you can easily create a file dialog using the `QFileDialog` class.

3. Is it possible to select multiple files?

Yes, just use the `QFileDialog::getOpenFiles()` function (note the ending s).

4. Why would you want to let the user select a color?

If you're creating a drawing program, the user might need to select which color to use.

5. What class should be used to create a font dialog?

The `QFontDialog` class.

6. Which dialog should you use if you want to ask the user a simple question?

The easiest way of doing this is to use the `QMessageBox` dialog. You could, however, also create a custom dialog for this.

7. If you were about to open 50 files, what should you set the maximum progress value to?

50, of course. Then you simply call `QProgressDialog::setProgress()` every time a file has been opened.

8. Can you use the base class `QDialog` to create your own tab dialog?

Yes, but you shouldn't. Although it is possible to do this with `QDialog`, you should use `QTabDialog` instead. After all, the Qt developers have already done most of the work for you.

Quiz Answers for Hour 11

1. What is a layout manager?

A layout manager is a class that can be used to lay out widgets.

2. How can layout managers help you in your work?

By using a layout manager, you don't have to define the widget's location-coordinates by hand and by this save a lot of work.

3. How does `QVBoxLayout` organize its child widgets?

QVBoxLayout organizes its child widgets in a column.

4. How does `QHBoxLayout` organize its child widgets?

QHBoxLayout organizes its child widgets in a row.

5. How does `QGridLayout` organize its child widgets?

QgridLayout organizes its child widgets in a grid.

6. Which two numbers represent the upper-left widget in a `QGridLayout` layout manager?

`0` and `0`.

7. When do you need to use nested layout managers?

To achieve a more original, and many times more complex, layout.

8. When do you have to call the `QLayout::Activate()` function?

In the old 1.4x versions of Qt, you had to call to function to activate the layout manager.

A

Quiz Answers for Hour 12

1. Which class represents a file in Qt?

   The class QFile.

2. What is the QTextStream class used for?

   It's used to create a stream between the file and the program. This stream can then be used to transfer information from the file to the program.

3. What does the QDir class do?

   It reads a directory and creates a vector with one element for each directory item (Remember, in a vector, each element can be accessed with the [] operator).

4. How would you get the name of the fifth item in a directory?

   By calling myQDirObject[4]. Remember, the 4 represents the fifth argument because the numbering starts at 0.

5. When would you need to use the QFileInfo class?

   When you need information about a file (such as its size, for example).

Quiz Answers for Hour 13

1. Why do you think QValidator is such an abstract class?

   Simply because it's impossible to predict all the different ways you, the programmer, would want to use a validator.

2. Are there any predefined validator classes at all?

   Yes, QDoubleValidator and QIntValidator.

3. If you answered Yes in the previous question, can you tell what this validator (or these validators) can be used for?

   For validating floating-point numbers and integers.

4. Which Qt classes can use a validator?

   QLineEdit, QSpinBox, and QComboBox.

5. Which function do you need to call to tell an object to use a validator?

   The setValidator() function.

6. When creating your own validator classes, which virtual function do you insert the actual validation code in?

   The validate() function.

7. There's one certain virtual function that you can use to fix strings that are almost acceptable. What function is it?

   The `fixup()` function.

Quiz Answers for Hour 14

1. When should you use the `QStack` container class?

   When you want to create a list of elements and then retrieve them in reverse order.

2. When should you use the `QQueue` container class?

   When you want to create a list of elements and then retrieve them in the same order as you inserted them.

3. What is a hash table?

   A *hash table* is a list of elements in which every element can be accessed through a string key or an integer key.

4. Which class would you use if you want to create a hash table with integer keys instead of string keys?

   The `QIntDict` class.

5. What is the `QCache` used for?

   It's used to create a hash table that you can control the size of.

6. What happens when the maximum total cost value is reached in a cache?

   The element that's least recently touched will be deleted.

7. When are you required to use an iterator?

   When you want to traverse one of the dictionary classes (`QDict`, `QIntDict`, `QCache`, or `QIntCache`).

Quiz Answers for Hour 15

1. What's the first thing you need to do before you can show a GIF animation?

   You need to make sure you compiled Qt with GIF support.

2. Is there any way you can speed up an animation?

   Yes, you can set the speed of the animation with the `QMovie::setSpeed()` function.

3. Is there any way you can get the current speed of an animation?

   Yes, by calling the `QMovie::speed()` function.

A

4. Does Qt have its own image format?

Yes, you can save and load images of this format with the `QPicture` class (usually saved with the `.pic` file name extension to verify that the Qt's image format is used).

5. Why should you use Qt's own image format?

Because it's a platform-independent format that's supported on all Qt platforms.

6. Is it possible to use JPG images with Qt?

Yes, if you have the JPG library installed on your system. You should not use JPG images if you're not absolutely sure that all users of your program have the JPG library.

Quiz Answers for Hour 16

1. What do you need to do to be able to copy and move text with the standard key combinations?

You don't need to do anything extra.

2. Is it possible to cut and paste images with the standard Qt Clipboard function?

Yes, by using the `QClipboard::setImage()` and `QClipboard::image()` functions.

3. Which class should you base your class on if you want to be able to use it with the Clipboard?

The `QMimeSource` class.

4. Is it possible to make only certain areas of a widget able to receive drag-and-drop objects?

Yes, that can easily be done by using the `mouseMoveEvent()` function.

5. Which function is called when you drop an object on an area that can receive the object?

The `dropEvent()` function.

6. Is it possible to make widgets that you can only drag objects from and not drop objects on as well as other widgets that you only can drop object on and not drag them from?

Yes, simply don't define any functions for either dragging or dropping for the widget, as appropriate.

Quiz Answers for Hour 17

1. What is KDE?

   KDE is a set of GUI programs that together make a full-featured desktop environment.

2. When writing a KDE program, which class should you use instead of `QApplication`?

   The `KApplication` class.

3. What is kapp?

   kapp has the same function that qApp has in a normal Qt program. It's a pointer to the uncreated `KApplicaion` object.

4. Which class should you use to create the main window in a KDE program?

   The `KTMainWindow` class.

5. What can you use the `KApplication::getHelpMenu()` for?

   For creating a Help menu that follows the KDE standard.

6. Is there a good way to show an HTML document in a KDE program?

   Yes, this is very simple if you use the `KHTMLWidget` class.

Quiz Answers for Hour 18

1. What can be found in the KDE core library?

   The most low-level classes, such as `KApplication` and `KProcess`.

2. Which class should you use if you want to start a subprocess in your program?

   The `KProcess` class.

3. If your subprocess happens to be a shell command, which class should you use?

   The `KShellProcess` class should be used.

4. What advantages does `KPixmap` have over `QPixmap`?

   `KPixmap` includes two new color modes that make your program work better on 256-color displays.

5. Is it possible to minimize a window from within a KDE program?

   Yes, this can be done with the `KWM` class. Actually, you can manage all window manager operations through this class.

6. What type of classes do you find in `libkdeui`?

   `libkdeui` holds the user interface classes. These classes can be used to create the actual user interface.

A

7. When you're writing a KDE application, is it required that you always build the user interface with the classes in `libkdeui`?

Absolutely not. You can use Qt classes for this and still make your program KDE compatible.

8. Should you use the classes in `libkfile` when you want to perform some file I/O operation?

No, there are no such classes in `libkfile` at the moment.

Quiz Answers for Hour 19

1. What is OpenGL?

OpenGL is a library for creating high-performance 3D graphics.

2. What is MESA?

MESA is a free implementation of OpenGL.

3. What is `libqgl`?

`libqgl` is the name of Qt's OpenGL extension. Qt's OpenGL classes are defined in this library.

4. When should you use OpenGL?

When you want your program to do some graphic-intense operation. For simple drawing operations, it's safest to stick with `QPaint`.

5. What is OpenGL's weakness?

OpenGL's most obvious weakness is its lack of functions for user interaction. It's hard to implement buttons, menus, and such in an OpenGL program.

6. What is the `QGLWidget` class used for?

The `QGLWidget` class represents the OpenGL widget. You should add your OpenGL code to a subclass of `QGLWidget`.

Quiz Answers for Hour 20

1. Why should you use Qt to develop Netscape plug-ins?

Because it lets you use a library that you're already familiar with and because you don't have to learn how to use the API provided by the Netscape Plugin SDK.

2. What does the `QNPlugin::getMIMEDescription()` function do?

The `QNPlugin::getMIMEDescription()` function is used to set the MIME type, the filename extension, and the MIME description.

3. What is a MIME type?

MIME provides a way giving a file or stream of data a special type so that the browser know how to deal with it.

4. Suppose you've created a plug-in for showing BMP images. You open a document with many BMP images in it. How many QNPlugin objects are created?

Just one. Always only one.

5. In the scenario from question 3, how many QNPInstance objects are created?

One for each BMP image.

6. What is the QNPInstance::newWindow() function used for?

The browser uses the QNPInstance::newWindow() function to get a new QNPWidget object (actually, a subclass of QNPWidget).

7. When does the browser call the QNPInstance::newStreamCreated() function?

The QNPInstance::newStreamCreated() function is called when the browser has some data to feed the plug-in with.

8. What kind of code should you find in a subclass of QNPWidget?

Regular Qt code.

9. When do you need to create a subclass of QNPStream?

When you want your plug-in to receive data through a stream.

10. What is the <EMBED> HTML tag used for?

The <EMBED> tag is used to embed a plug-in into a HTML document.

Quiz Answers for Hour 21

1. What is user-space text?

User-space text is all text that's visible to the user.

2. Why should you use QString for all user-space text?

Because QString uses Unicode encoding, that guarantees your text is presented in the correct way. Using QString can also improve performance in some cases.

3. When do you need to use the tr() function?

The tr() function must be used whenever there's a string that you want to translate.

4. What is the `findtr` utility used for?

   The `findtr` utility is used to create a database of all translations in one or more files. It simply finds all calls to the `tr()` function and adds an entry for each new string.

5. When do you need to use the `msg2qm` utility?

   Always, when you want to use the translation function.

6. When can the `mergetr` utility be useful?

   `mergetr` can be useful when changes have been made to the source file(s) and you want to merge these changes to the language-specific PO files as well.

7. Which class takes care of the actual translation inside your program?

   The `QTranslator` class.

8. What does the `QApplication::installTranslator()` function do?

   The `QApplication::installTranslator()` function tells the `QApplication` object that there's a translator available and that it should be used.

9. Why is it required that you call the `Q_OBJECT` macro and use the Meta Object Compiler on a class that uses translations?

   Because the translation functions are implemented by `moc`.

10. What can the `QDate` class be used for?

    The `QDate` class can be used to show the current date or to work with date values in general.

11. What can the `QTime` class be used for?

    The `QTime` class can be used to show the current time or to work with time values in general.

12. When should you consider using the `QDateTime` class?

    The `QDateTime` class should be used when both the date and time need to be shown. You could use two separate `QDate` and `QTime` objects for this, but `QDateTime` is more convenient.

Quiz Answers for Hour 22

1. Is it possible to write network applications with Qt?

   Yes, by using the Qt network extension.

2. What is POSIX?

   POSIX is a standard for operating systems. All UNIX variants as well as Windows NT support this standard.

3. What is POSIX.1?

POSIX.1 is the part of POSIX that's most interesting to programmers. It defines how to access system-specific features on the function level.

4. Are there any functions in Qt that are not fully compatible between UNIX and Windows.

Yes, there are a few, but the differences are very small and usually don't cause any problems.

5. What is `tmake`?

`tmake` is a neat little utility that helps you create makefiles for all the different Qt-supported platforms.

6. What is a project file?

A *project file* is a file in which you give `tmake` certain instructions about your project—for example, which files are included.

7. What is `progen`?

`progen` is a great utility that helps you create project files. `progen` is especially useful when you're working with larger projects.

Quiz Answers for Hour 23

1. When should the `qDebug()` function be used?

The `qDebug()` function informs you about a certain program event (that is, when a certain event occurs).

2. When should the `qWarning()` function be used?

The `qWarning()` function informs you that something unexpected has occurred in the program.

3. When should you use the `qFatal()` function?

The `qFatal()` function is used when a rather serious error occurs in the program and it therefore needs to exit.

4. What does the `ASSERT()` macro do?

The `ASSERT()` macro can be used to inform you when a Boolean value is not what it should be.

5. What does the `CHECK_PTR()` macro do?

The `CHECK_PTR()` macro can be used to check whether a pointer is null. This macro is perfect for determining whether an object is created correctly.

A

6. What is a debugger?

   A *debugger* is a program you can use to get detailed information about what's happening inside a program. With many debuggers, you can also control exactly which parts of the program are executed and check the states of the variables.

7. How do you tell gdb which file you want to work with?

   You tell gdb which file you want to work with by entering the filename as an argument to gdb.

8. With what gdb command do you set a breakpoint?

   You set a breakpoint with the gdb command break.

9. What does the command run do in gdb?

   The run command starts the program.

10. If you were to guess, which command do you think quits the gdb debugger?

    The quit command, of course.

Quiz Answers for Hour 24

1. What is a GUI builder?

   A *GUI builder* is a program that graphically lets you create a GUI interface.

2. Is there more than one Qt GUI builder available?

   Yes, there are a few. Three of them are covered in this hour.

3. What can't a GUI builder help you with?

   A GUI builder can't write functions that don't have anything to do with the GUI. The primary use of a GUI builder is to build GUIs, although some GUI builders also include some other features.

4. Why do you still have to know how Qt works even though you're using a GUI builder?

   To do those things that a GUI builder can't do automatically for you. You also need this knowledge to fix GUI problems that might come up when using a GUI builder.

INDEX

G